The Buzz about *This Is Not The Career I Ordered...*

"Any woman interested in reinventing her career should read thi' 'k. Caroline Dowd-Higgins is a breath of fresh air. Her ~ ɔ reinventing your career will show you how an' ' ward."

—Debra Fine, bestselling autl

"Most of us will have seven to ten jobs over ᵕur lives, so how to recharge, reignite and reinvent ourselves ᵢ. something *everyone* needs to know. And, if you're lucky enough to already have the career you ordered, you should read this book because it will definitely ensure your success!"

—Peggy Klaus, Executive Coach and author of *BRAG! The Art of Tooting Your Own Horn Without Blowing It* and *The Hard Truth About Soft Skills: Workplace Lessons Smart People Wish They'd Learned Sooner*

"Landing a job is one thing; finding personal and professional fulfillment through working your passion is another entirely. *This Is Not the Career I Ordered* is a must-read for anyone who has not yet found that 'sweet spot' in their career. It is a friendly, easy read, but not at all simplistic, with valuable insights for first-job seekers through seasoned professionals."

—Kathryn Marion author of: *GRADS: TAKE CHARGE of Your First Year After College!*

"Caroline Dowd-Higgins challenges us to find careers we are passionate about and provides the practical tools, resources and strategies to do just that. The book is full of real life engaging success stories that we can all learn from and be inspired by."

—Ruth Stergiou, CEO Invent Your Future Enterprises

"Caroline Dowd-Higgins captures the essence of entrepreneurship – fearless authenticity, crazy creativity and radical reinvention. Sitting down to read *This Is Not the Career I Ordered* is like listening to 20 amazing mentors share the secrets of their success. Whether you are contemplating a reinvention or whether you are already in the middle of one, there is no reason to do it alone – let the women in this book inspire you, push you and give you the strength to take the next step.

—Starla Sireno, Founder, CEO Fearless Women Network

"Extraordinarily relevant, on-point, and thoughtful message for individuals in any stage of their career journey. Working closely with college students of all ages, I shall certainly recommend this book to them and to our alumni."

—Julia M. McNamara, PhD, President Albertus Magnus College, New Haven, Connecticut

"Wonderfully written and easy to read, Caroline Dowd-Higgins', *This Is Not the Career I Ordered*, prepares women for career change with anecdotes, concrete suggestions and superbly informational web sites highlighting many new products and services. For women in the medical, or any field contemplating a career change, this book is a must have resource and a great gift for friends, family, and colleagues. The stories of women who are successfully recharging, reigniting and reinventing their careers prove the adage 'If you love your job you never work a day in your life.'"

—Dr. Kathleen Toomey, Medical Director at the Robert Wood Johnson University Hospital and a Medical Oncologist in Private Practice

"Career success in the second decade of the 21st century belongs to those who courageously move beyond the boundaries of their comfort zones toward exploration of possibilities. Dowd-Higgins masterfully weaves together anecdotes of women who have done precisely this with solid tools and tips for parlaying who you are into what you can become."

—Lois P. Frankel, Ph.D., author of *Nice Girls Don't Get the Corner Office* and *See Jane Lead*

"This much needed book provides practical advice and action steps to recharge an existing career or execute a major career reinvention. The inspiring stories of women who are thriving in their new careers, many as entrepreneurs, provides insightful wisdom that is just as applicable to men. Caroline Dowd-Higgins captures the essence of finding passion inspiration in our work that leads to ultimate career satisfaction."

—Dr. Donald F. Kuratko, *The Jack M. Gill Chair of Entrepreneurship Professor of Entrepreneurship & Executive Director* Johnson Center for Entrepreneurship & Innovation at the Kelley School of Business, Indiana University - Bloomington

"STOP THE PRESSES!!! Caroline Dowd-Higgins' book: *This Is Not the Career I Ordered* is a HIT! Everything you want to know and more in this authentic, revealing, funny, inspiring book. With practical career advice, who doesn't want to move forward in their careers! Let's order seconds on this book."

—Sallie Felton, Life Coach/Transition Specialist, International Talk Radio Host

THIS IS
NOT THE
CAREER
I ORDERED

SECOND
EDITION

All the Best to you, Alma! Cheers,

THIS IS
NOT THE
CAREER
I ORDERED

*Empowering
Strategies from
Women Who
Recharged,
Reignited, and
Reinvented
Their Careers*

SECOND
EDITION

CAROLINE DOWD-HIGGINS

REINVENTION PRESS
BLOOMINGTON, INDIANA

Published by
Reinvention Press
P.O. Box 6043
Bloomington, IN 47407

ISBN: 978-0-9827318-1-9

Editor, Amy Gifford Hume
Copy editor, Ann Michalsen–ADM Edits www.admedits.com
Text & cover design, Mayapriya Long–Bookwrights www.bookwrights.com

Printed in the United States of America

66You've got to follow your passion. You've got to figure out what it is you love—who you really are. And have the courage to do that. I believe that the only courage anybody ever needs is the courage to follow your own dream.99

—Oprah Winfrey

CONTENTS

Acknowledgements   xii
Preface   xiv

1. Learn to Sing a New Tune   1
   1. Trading Stages: From Opera Singer to Career Coach   1
   2. Career Reinvention Is an Art   4
   3. Begin With What You Value   5
   4. Find What Makes You Tick   9
   5. Why Personality Matters   11
   6. Learn From The Queen of Transferable Skills   13

2. Utilize the Power of the Women in Your Back Yard   17
   7. These Are Not the Careers They Ordered   17
   8. Inspiration to Pay-It-Forward   18
   9. Build Your Personal Board of Directors   20
   10. Unlock Your Passion   21
   11. Why Every Woman Needs a Reinvention Toolbox   23

3. Turn Survive into Thrive   25
   12. Jessi Walter Brelsford: When Life Hands You Lemons…
       Make Cupcakes   25
   13. Christine Clifford: Don't Forget to Laugh   28
   14. Mary McManus: A Gift From the Heart   35
   15. Carole Brody Fleet: A Widow Learned to Heal in High Heels   42
   16. Claire Gillenson: Making Peace With Grief   47
   17. Take a Step Forward   54
       Reinvention Toolbox: Know Thy Self; Showcase Your
       Resiliency; Utilize Soft Skills   55

4. Become a Member of the Creativity Club   58

18. Stacey Kannenberg: Mom-on-a-Mission Builds Publishing
    Empire   58

19. Carla Falcone and Romy Taormina: Turning Morning
    Sickness Into a Business Empire   64

20. Heidi Roizen: Get into Your Skinny Jeans   67

21. Grace Chon: From the Ad Agency to Puppy Love   72

22 Tana Poppino: Never Wanting to Wonder What If?
    Rodeo Cowgirl Goes Pro   77

23. Take a Step Forward   81
    Reinvention Toolbox: Build Relationships – Not Networks;
    Tap into Your Resource Team   82

5. Learn a Lesson from the Recovering Lawyers   85

24. Ellen Covner: From Law to Landscaping   85

25. Tonya Fitzpatrick: Turning a Passion for Travel into a Career 91

26. Beth Patterson: Law and Enlightened Order   96

27. Liz Williams: Legal Eagle Forges New Path with Food   100

28. Lisa Montanaro: Organizing Geek Launches
    Online University   107

28. Take a Step Forward   115
    Reinvention Toolbox: Own Your Passion; Take
    Calculated Risks; Be Authentic   116

6. Make Way for the Artists   119

30. Angela Jia Kim: Understand the Power of an Itch   119

31. Danielle Bobish: Making the Most of Your Curtain Call   124

32. Ginger Hodge: When Donkeys Fly   128

33. Jo Laurie: Do You Live to Work or Work to Live?   136

34. Melani Lust: Renaissance Woman Sees Life Through a
    Creative Lens   140

35. Take a Step Forward   147
    Reinvention Toolbox: Recognize Your Transferable Skills;
    Develop Your Professional Poise; Give, Give, Get   149

7. Let's Hear it for The WAHMs: Work-at-Home Moms 152

36. Vianesa Vargas: First, Take Care of Yourself 152
37. Pam Beattie: Friendly Fur Leads to a Business with Repurpose 157
38. Candace Alper: Name Your Tune 162
39. Lara Galloway: Be Proud to Make Your Family the #1 Priority 167
40. Monica Castro: Spanglish and the Healing Power of Bees 173
41. Take a Step Forward 178
    Reinvention Toolbox: Earning versus Getting; Employing
    Effective Communication 180

8. Connect with Wise Women 183

42. Alma Bond: Forget Everything You Ever Learned About
    Retirement 183
43. Beverly Solomon: Object d'Art: Model to Marketing Maven 187
44. Meg Nollen: Navigating the Corporate Labyrinth 191
45. Susan Vernicek: Identity Check 199
46. Karen Kibler: Earning a PhD at Forty-Something 203
47. Take a Step Forward 208
    Reinvention Toolbox: Use a Portfolio as Your Secret Weapon;
    Embrace Change 211

9. Everything Has Its Place: How to Find Yours 215

48. Kari DiFabio: Say "Cheers"…to a New Career 215
49. Debbie Waitkus: Hole in One 220
50. Stacy Breurers: From M & A to Cabernet 226
51. Kim Daly: The Urbane Concierge 231
52. Jeannie Montagano: South Paw Becomes a Professor 238
53. Take a Step Forward 244
    Reinvention Toolbox: The Art of Self-Promotion;
    Leadership Lessons; Play Nice in Your Career Sandbox 247

10. A Call to Nurture 252

54. Jacqueline Edelberg: Harnessing the Goodness of
    Her Neighborhood 252
55. Joyce Boyd: There is More to Life Than Being the
    Maytag Woman 261

56. Ellen Palmer: Tap Into Your Feminine Side   266
57. Carol Covin: A Cure for Cancer in Her Desk   273
58. Holly Lemon Batterton: A Circuitous Route to Career Bliss   279
58. Take a Step Forward   283
     Reinvention Toolbox: Using a Coach – Best Practices;
     Honor Thy Self   286

11. The Force of the Sisterhood   289
60. Empowerment, Optimism, and Humble Confidence   289
61. Running Your Career Marathon   290
62. Setting and Achieving Goals   291
63. Work/Life Balance and Making Choices   292
64. Celebrate the New You: Recharged, Reignited,
     and Reinvented   293

Resources   296

About the Author   297

ACKNOWLEDGEMENTS

I am indebted to the many women who shared their amazing stories for my book. Their contributions have changed my life, inspired me with hope, and solidified my belief that great things happen when women come together in community. Thank you for sharing your trials and tribulations as well as your triumphs – we can all learn from your journeys.

This second edition showcases the continuing journeys of the women from my original book as well bonus stories from new women who inspired me. My longtime friend and colleague, Amy Hume came onboard for the second edition as my editor and also conducted many of the What's New? section interviews with the women featured.

As a fellow career coach, Amy has been through a career reinvention herself and knows the power of transformation. I could not have completed this second edition without her and I am eternally grateful for her extraordinary work.

My mentor and sponsor, Deborah C. Stephens continues to hold a special role on my Personal Board of Directors and in my life. She empowered me to write the first book, which propelled my career in ways I would have never imagined. Thank you, Deborah.

To the fabulous Stacey J. Miller, my publicist extraordinaire, whose constant support and enthusiasm is palpable and motivating. Kudos to Bill Kamper, Tom Casale, and Monika Arturi from Simplified Solutions, who created my website. Special thanks to the award winning, Mayapriya Long of Bookwrights, who designed the cover and interior of the book and to Ann Michalsen for her copy editing expertise.

To my friend and colleague, Nancy Hutchens – thank you for your coaching expertise and dreaming big with me as we create new materials to help women thrive.

Shelley Spencer has made a profound impact on my life and career and I look forward to continuing my work with her for a long time to come. Thank you for being an executive producer extraordinaire as well as the best dot connector I've ever encountered for the myriad of projects we are pursuing together.

I want to acknowledge my family for their patience and understanding during the creative process. To my husband, C. David Higgins, who taught me to be ready when opportunity knocks and serves as my constant inspiration. To my parents, Marty and Nancy Dowd, who provided unconditional support as their opera-singing daughter reinvented herself, and for believing in me, and this project. To my sister, Jennifer Bruner, who is a master connector and graciously promotes my work to her expansive network. To my brother, Thomas Dowd, who is willing to let me impart my career development wisdom as he navigates his professional journey.

To the many friends and colleagues who have touched this project in a variety of ways: Nichole Williams, Rebecca Keith, Michelle Richardson, Joni McGary, Jerri Rusnak, Caryn Castellan, Carolyn Broughton, Maureen Berkner Boyt, Steve Bennett, Dr. Lois Frankel, Gail Sheehy, and Marshall Goldsmith. And to the myriad of people who are not on this list but helped in so many ways – thank you!

PREFACE

I came to this book project by an unexpected route. A friend of mine heard a fabulous speaker at a women's event and called to tell me about her. She said the speaker and author, Deborah C. Stephens, relocated from California to Indiana and was looking to build her network of women in the Midwest. I reached out to Deborah and set up a lunch meeting and we've been friends ever since.

To my great fortune, Deborah became one of my mentors and later my sponsor. She is part of my resource team and the catalyst for this book. She co-authored the women's book: *This Is Not the Life I Ordered* (one of her eight bestselling books) and was looking for experts to pen additional books with the *This Is Not The* (fill in the blank) *I Ordered* theme. She quickly encouraged me to write *This Is Not the Career I Ordered* because of my passion and expertise in the career development arena.

The two-year journey started at Deborah's kitchen table much like the gatherings with friends she describes in her women's book. I began interviewing women I knew who had experienced a career transition. In the spirit of great networking, these women connected me to their friends, colleagues, and family members who also had stories to share. Within a year, I had spoken with hundreds of women in the USA, Canada, and England as a result of national press inquiries and good old-fashioned relationship building.

The second edition features follow-up stories from most of the women from the original book. The *What's New?* section of their stories shows where they are now and how they have evolved in their lives and careers during the past few years. Their journeys further illustrate that it's OK to change your mind and your career as often as you like. This new book also features bonus stories with women I have encountered that will inspire you with their reinvention moxie!

Survival Guide

Since I have experienced my own career transition and reinvention, I have a personal stake in this project. I was inspired by the women I interviewed, and their commitment to helping others learn from their experiences, to make your journey a little less rocky. The power of women in community is extraordinary.

While the career advice and action steps I present are applicable to men as well, the book is told through the eyes of women, who have become stronger and more confident in their quest for reinvention. You will laugh and cry and be motivated by their experiences, but most importantly, you will learn from these women.

My goal is to provide you with a survival guide in the form of a *Reinvention Toolbox* that shows you how to implement your own personal career reinvention. Some readers will want to recharge, or reignite an existing career with small tweaks, while others will pursue a major overhaul. The action steps for success are in this book.

Empowerment

Working in a university setting for over a decade, helping students and alumni forge their personal career paths, has been a rewarding experience for me. My private coaching practice and public speaking engagements have also given me opportunities to work with amazing people around the globe. But the most gratifying moment for me is when a woman begins to walk tall with a renewed self-confidence and the ability to own her strengths and articulate her passions and values. That is true empowerment and the ultimate message of this book.

Think of this book as your personal career development journal. Take notes on the pages and fill out the exercises right in the book, so that you have a resource to refer to later. Some of the steps in the *Reinvention Toolbox* require self-reflection, time, and planning but many are quick how-to steps to energize you and get you started on your path to reinvention now. The wisdom at the end of each individual woman's story, and each chapter, is a wealth of information – all of which can help you take a step forward on the journey to achieving your goals.

Pay-it-Forward

Think about the other women in your life (mothers, daughters, sisters, friends, etc.) who can learn from the resources assembled by the women showcased in this book. I hope you will join me in sharing the generational wisdom with others so that we can support each other and serve as champions for those struggling to find peace, happiness, and prosperity in a career.

We all know that these are difficult times and that the employment landscape has changed dramatically. The reality is that you may have to stay in your current job for a while to make ends meet or until you land the new position that better matches your values, interests, personality, and skills. That's okay – my goal is to help you get started on this journey of reinvention so that when the time is right, you'll be ready!

Tap into the power and enthusiasm of the sisterhood and enjoy the steps in creating a new you – one that is recharged, reignited, reinvented, and ready to take the world by storm. Women in community are amazing – enjoy the journey!

Second Edition

The original *This Is Not The Career I Ordered* was a labor of love in every possible way. It began my journey as a published author and has connected me with thousands of women worldwide. Not a day goes by that I don't hear another wonderful reinvention story from a new woman I meet or through the power of the women's network.

I decided to write the second edition because I wanted to illustrate how change is constant in all of our lives. The original women whom I showcased continue to experience change as their career and life journeys evolved. The women from the original book have a section titled: *What's New?* at the end of their story so you can see how life has progressed for each of them. The bonus stories are new to the second edition and feature additional women with fascinating stories and career trajectories.

I hear over and over again that certain stories resonate with certain women so I have purposefully written about a broad and diverse group of women with the hope that at least one of these stories will speak to you on a personal level.

If you have read the original book then you will enjoy catching up with old friends to see where they are now. If you are new to *This Is Not The Career I Ordered*, you can start fresh and get to know some amazing women who have taken control of their career destinies and are thriving!

LEARN TO SING A NEW TUNE

1. TRADING STAGES: FROM OPERA SINGER TO CAREER COACH

Performing is like oxygen for me – I love the energy of a live audience and honed my talents to become an opera singer. I was a professional Diva – the good kind that is, since there is no room for inflated ego or bad attitude in the ultra competitive musical job arena. I enjoyed the intellectual stimulation as well: mastering foreign languages, embracing new cultures, and being a savvy self-promoter and negotiator. My musical career took off and I was living my dream.

Over the course of several years, the lack of financial security, benefits, and living the life of the proverbial starving artist was taking its toll, financially and emotionally. It takes a lot of money to sustain a career in the opera world since the voice lessons, musical coaching, and accompanist fees are a constant part of keeping yourself fit and at-the-ready for the next gig. Additionally there is the long distance travel for auditions, being away for months at a time, and the reality of missing my husband who was back at home. So, I knew I needed more in my life to make it complete; but how does an opera Diva with degrees in music find a new career?

What's a Diva to Do?

I would be remiss if I didn't own up to the fact that my personal career reinvention journey was an emotional and difficult one. I went through the full gamut of emotions from fear to rage when my career did not go as I had planned. I couldn't figure out what I was doing wrong until I finally realized that I wasn't doing anything wrong – perhaps this just wasn't the best fit. That epiphany did not come easily or quickly so my goal is to help make your career transition a smoother one.

You're Not in Kansas Anymore, Dorothy!

As I looked back, I realized that I was the type of kid that was incredibly focused at a young age. I fell in love early with performing, and developed the requisite thick skin, honed my craft, and earned an undergraduate and Master's degree in music to complete my package as a professional singer.

I paid my dues with blood, sweat, and tears, and in my mind I was destined for a glamorous life as a performing artist who would enjoy the jet setting travel and perhaps even taste a modicum of fame. When I took off my rose-colored glasses, I realized that truly living the artistic life was not what I expected. Even though I still loved performing, continuous travel became exhausting, as did living in hotels and billeted rooms in the homes of Opera Company board members. I was lonely.

Perseverance or Denial?

The life of a performing artist for me was feast or famine and while the feasts were delicious, the famines were extremely debilitating emotionally. While I did achieve recognition and earned accolades for the work I was performing, deep down I knew something was missing. For far too long, performer's guilt kept me from admitting what I was missing. I forged ahead, trying to convince myself that my next big break would bring the recognition and solvent lifestyle I really wanted. I was not about to give up – that went against every fiber of my being. I was bound and determined to make this work, come hell or high water.

Looking back, I realize that I was ignoring the red lights in my way, not seeing them as signs that I was possibly on the wrong path. I was always taught to persevere and a performer has to suffer for her art, right? **Let me tell you very clearly that nobody has to suffer for his/her career.** You should be joyful in your work and once I came to terms with that notion, my entire world opened up.

Giving Up Guilt

After some serious soul searching, I realized that singing opera was something I did but it did not entirely define who I was as a person. That was liberating, but how was I going to make a living? Last time I looked, opera singers were not high on the list of sought-after nonmusical job candidates. Or so I thought….

Now, years after my personal career reinvention, I consider myself Jill-of-all-Trades since I have enjoyed a myriad of career opportunities in television, radio, and theatre using my voice and stage presence professionally. My career repertoire also includes event planning, marketing and communication, public speaking, employer development, recruiting, career and executive coaching. Now I can add author, entrepreneur, journalist, and media host to that list and I am confident that I will continue to add experiences that play to my strengths since I am empowered with the knowledge that I can do many things well.

A Grateful Diva

I am still performing, but now I don't have the stress of earning my living as a singer. I founded a professional singing group, *The Grateful Divas*, with fellow singer friends and I perform solo and ensemble shows to raise money for nonprofit and charitable organizations nationally. I'm now a Diva on a philanthropic mission and I have been liberated to enjoy myself as a musician in ways I never thought possible.

Currently, I have the great privilege of serving as a Director of Professional Enrichment at the Indiana University Alumni Association. I am developing career and leadership resources for IU alumni across the globe based on a lifetime engagement model because career needs evolve over time. I also have a vibrant career consulting practice and speak nationally on career and professional development issues.

I truly believe that anyone can learn to sing a new tune and have proven it true in my own life. Taking what I have learned on a personal level, and with the myriad of clients I have worked with, I have created a navigational system for career change and reinvention. In this book, I will introduce you to amazing women from around the world and a variety of job fields who have mastered the art of change by recharging, reigniting, and reinventing their lives and their careers.

2.   CAREER REINVENTION IS AN ART

In this tumultuous economy, many women have been forced to reinvent themselves due to downsizing and workforce cutbacks. Others have realized that their careers did not honor their values and they were on a live-to-work carousel and could not get off. We have a *new normal* in our present day career world so I know how scary a career transition can be at this time. My goal is to empower you with strategies and action steps so that you can make career choices that suit your unique situation.

I have interviewed hundreds of women across the globe for this project and several of their stories appear in this book. After talking with so many women, I was relieved to know that many of them also struggled with the guilt of giving up one career to pursue another, especially if their education or training supported the original career. I can tell you from experience, it's a scary step to take; but once you let go of the guilt, it will be very liberating and eventually, confidence-building.

The Reinvention Journey

We all have a myriad of transferable skills that we can utilize for a variety of careers regardless of our educational backgrounds. Heidi Roizen, one of the women I interviewed, shared that a career is like a marathon over the course of a woman's life. It's rare that we have the same career for the entire journey so consider new opportunities that match your passion as you travel the personal mile markers in your life.

Career reinvention is truly an art, one that you alone control. Nobody can reinvent you, except you. It is a powerful concept and one that I hope will bring you self-confidence once you learn more about the steps and strategies to help you move forward towards your individual goals.

3.   BEGIN WITH WHAT YOU VALUE

Choosing the women to feature in this book was a difficult task since I truly cherish each woman's unique story. I picked the stories for the book to showcase a variety of career fields and diverse experiences amongst the women. These ladies shared their hopes and dreams as well as failures and emotional journeys so that you could learn from their experiences. Amazing things happen when women come together in community and now you are part of the strong contingent of women who are contemplating, or have undergone, a career change. These women are a resource you can turn to for advice and inspiration and they personify the power of the sisterhood.

The first step in a career reinvention is to get quiet with your SELF and assess your **values, interests, personality,** and **skills.** In career development jargon, we call these VIPS. First, we'll focus on values. A thoughtful self-reflection can help you determine your plan of action for a career transition. We all know people who are unhappy in their jobs. So take the time to thoughtfully consider what you value because **research shows that values are the biggest predictor of career satisfaction.**

You Alone Can Identify Your Values

We each value different things and there are no judgments about which are better or worse. You are in control of what you value as well as how you pursue new opportunities that match your passion.

Some people value variety, autonomy, security, prestige, or flexibility in the workplace – the options are endless. Think about what motivates you and why.

- What are your peak experiences?
- How do you spend discretionary money?
- Whom do you admire?
- What reasons have driven your past decisions?

Being aware of what you value in your life is important because a career choice that is in line with your core beliefs and values is more likely to be a lasting and positive choice.

Values – Palooza!

My values epiphany came when I realized that I value security in my work. I was an emotional wreck when I worked from audition to audition, not knowing where my next paycheck was coming from. I also value variety, which is why I work many different jobs as a consultant, writer, public speaker, university director, etc., which make up my comprehensive career picture. When I was able to recognize what I valued and what I was missing in my performance career, I could move forward with a plan for my new career possibilities.

Below is a brief list to get you started thinking about what you value. Remember, the values possibilities are endless.

Take the time to consider your top values based on what you want in your life now. Values change as we progress through life so what you value now may be completely different from a career you had in the past. I talk with many women who leave and re-enter the workforce before or after they have children, or take care of elderly parents. This is a great example of how your values can change with different circumstances in your life.

Write it Down!

I encourage you to utilize this book as a personal career development journal where you can start to map out your values and take additional notes as I guide you on your unique career discovery journey. You will begin to connect the dots and see a clearer picture of what is important to you so that you can pursue a career path that's right for you.

SAMPLE VALUES

Intrinsic Values

Achievement	Equality	Power
Balance	Giving to Community	Respect
Belonging	Honesty	Responsibility
Commitment	Independence	Self-Respect
Contributing	Influence	Spirituality
Environmental Awareness	Integrity	Status

Work Environment Values

Aesthetics	Flexible	Quiet
Autonomy	High Earnings	Relaxed
Benefits	Learning	Sense of Community
Comfortable Income	Location	Structured
Excitement	Personal Safety	Time Freedom
Fast-Paced	Predictable	Security

Work Content Values

Adventuresome	Decision-Making	Physical
Advocacy	Detailed	Problem-Solving
Analytical	Helping	Public Contact
Challenging	Initiating	Research
Conceptualizing	Leading-Edge	Risk-Taking
Creative	Organizing	Variety

Work Relationship Values

Caring	Harmony	Open Communication
Competition	Individualism	Recognition
Cooperation	Leadership	Support
Diversity	Loyalty	Teamwork
Friendships	Management	Trust

From the values list, circle at least one (the more the better!) career value in each of the four main categories: **Intrinsic Values**, **Work Environment Values**, **Work Content Values** and **Work Relationship Values**. Take some time to think about why these are important to you and how you can fit them into your career plan. Eventually, you will rank them in order of priority so you can refer to this when you have done a full values, interests, personality, and skills (VIPS) self-assessment.

It's rare to find a career that meets all of your values all the time. But having an awareness of what you value will help you look for, or create, new opportunities that are gratifying. Having an accurate understanding of what you value will help you answer the question: Why should I engage in *this* line of work?

Honor Your Values

Values mean different things to different people so be sure to honor what **you** value in this self-reflection process. If I queried five of my clients who identified the same value of *financial success* and asked them to define it they would each articulate very different answers, and that's a good thing! You alone can determine what you value, so put your blinders on and tune out the advice of well-meaning family and friends for the purpose of this exercise. Really consider what would satisfy **you** in a career.

From the time I was a little girl, I remember my grandfather talking about the importance of finding a job with good benefits. He worked his entire career at General Motors and valued the healthcare and retirement benefits from that company. Before I was old enough to work, I had absorbed my grandfather's career values by family osmosis. I caution you to discover what is important to you so that you are not steered off your personal values course by outside sources. Take the time to make your own values decisions. While I have great respect for my grandfather, over time and with serious self-reflection, I was able to identify my unique career values. I discovered that although we shared the *benefits* value, my complete values list, and how I ranked *benefits*, was much different from that in his viewpoint.

Think about the jobs you have disliked during your career and reflect on the values that were not being met in those situations. This may help you find harmony in a future career opportunity and give you a better understanding about why values predict satisfaction at work.

4.   FIND WHAT MAKES YOU TICK

Now that you have an understanding of what values are and how they drive your career gratification, you can begin to explore how you can match your values to a potential job. The next predictor in your personal self-assessment is **Interests.** Knowing your interests can help you discover your passion and give you clarity about choosing a career. **Interests are the biggest predictors in career selection since we gravitate towards doing what we like.**

One of my favorite assessment tools is the **Strong Interest Inventory® (Strong)** which measures career and leisure interests. Working with a career development professional who is certified to administer and interpret your Strong assessment results can help give you clarity about how your interests impact your career choices.

The Strong tool breaks interests down into six categories:

Realistic – (Doers) People who have athletic or mechanical ability, prefer to work with objects, machines, tools, plants, or animals – or to be outdoors.

Investigative – (Thinkers) People who like to observe, learn, investigate, analyze, evaluate, or solve problems.

Artistic – (Creators) People who have artistic, innovating or intuitional abilities, and like to work in unstructured situations using their imagination or creativity.

Social – (Helpers) People who like to work with people – to inform, enlighten, help, train, develop or cure them, or are skilled with words.

Enterprising – (Persuaders) People who like to work with people influencing, persuading, performing or leading, or managing for organizational goals or for economic gain.

Conventional – (Organizers) People who like to work with data, have clerical or numerical ability, carry things out in detail, or follow through on others' instructions.

There Is No Magic Bullet

While assessments are not meant to give you all the answers and identify perfect career options, these tried-and-true career development industry tools can take you on a deeper guided self-reflection than you might be able to do by yourself.

When I discovered that my Strong code was SAE – Social, Artistic, and Enterprising, it confirmed my love for all things creative, but gave me a new awareness about my interest in helping people. It also identified my interest in persuading and influencing others and helped me discover how I could *perform* in a different way on the job.

I remember fondly a client of mine who worked in the television industry. After a year working at a national affiliate TV station, she came to me because she was unhappy working the news beat and considered changing fields altogether. I encouraged her to think about what she loved about her job as well as what she disliked. It turned out that the news beat was not a good match but the day-to-day tasks at the station in her capacity as a producer still gratified her. After an interests self-reflection exercise she articulated that she loved food, cooking, and products related to the culinary industry. If only she could find work that celebrated her interests.

Rediscover Your Interests

We began to look at ways to match her interests to her skills in telecommunications and eventually discovered that she could marry both in a career. She now works for a Food Network TV program as a producer and is thrilled to go to work every day because her foodie-loving interests are being met.

Keep in mind that your interests may indeed lead to a career opportunity. Why not rediscover what really interests you and begin to look for, or develop, career opportunities in this arena? Here are some action steps to get you started:

- Make a list of your interests (past, present, and a future wish list) and be ready to add to this inventory as you continue with your career self-reflection.
    - ✧ Consider these interest sources, the possibilities are endless:

✓ TV shows, movies, books you read for pleasure, news papers, magazines, etc.

✓ Classes you take for fun, volunteer work, sports, arts, community activities, etc.

✓ Websites or blogs you frequent, things you do when not working, family activities, etc.

What are the patterns you see with your interests? Are there ideas you have about a dream job and how you could incorporate your interests into a career? Remember that your interests change over time so perhaps you are craving a new career opportunity that speaks to your current interests. Keep adding to your interests log and be sure to update it as your interests change. Career development is a journey and you may have many different occupational chapters during your work life.

If the Strong Interest Inventory® is appealing to you, I can help you find resources available in your geographic area to take this assessment. I can also guide you on a customized interest self-discovery so feel free to contact me at www.carolinedowdhiggins.com.

5.   WHY PERSONALITY MATTERS

Following the career development steps of self-evaluating your VIPS (values, interests, personality, and skills) it's time to focus on personality. This happens to be one of my favorite parts of the career reinvention and self-reflection journey. Personality refers to your unique patterns of mental, emotional, physical, and behavioral characteristics.

You may have heard of the **Myers-Briggs Personality Type Indicator™ (MBTI)**, an assessment tool that breaks personality down to four preferences.

- Where do you draw your energy? Do you prefer to focus on the external world of people and actions or are you energized by ideas and feelings of the inner world?

- How do you perceive information? Do you focus on the realities of the present or the possibilities of the future?

- How do you make decisions? Are you guided by objective, analytical reasoning or subjective, personal values?

- What is your need for order in life? Do you prefer to be organized and planned or spontaneous and flexible?

If you have project envy for another colleague's work, it may be time to consider a change.

Channel Your Personality

My MBTI assessment shows that I am an extrovert as one of my four preferences. I am energized by people so I'm happiest in my work environment when I am working with, or presenting to, groups of people. A flashback to my performance days – clearly, I still love an audience! Introverts might enjoy working in smaller groups or one-on-one with people, since their batteries are recharged when they spend time alone. Personality plays a huge role in how you interact and communicate with people in your work environment.

A former colleague of mine thought she had landed the perfect new dream job that enabled her to work from home. Quickly she became lonely in her home office and missed interacting with people on a regular basis. She needed stimulation and variety from interacting with people to be gratified in her work environment. She is now in a similar job but is working in an organization outside of the home, where she comes in contact with people every day. This is a much better match for her personality.

Know Thy Self and honor your inborn personality type to help you find a career that matches your natural tendencies. There are many fabulous career coaches certified to administer and interpret the MBTI, but I caution you to find experienced practitioners who can guide you through this exciting self-reflection. The unofficial online versions cannot give you the full picture of the instrument and how personality plays a role in your career world. Take the time to find someone with credentials, or contact me via my website www.carolinedowdhiggins.com, and I can assist you.

The MBTI now has expanded versions (Step II and Step III) that delve even more deeply into additional competencies and personality traits that may help you further discover your ideal career fit.

6. LEARN FROM THE QUEEN OF TRANSFERABLE SKILLS

My Diva training has actually served me well in all my career endeavors. When I first contemplated a career change, I was paralyzed with fear because I didn't think I was marketable in any other field. My degrees were in music – how was I going to convince an employer that I had other assets to make me a value-add in an organization! In the beginning, I didn't own the various skills in my professional toolbox and took for granted the fact that I was a skilled communicator, writer, marketer, and promoter since these were competencies I employed regularly and easily for my singing gigs.

I also learned the importance of my stage presence and realized that when I spoke, people listened. My trained singing voice translated well into a compelling speaking voice and I was able to get people's attention and keep it by using my voice in a different way. My multicultural awareness, knowledge of foreign languages, and travel savvy also helped me connect with people and relate to diverse constituents. I had a plethora of skills I never showcased consciously and it was exciting to learn how to articulate these with prospective employers.

The Power of my Voice

Every day I speak with women who have no real sense of what their skills are. Simply put, a skill is an ability, based on training or experience, to do something well. We all have skills and the trick is to discover what they are and market them with humble confidence to make ourselves attractive to employers (and beyond) so that we can utilize these skills in the workplace and in life.

As a trained opera singer turned Career and Professional Development Coach, I like to think of myself as the Queen of Transferable Skills. When I was making my unique career transition, most employers were very dubious about what I had to offer. In time, I became my own best advocate and was able to market to others what I did well. Over the years, I have worked with thousands of students, alumni, and clients who have studied everything from Creative Writing to Analytical Chemistry and when they own the transferable skills in their professional toolbox, they understand how degrees and credentials are significant, but only play a part of their overall package in the job market.

I guarantee that you have hidden skills you have not yet owned and embraced. Once you discover your skills you can start to connect the dots with your other VIPS (values, interests and personality) and find opportunities that are a true match for you career-wise.

Skills Treasure Hunt

Since it can be hard to consider your skills alone, I urge you to ask people in your circle of trust (family, friends, and colleagues) to share what they think you do well. Having others help identify your skills can be very powerful, but ultimately you are in control over which skills you choose to market on your new career path.

Ask five trusted individuals who know you well to write down a list of skills they believe you possess. It's best to give them some lead time so they can give serious thought to your unique skill set. Having multiple written lists will allow you to compare what others believe you do well with the list you develop about your own skills. See if you can detect a pattern among the lists.

To get you started, skills fall into three main categories:

Transferable Skills – these can be taken from job to job and are important in many career sectors. Examples include: communication (verbal and written), critical thinking, analysis, leadership, and project management.

Specialized Knowledge – these are skills relevant to a particular job or career field. Examples include: operating laboratory equipment, computer program proficiency, French Cuisine cooking, and foreign language fluency.

Adaptive Skills – these are personal attributes you bring to the professional environment and often the most sought-after by employers. Examples include: motivation, initiative, integrity, flexibility, resilience, and self-management.

Here is a list of sample skills. Take the time to consider what skills are in your toolbox, as well as those you may want to develop. Circle all the skills on the list that you believe you have now. Identify skills you want to develop with a different mark. Use a third notation to indicate the skills you love to use – those that give you strength.

Reflect on multiple skills that show up in the individual categories: **Communication Skills, Humanitarian Skills, Physical Skills, Creative Expression, Mental/Creative, Mental/Analytical,** and **Leadership/Management** to determine if your skills cluster in a particular area.

SAMPLE SKILLS

Communication Skills

Facilitate Groups	Speak Before Groups	Explain
Sell	Interview	Meet the Public
Influence/Persuade	Consult	Promote
Serve as Liaison	Write	Motivate

Humanitarian Skills

Take Care of Others	Listen	Coach
Provide Hospitality	Advocate	Counsel
Train	Instruct	

Physical Skills

Use Body Coordination	Operate Equipment	Repair/Restore
Work Outdoors	Hand Dexterity	Build/Construct

Creative Expression

Produce Events	Food Production	Perform
Compose/Author	Display	Craft-making
Invent	Design	Create Images

Mental/Creative

Use of Memory	Synthesize	Conceptualize
Visualize	Use Intuition	Demonstrate Foresight
Improvise	Brainstorm	

Mental/Analytical

Budget	Manage Records	Evaluate
Calculate	Solve Problems	Analyze
Observe	Monitor	Research
Categorize	Edit	Compute

Leadership/Management

Mediate	Implement	Supervise
Negotiate	Coordinate	Initiate
Organize	Plan	Determine Policy
Delegate	Decision-Making	Follow Through

Rediscovering what you do well can be an exciting journey. Since most jobs require utilizing these skills at least 40 hours per week, you want to make sure that you are employing skills you enjoy that also give you strength.

The VIPS discovery process is very empowering, and positively influences your decisions and actions on the path to finding a great career fit. Awareness about your values will bring you satisfaction. Refining your interests will lead you to a career that is gratifying. Learning about your personality will help you to make occupational choices that suit your preferences. Owning the skills that give you strength will allow you to market yourself as a valuable commodity in the world-of-work.

UTILIZE THE POWER OF THE WOMEN IN YOUR BACKYARD

7. THESE ARE NOT THE CAREERS THEY ORDERED

The research for this book began several years ago when my mentor introduced me to this project. The world was entering a perfect career storm as people were being let go from long-term jobs and dissatisfaction at work was at an all-time high. I set out to interview women who made a transition from one career to another with the hopes of helping others who were considering a move and to provide them with sound advice and action steps.

To date, I have interviewed hundreds women across the USA, Canada, and England. Women came out of the woodwork to answer press inquiries and they shared their wisdom in order to help you learn from their mistakes, as well as their successes. The network is alive and well and almost every woman with whom I spoke recommended another amazing woman from her personal set of contacts that was ideal for this project.

I spoke with women from all walks of life from entry-level twenty-somethings to a woman in her 80s who feels too young to retire. Some changed careers because they were forced to do so after a downsizing or lay-off. Others were looking for new challenges and opportunities to really play to their strengths. Many tapped into their entrepreneurial spirit and embraced an opportunity to be their own boss while others had experienced burn-out or illness from a job that was debilitating.

The Only Thing Constant is Change

Not every change was from a negative work environment. Some of these women sought new ways to stimulate and challenge themselves. Many found innovative opportunities after retooling or seeking additional credentials to empower themselves with more focused skill sets.

The common denominator in all the women I interviewed is that they took matters into their own hands and became their own change agents. It was scary, exhilarating, challenging, and gratifying, running the full gamut of emotions. But in the end – all these women are happy that they pursued a change.

Life is too short to be miserable or unsatisfied at work. We spend the greater part of our waking hours on the job, so I want you to find work that gives you an opportunity to thrive. How you function at work plays a significant role in your happiness at home. My goal is to help you recharge, reignite, and reinvent your career so that you can lead a more satisfying life.

Check out my website: www.carolinedowdhiggins.com as a continuing resource for career and professional development tools and inspiration.

8.   INSPIRATION TO PAY-IT-FORWARD

One of the most gratifying things about interviewing all the women for this book was the realization that they wanted to help others learn from their personal journeys. Many have incorporated a give-back plan in their work environments and others are committed to paying-it-forward and helping others as mentors and advisors.

Throughout my life, I have been fortunate to have mentors who have provided me with expert guidance and I am so pleased to share with you what I have learned. Women are nurturers and I encourage you to look to the women in your life and discover how you can cultivate them. I guarantee that they will reciprocate and support you someday when you are in need.

Career Karma

I believe it takes a village to develop a career in the professional world and the first step is to surround yourself with people you respect and trust. The next step is to be conscious of how you can pay-it-forward and help others in return. We introduce new relationships into our lives every day whether consciously or not, and having the awareness that you can help others is not only good for the karmic circle of life, it's just the right thing to do.

Angela Jia Kim, my very first book interviewee, is CEO and Founder of **Om Aroma & Co.** and Co-Founder of **Savor the Success. com**. She has built her businesses on the *Give, Give, Get* rule when networking. Nothing is more of a turn-off than someone who is in it just for themselves. When you are a genuine networker and operate from a position of authenticity, people are more apt to help you. After all, business is all about human interaction, so considering how you can help others will increase your personal capital.

Paying-it-forward is not just applicable to networking. Whether it is volunteering your time and expertise or donating a percentage of targeted proceeds towards a worthy cause, generosity and the spirit of community are being celebrated on a grand scale.

It's Not the Destination but the Journey

Careers are a lifelong journey and we've all had people that were instrumental in helping us along the way in good times and in bad. Make an effort to be conscious about how you are helping others because what goes around really does come around. It may require a new mindset, behavior, and strategy, but at the most basic level, all it requires is that you make a choice. By giving back, you just might be a role model for someone else and help make the pay-it-forward conduct become the norm for everyone.

9. BUILD YOUR PERSONAL BOARD OF DIRECTORS

It's no secret that a mentor can be a terrific resource as you navigate your personal career path. Some organizations assign mentors; other relationships develop naturally when like-minded people hit it off. If you are your own boss, or don't have a company to connect you with a mentor, you can and should pursue mentors on your own.

Seeking a mentor starts simply with asking for advice from a trusted professional who has *been there and done that* in your desired industry. Start by asking for information and advice and see how the relationship develops. You will know when you have made an authentic connection with someone and taken the relationship beyond colleague to personal guru.

Mentors help to improve upon your strengths and guide you along your path to success, providing inspiration and resources that come from experience. A mentor can also help you set and accomplish your goals. Mentors will guide you and offer practical ideas about how you might do things differently. We all need at least one mentor who can speak candidly and offer constructive criticism, even when we don't want to hear it.

Build Your Personal Resource Team

Mentors should help boost your self-confidence and empower you to achieve and overcome obstacles. But don't think that you need one perfect mentor to help you on your professional way. In reality, life is full of mentors that can advise you day by day, sharing important bits of wisdom incrementally over time. I encourage you to take a close look at the many people in your life and reflect on how they may actually be mentoring you right now. Build your own personal Board of Directors, your personal posse to guide you in your career pursuits.

You can gain a wealth of support and resources with a team. Sometimes these relationships develop organically and sometimes you need to take the driver's seat and ask others for help. Mentors volunteer their time and experience, so always show them your respect. Listen, don't argue – and always follow up with personal thank-you note or gesture of gratitude. The mentor relationship is powerful and valuable, so cultivate it wisely and be mindful of how you can help others and keep the circle of wisdom continuous by becoming a mentor yourself.

I know that many of you reading this book will make a connection to at least one woman who has been showcased. I urge you to reach out to these women and incorporate them into your personal resource team. They understand the power of positive relationships and have all benefitted from the guidance of others. At the end of their stories in each chapter, they provide valuable resources which they utilized during their career transition that may be advantageous to you.

10. UNLOCK YOUR PASSION

A recurring bit of career advice from the women with whom I conducted interviews across the globe was to *find your passion*. It sounds simple but I am shocked at how few people are actually in tune with their personal passions. I'm not talking about romance; rather, I'm asking you to consider what motivates and inspires you on a regular basis and how you can incorporate this into your career.

In his book, *The One Thing You Need to Know About Great Managing, Leading and Sustained Individual Success*, Marcus Buckingham shared a statistic:

"Only twenty percent of people report that they are in a role where they have the chance to do what they do best every day, and the rest of the world feels like their strengths are not being called upon every day."

The operative word is *role* – those in the rest of the eighty percent are not mediocre or incompetent, they are just not in the right role. I challenge you to consider what gives you strength and by doing so, discover your passion.

How Do I Find My Passion?

First you need to understand what passion in this context means. Passion can be expressed as a feeling of excitement, enthusiasm, or compelling emotion towards something. A person is said to have a passion for something when she has a strong positive affinity for it. In the career world, passion is something for which you are extremely enthusiastic and can imagine pursuing as a vocation without calling it *work*.

Answer these questions to help discover your possible career passions:

- What do you love to do in your free time?
- What are the skills that come naturally to you without much thought or effort?
- If you had no limitations (financial, education, location, etc.) and could do any job, what would you choose?
- What types of things energize you?
- What activities, subjects, or causes have you been deeply involved with?
- What are some areas in which your family and friends consider you an expert?
- When you are online, or at a bookstore, what subjects most appeal to you?
- Do you possess deeply held beliefs for which you have a calling in life?
- What are the types of things that people ask you for help with?
- What are some of the big goals you want to achieve in life?

I have always been passionate about public speaking. Perhaps it's part of my performance gene. I am energized by opportunities to teach or present to groups where I can tap into my enthusiasm for commanding an audience. My passion has been monetized by speaking nationally, giving workshops, writing, and developing a robust coaching practice. When I am speaking to a group of people and engaging them in a conversation about a special topic, time flies for me, and it never feels like work. My goal is to create more opportunities to play to my passions and to deliver messages that help people own their strengths and self-confidence in the workplace.

By adding your passions to your self-assessment results you will begin to see what you are best at, what you enjoy most, and what areas of advice and expertise people seek from you. You can now begin researching careers that honor your passions and your VIPS.

Who is in Your Circle of Trust?

A small step in owning your strengths is to query the people in your circle of trust. As I mentioned in the previous chapter, find friends, family members, or colleagues whom you believe will give you authentic feedback. Ask them to share at least five things they believe you do well. It can be very empowering to see how others perceive your strengths. Ultimately, you are in charge of what you believe you do well, those things that actually give you **strength,** but the feedback is a great point of departure on your personal strengths quest.

If you prefer a more structured approach, I recommend: *Strengths Finder 2.0*, a book by Tom Rath, coupled with an online resource tool that will take you through a personalized strengths assessment.

It can be very liberating to focus on your strengths and not fixate on your weaknesses. After all, you are not broken – it's possible you simply need to unlock your passion by discovering your strengths to find the right career role.

11. WHY EVERY WOMAN NEEDS A REINVENTION TOOLBOX

It's fine to learn about great career reinventions from other women's stories. But my goal for this book is to provide you with resources and action steps so that you can create the change in your life you want to achieve.

Some career changers will recharge and reignite their careers with small-scale tweaks and strength-building opportunities. Others will undergo a full-scale reinvention. At the end of each chapter, I have created a *Reinvention Toolbox* packed with exercises and action steps to empower you with self-confidence and strategies to achieve your goals.

I will take you on a guided career development journey to help you get to know yourself, and to understand the importance of emotional intelligence and resiliency in the work place. I will teach you to build and steward relationships and to tap into the power of your personal resource team. You will learn from me and many fabulous women who have done it themselves, how to own your passion, take calculated risks, and live an authentic career life.

Your Guided Tour for Reinvention

You will also learn to navigate the *new normal* of this career world and become your own best advocate with the art of self-promotion. Should you decide to utilize a career coach, I will share tips and best practices to get the most from your coaching relationship. My goal is to help you make excellent choices and prioritize yourself so that you can continue to nurture your families and loved ones.

I will empower you to have the courage to put yourself first so you can thrive in a career that fits your passions and your values, interests, personality, and skills. The *Reinvention Toolbox* will help celebrate the new you – recharged, reignited, and reinvented!

Now it's time to meet, and learn from, the amazing women who have successfully transitioned and are leading gratifying new career lives.

3

TURN SURVIVE INTO THRIVE

The women in this chapter have all dealt with extreme adversity that impacted their careers. Through perseverance, positive energy, hard work, and tapping into their passions – they have turned survive into *thrive*.

12. JESSI WALTER BRELSFORD: WHEN LIFE HANDS YOU LEMONS...MAKE CUPCAKES

A Harvard graduate with an Economics degree, Jessi Walter Brelsford was the picture of success in her Vice President, six-figure position at Bear Stearns in New York City. She was young, thriving in her corporate career, and enjoying the life of an executive woman when one day everything changed. Bear Stearns and JP Morgan merged, and Jessi was laid off. In a matter of moments the rising young executive in the New York financial district became an unemployed Ivy League grad looking for work.

From Corporate Maven to Cupcake Queen

As so many have experienced in the largest unemployment recession since the Great Depression, diving back into another job in the corporate world was not so easy. While Jessi enjoyed her Wall Street job, this new setback was really an opportunity for her to reassess her values and interests and reflect on what was really important in her life.

When life gives you lemons you make lemonade – well in this case, Jessi made cupcakes and a myriad of other delicious foods! She decided to combine her love for kids and food in a practical way. She always enjoyed cooking and, although she does not have kids of her own, her family considers her the Pied Piper for kids, who enjoys spending time with her 23 first cousins. *Cupcake Kids* started as a hobby and blossomed into a full-fledged business soon after. (*Cupcake Kids* was later renamed **Taste Buds Kitchen**.)

At first it began with birthday parties where she would share her culinary talents with friends who wanted to make their child's party extra special. In came Jessi, who showed the kids how to cook well-balanced and healthy foods, teaching them about math, measuring, nutrition, and following directions with this hands-on birthday celebration. The parents and the kids loved Jessi's events and soon she was sought after for the kid party circuit.

Happy Kids and Katie Couric!

Tapping into her entrepreneurial spirit, Jessi developed a business plan utilizing her Harvard degree and her tenure on Wall Street. She created a company that provides experiential cooking opportunities designed to be fun and informative so kids can learn about food and nutrition. Jessi believes that creativity plays a vital role in childhood development by helping to build self-confidence and independence.

As a Division I swimmer at Harvard, Jessi developed a competitive edge, a strong work ethic, and impeccable technique. These transferable skills have served her well with **Taste Buds Kitchen** as did the countless classes she took at the Institute of Culinary Education and the French Culinary Institute.

"I use tons of the skills that I learned on Wall Street. Everything from working with clients to building modeling spreadsheets, to managing people. Wall Street was a great learning experience for me where I was able to delve into the business world of financing and operations. That experience has helped me immensely as I work to develop my own company. I also love connecting with people and telling them about my business. I truly believe in what I'm doing and I know firsthand all of the benefits that **Taste Buds Kitchen** has to offer to so when I meet someone new, I find it natural to tell them all about it."

Feeding the Business

But what about the financial challenges of starting a new business? Jessi says that she is supporting herself partly from the business profit and in part from her savings as she continues to pour most of her proceeds back into the company. She has big plans in store and this company is an investment in her future.

Reflecting on what she knows now that she did not know when starting her business, Jessi shares that she would try to narrow her market sooner. "I've spent a lot of time trying different lines of my business. The more focused and organized a business, the better brand you build and the better your success."

While Jessi admits that time is the biggest challenge for her one-woman business, she relies on the advice and wisdom from her Dad and Grandfather – fellow entrepreneurs who have mentored her throughout this process. Jessi appeared on CBS Evening News with Katie Couric and it's fair to say that **Taste Buds Kitchen** is really cookin' now!

What's New?

A lot has changed since I first spoke with Jessi. An important change was the name of her business – it's now **Taste Buds Kitchen**, which doesn't limit her to a cupcake theme. One of the lessons Jessi shared is the importance of researching a business name, finding the right one, and sticking with it. It's important to do it right the first time, but this hiccup didn't derail Jessi's efforts.

Although the business changed names, it kept growing under Jessi's diligent care. **Taste Buds Kitchen** now enjoys a specially-built kitchen in New York City where their parties and lessons – for kids and adults – are held. Also, **Taste Buds Kitchen** was able to land a coveted spot in kid-famous retail store FAO Schwarz. And to keep the business growing, **Taste Buds Kitchen** now offers franchise opportunities for passionate, want-to-be-business owners across the country.

To support all this growth, Jessi added new team members. On staff are a Class Director & Executive Chef, an Events Director, a School Program Director, and the FAO Manager and Retail Specialist. And it's through the development of this team that Jessi learned her next lesson – the importance of delegation and prioritization. Since time management is still a big challenge, Jessi has focused on learning to let others do things so she can focus on leading the business. "I have to do what only I can do, and get help where I can." Also important is staying focused on what needs to be done now, and knowing what can wait. Early in the company's history, all her time was spent "on the basics." With the growth of her business comes many other activities – "choices" that have to be made concerning where to spend time, attention, and dollars.

Jessi knows that her high tolerance for risk was a strength for her in her career growth. She "didn't need a lot of security," so she felt free to charge forward with her passion. And while she appreciates the flexibility of having her own business, she "has worked harder than ever," to make it a success. Jessi noted that "it took four years of constant, hard work" to get her idea from paper to reality.

But the hard work doesn't always feel like work to Jessi, She defines career success as "supporting myself doing something I love, and having the flexibility to fit it into my life." It's no wonder that **Taste Buds Kitchen** is thriving and growing. "I'm so thrilled I did it," said Jessi, "and I would love to keep growing and expanding in the future."

Jessi's Advice and Action Steps:

- Take the time to develop your business plan/strategy; you can't be everything for everyone so know your market. Seek out help if you need it. This is your foundation and extremely important for new entrepreneurs.
- Do your best every day – you can always turn a negative into a positive.
- Market your new business – utilize your network. It's essential that everybody you know helps you promote your business.

- Be prepared to work harder than you ever thought possible if you start your own business – you have only yourself to rely on.
- Consider people you can hire for freelance work as needed. I hire school teachers and Chefs to help me with large parties and events. They are good with kids and appreciate the additional work on weekends and after school – it's a win-win for all.

Jessi's Resources:

Taste Buds Kitchen: www.tastebudskitchen.com
Savor the Success: www.savorthesuccess.com
Ladies Who Launch: www.ladieswholaunch.com

66Knock and the door will be opened to you.99

– Book of Matthew 7:7

ↄ ↄ ↄ ↄ

13. CHRISTINE CLIFFORD: DON'T FORGET TO LAUGH™

Christine Clifford's story is new to the second edition and will resonate with so many women who have experienced divorce, cancer, or both. Her reinvention has impacted her mind, body, spirit, and career. Her sheer grit, determination, and resilience have inspired me from the first time we spoke and no matter how hard things get, she has taught me how to laugh.

A Senior Executive Vice President for The SPAR Group out of New York, Christine Clifford was also the top salesperson in this multi-million dollar retail services firm and seemed to have it all. But at age 40, she was diagnosed with breast cancer and her life changed – forever. She felt as if her life had changed direction suddenly and with no notice, as if someone had unplugged the treadmill while she was still running on it.

She may have cracked the glass ceiling with her executive rank in a male driven industry, but navigating cancer was her toughest challenge ever. Throughout her career at SPAR she was negotiating multi-million dollar contracts and traveling extensively. One year she clocked 298 days on the road and admits that she missed a big part of her young children's lives because her focus was on work.

Priority Epiphany

After a year of surgery, aggressive chemotherapy, radiation, and the loss of her hair, Christine had a dramatic change in her priorities. She wanted a career that would allow her to travel less, spend more time with her kids, and still provide her with significant earning power.

Four weeks after surgery, she awoke in the middle of the night with a vision - of cartoons. Over 50 cancer-related cartoons started popping into her head. Christine realized that in all the support, gifts, calls and messages she'd received, no one ever brought her anything that made her laugh. In fact, she noticed that people were actually careful to avoid humorous conversation or topics around her. Yet, she recognized that laughter provided a necessary release from the tension and even promoted recovery.

So, Christine decided to do something about it and created **The Cancer Club®** which is now the world's leading source of gifts and inspiration for people dealing with cancer. It took a little over 2 years for Christine to phase out of her SPAR career since she still needed the health care benefits until her new business venture was profitable. But she built a strong foundation during those early years and the company thrived.

Don't Forget to Laugh™

Not only is this tag line trademarked by Christine for **The Cancer Club®**, it represents the heart and soul of her company. She firmly believes that laughter is the best medicine and has written many books that will inspire and bring a smile to the face of those dealing with cancer.

Her books: *Not Now...I'm Having a No Hair Day*; *Our Family Has Cancer, Too!* (written for children); *Cancer Has Its Privileges: Stories of Hope & Laughter*; *Your Guardian Angel's Gift*, and *Inspiring Breakthrough Secrets to Live Your Dreams* are filled with award winning cartoons that are a signature of **The Cancer Club®** and Christine's commitment to healing with a smile, a lift, and a laugh!

The Cancer Club® website is an amazing resource with tips and products – such as healing hats, inspirational DVDs, and an exercise video for women recovering from breast cancer – to help people cope with the realities of cancer. Christine also travels nationally giving talks and workshops to spread her message of healing and hope.

One Move at a Time

Always the savvy business woman, Christine had a breakthrough deal with **The Cancer Club®** when her exercise video (*One Move at a Time*), developed exclusively for women recovering from breast cancer, sold over 25,000 copies to a major pharmaceutical company. But the challenge of running your own business is that you also wear all the hats, all of the time.

Christine does everything for **The Cancer Club®** from the inspirational speeches to posting products purchased on her site. She calls herself a 99.9% one-woman band but does have 2 graphic designers and a virtual assistant whom she contracts for some tasks.

She shared that having her freedom is amazing. Running her own company, she can prioritize life and family around her work schedule. She walks 4 miles every day – in sun, rain, and even snow – and is accountable to no one but herself. Christine also doesn't take life for granted and feels so blessed to have this second chance.

Be Your Own Valentine

One of Christine's mottos is that *everything happens for a reason* and she lives that philosophy in multiple ways. Now a two-time divorcee, Christine is on a mission to empower other women who are divorcing so they may heal, grow, and gain the confidence they need to be in charge of their lives again.

She is the co-founder of **Divorcing Divas®** and is working to help other women live happily ever after knowing that divorce is not the end…it's the beginning. Through support, education, resources, and hope, Christine and her business partner Barb Greenberg present seminars and support groups to help women in need. She is also working on a humorous book about divorce.

They have developed 10 Divorcing Divas Tips that others may find helpful:

1. Don't Panic
2. Take Four Steps Forward
3. Surround Yourself With Supportive Friends and Family
4. Realize Your Life Will Never Be the Same
5. Research all the Possibilities
6. Do Something Special for Yourself
7. Don't Beat Yourself Up
8. You are the Source of Your Happiness
9. Learn to Forgive
10. Don't Forget to Laugh

Give Yourself Permission

As if one successful business was not enough, Christine is at the helm of **The Cancer Club®**, **Divorcing Divas®** and **Christine Clifford Enterprises®** where she manages her public speaking career and consulting practice. Christine has earned the prestigious Certified Speaking Professional (CSP) credential from the National Speaker's Association and has received accolades from audiences and speaker bureaus nationwide. She reinvented herself and her life to focus on what really matters.

Having a disease like cancer gave Christine permission to make a change. She believes the trade- off of the mega corporate career and salary is well worth it for her new multi-faceted career. While the income is not the same, she is making a good living doing what she loves.

Christine shared with me that this is her one and only shot at life and she intends to make the best of it. She has made herself, her adult kids, and laughter her top priorities. Waking up every day, Christine can't wait to see what happens because life is grand!

Resilience Personified

In my original conversation with Christine, she talked about how unpredictable life can be, and that she was determined to make the best of the time she has. That unpredictability showed itself again when Christine's cancer recurred 20 years after her first diagnosis. When we spoke recently, she was in the hospital, fighting for her health with her characteristic optimism and sense of humor. Christine told me that "her cancer story" (from the first diagnosis) was getting old, and that this recurrence will give her new material to use in her books and talks.

In the recent past, Christine had been spending more of her time on her consulting business. She is an expert in marketing businesses using a three-part process – developing a "brand brief", creating "knock-your-socks-off" marketing pieces, and creating strategies to get business. The **Divorcing Divas®** business is also going strong. From her hospital bed, Christine was working on an upcoming conference for **Divorcing Divas®.**

Asked to reflect on her career change many years ago, Christine is clear that she has no regrets and would change nothing. Understandably, cancer is Christine's primary focus now. She explained that this journey is very different from that last time – "I'm 20 years older, not married, and I don't have small children to worry about. Unlike last time, I've had to undergo major surgery and have had complications from chemotherapy treatment. It's challenging to juggle three businesses while going through treatment!"

Christine laughs as she tells me that, although she is a branding and marketing expert, she didn't follow her own advice. "You should put all your time, money and resources into one endeavor until you become expert in your field. Instead, I've been supporting three businesses!" She goes on to explain that she loves the variety of managing and growing three different businesses, and that she loves all three.

I asked how she gets any work/life balance with the demands on her time. "I never handle a piece of paper, email, or phone call more than once. This has worked flawlessly for me and gives me the free time to walk four miles five times per week, and play lots of golf. I must be conscious about making time for myself," to achieve that balance.

Life is uncertain and brief. Make the most of the time you have, and keep your sense of humor intact through the journey. Christine's story is an inspiration to us all.

Christine's Advice and Action Steps:

- If you believe in your product, your service, and your company – anything is possible.
- Make good hiring choices with outside vendors and contractors.
- Solicit feedback but don't let negative input stop you from moving forward – trust your gut.
- Use humor to deal with adversity.

Resources:

Christine Clifford Enterprises: www.ChristineClifford.com
The Cancer Club: www.CancerClub.com
Divorcing Divas: www.DivorcingDivas.net

66 It's always ok in the end – if it isn't ok, it isn't the end. 99

– Anonymous

❧ ❧ ❧ ❧

14. MARY McMANUS: A GIFT FROM THE HEART

Mary McManus, Boston Marathon finisher, yogini, inspirational speaker, published poet, entrepreneur and former award winning social worker turned adversity on its head after being diagnosed with post-polio syndrome in mid-life. Mary turned to writing inspirational poetry and then yoga to heal her life. She never imagined the path that would unfold before her.

A Brave New World

At the age of 53, Mary was diagnosed with post-polio syndrome, a result of her original polio affliction that began when she was just five years old. Four years into her healing journey, Mary discovered that unresolved trauma from her childhood was a factor in the debilitating symptoms of post-polio syndrome. She always persevered and made the best of a very difficult physical situation, getting around with a cane or a wheelchair when her condition got worse.

After 25 years as a social worker, Mary was eager to finish 3 more years at her job with the Department of Veterans Affairs in Boston, MA, so she could retire with full benefits. The post-polio syndrome became increasingly debilitating and there were days when Mary literally could not get out of bed. She worked with a team of occupational and physical therapists to help get her to the 3 year retirement goal, but ultimately, continuing to work at the VA was counter-therapeutic to the gains she was making in rehab.

Her job as a social worker at the Department of Veterans Affairs was incapacitating both physically and emotionally, so based on the advice of her doctors, Mary left her award-winning career with a heavy heart. But Mary is a deeply spiritual person; she believed that divine intervention was part of her new life and began to write as part of her catharsis and personal therapy.

Poetic Justice

Mary always loved to write. She created original poetry to commemorate and celebrate special occasions for family and friends. The poems just flowed out of her after she left her job as a social worker and she knew then that there was a bright future ahead and a new career opportunity. Mary's husband encouraged her to create *New World Greeting Cards*, original poetry for every occasion.

For two years Mary grieved the loss of her career as a social worker. But, she has a dream team of support in her family and has created a new identity as a poet that has tapped her creative talents.

How does one make a living as a poet? This was a concern for Mary too, and she pulled out her entire retirement account to fund *New World Greeting Cards* with the blessing of her husband and her daughter, Ruth Anne, who said, "You can't afford not to pursue this new poetry business and you should write a book!" Mary believes that when you are on the right path and you believe in yourself, everything else will fall into place.

Poetry in Motion

Like any author, Mary promotes her books and her inspirational journey. She has tapped into social media resources including Facebook and LinkedIn. She subscribed to Help A Reporter Out (HARO) to pitch her story. She authors a blog and has found a wonderfully receptive audience for her gift in the yoga community.

Mary is a frequent guest on radio shows and also builds her audience through the yoga community. As a Boston University and Boston College alumna, Mary has also reaped the benefits of the alumni networks at both schools. She even took on a public relations intern from Boston University to help her initially grow the business. Mary has discovered 'non-traditional' venues to share her journey and her books. She was invited to host a table at the Hyannis Race Expo because of her charitable donations and inspirational journey. She was an exhibitor and inspirational speaker at Boston GreenFest to share her journey and her strategies for health and wellness.

Setting Sail

Mary's daughter was right about books being a part of her mother's new career. Mary discovered the gift of poetry in her soul. She has since written three books of poetry: *New World Greetings: Inspirational Poetry and Musings for a New World* and a sequel: *Set Sail for a New World: Healing a Life Through the Gift of Poetry*. When her business began to teeter and sales of her books were not forthcoming, Mary began to think that maybe this poetry path wasn't for her. She then met an amazing healer and teacher who, after a healing session with breath work, told her to go home and write a beautiful poem.

Mary once again felt the stirrings of creativity in her soul and gave birth to *Songs of Freedom: Poems from a Healing Odyssey*. She is currently working on Volume II. The relationship with her first publisher did not turn out as she had hoped. She realized she could self-publish and uploaded her book to Amazon Kindle and self published the paperback using Create Space where she has complete creative control and is paid royalties much higher than her first publisher paid her. She is so excited that she had her first international sale of *Songs of Freedom: Poems From a Healing Odyssey*.

While the new career journey is scary at times, especially without a steady paycheck and benefits, Mary appreciates many new work values such as freedom, autonomy, the opportunity to create a balanced day and being accountable only to herself.

> "I create how I want to measure success now. It's no longer by how many patients I saw in a day and believe me it's taken awhile to let go of those values that were instilled and drilled into me after almost 20 years at the VA."

Still, there are challenges for Mary in grieving the loss of her social worker role identity.

> "I was at the top of my game as a social worker at the VA. I received many awards and accolades. Stepping way outside of my comfort zone and doing something I had never done before with a business, as an author and now yoga, made me feel vulnerable. Starting a new business venture and new path in

life after just being diagnosed with a progressive neurological disease is a challenge but I'm up for the task!"

Words of Wisdom

Mary has learned to give herself quiet time to ask for direction and listen to her voice of intuition. When Mary left the VA, she used a 30 day journal with 3 sections for each day to write down her goals and action steps. She continually asks herself "What do I want to do if I know I can only succeed?" She uses a gratitude journal giving thanks for what she has achieved and to focus on guidance for next steps.

An avid reader, Mary seeks poetic inspiration as well as life lessons from authors like Dr. Bernie Siegel, Peter A Levine, Ana Forrest and Matthew Sanford. She finds an incredible font of wisdom from her yoga teachers. Mary has given herself the gift of following her joy and bliss and makes time for creative outlets in her life. She has discovered the health benefits of yoga to manage stress and fear, and to forestall the progression of post-polio syndrome. She was limited in what she could do physically during the initial phase of her transition due to post-polio syndrome so she turned inward to meditation and visualization to harness the power of her mind and her spirit.

Perhaps the greatest physical challenge Mary has accomplished was completing a Boston Marathon, one of the most difficult marathon courses in the country.

26.2 Miles

Mind over matter does not begin to describe Mary's tenacity and passion to overcome obstacles. She would not let post-polio syndrome get the best of her physically so she decided to face the lion directly and push her body to the limit by running the Boston Marathon.

Her daughter and husband joined her for this personal quest and trained and ran the event with her to lend their support and enthusiasm for her journey. Mary worked with a professional trainer and physical therapist to get her into marathon shape.

Team McManus crossed the finish line of the 113th Boston Marathon at 4:49 pm – 7 hours and 49 minutes after taking their start at

Hopkinton, Massachusetts with mobility and visually impaired runners. In the ultimate gesture of giving back, *Team McManus raised over $10,000 for Spaulding Rehab Hospital – the facility which helped Mary take the first steps on her healing journey.*

Conquering Heartbreak Hill

The Boston Marathon is known for the treacherous Heartbreak Hill segment of the course that challenges the most accomplished of runners. Mary crossed the finish line for the marathon and tackled Heartbreak Hill which is a metaphor for her life. She is a woman who overcomes obstacles.

Now that the marathon is over, Mary continues to manage her symptoms of post-polio syndrome and her social security disability is helping to resolve her financial challenges. She wished she would have applied for social security disability benefits sooner so that she would have freed up her creative energies rather than doing a lot of reacting out of fear about her finances.

Second Act of the Second Act

Mary's focus has shifted from New World Greeting Cards to delving deeper into her yoga practice, blogging, and promoting her latest poetry book, *Songs of Freedom: Poems From a Healing Odyssey.* She has become a voice for trauma survivors and healing the mind-body connection. She continues to delight in creating original poems and keepsake gifts for friends and family.

With the wisdom she now has, she wants to give back and help others to heal. Mary realized that she needed to heal herself – mind, body and Spirit. Her poetry in *Songs of Freedom* speaks to the journey that trauma survivors take as they heal and reconnect with their true selves. She looks forward to sharing her gifts as a healer and a poet as the curtain rises on the second act of her second act.

Mary has brought joy, hope, healing, and celebration to others through her gift of poetry. She has overcome monumental challenges in her life and is thriving in a new career that she never would have imagined just a few years ago. As far as an award winning career?

Mary was one of six finalists for Brookline Woman of the Year and was honored at their annual award ceremony "Women Who Inspire Us." She was interviewed by Boston's # 1 FM radio station, Magic 106.7, for their Exceptional Women Show. She publishes her blog daily, and one of the greatest honors Mary receives is when she gets feedback about how her journey and words of wisdom have blessed the lives of her readers. Indeed, it is a new world for Mary McManus and a brilliant reinvention.

What's New?

When I reconnected with Mary, things in her life had continued to evolve. Her third book of inspirational poetry, *Songs of Freedom: Poems from a Healing Odyssey,* is now available on Amazon.com, and she is working on a second volume of *Songs of Freedom.* Although she continues to write poetry, she learned that the greeting card business was not for her. "I'm not a business person," said Mary, adding that she came to realize that "it wasn't what I was supposed to be doing." Meanwhile, she pursued her goal of becoming a yoga instructor, and she is proud to share that she is now a certified yoga teacher.

Mary remembers being in a place when she needed the healing of yoga, but there was no one trained in how to work with her specific needs. Her focus now is to bring the healing of yoga practice to people who struggle with being at home in their bodies. Her future dream is "to bring yoga back to the population I had to leave for my healing" by working with trauma groups for veterans and the rehabilitation population in general.

Mary told us that the career change to yoga instructor was easier because she had been through the first career change in starting her greeting card company. Since she'd already "done something I'd never done before," it was easier to work with fear and doubt as it surfaced. What was different, however, was going out and experiencing social interactions with others. In the process, Mary said she "has fully integrated back into life - coming out from behind her computer screen – to rejoin the human race."

No change is without challenge, even if it was meant to be. Mary has to closely monitor her physical stamina. She also had to get beyond her internal perceptions of being " less-than, not good enough, the oldest person in her yoga teacher training class and practicing yoga with modifications." In general, it was the challenge of letting herself be vulnerable again, and it's a challenge she meets head-on, every day, in her practice and in her life.

When asked what she would have done differently, her answer was simple: "Not struggle as much against it. I would have let go of fear and relax more into the transition." A good lesson for us all.

Mary's advice for someone thinking about change is simple: "Go for it! Really allow the universe to support you… It's so there!"

Mary's Advice and Action Steps:

- Give some of your talents away and the rewards will come back tenfold.
- Be open to where the journey may lead. Remember when one door closes another door always opens. When it seemed as though my business was 'failing' it was an opportunity to explore another path which serves both my needs and the highest good. Be flexible. Stay tuned in to your intuition.
- Tune into your passion and tune out voices of negativity. When things don't seem as though they are moving forward, it's okay to take a break, but don't abandon your true passion and purpose.
- Develop a dream team of support and sever ties with people who are not supporting you in your new path.

Resources:

Mary's Blog: www.marymcmanus.com
South Boston Yoga: www.SouthBostonYoga.net

> "When you get a diagnosis, don't play to the result, take it day by day"

– Michael J Fox

෴ ෴ ෴ ෴

15. CAROLE BRODY FLEET: A WIDOW LEARNS TO HEAL IN HIGH HEELS

At the young age of 40, Carole Brody Fleet had a thriving career in the cosmetics industry. She built a new house from her Mary Kay Cosmetics earnings and became a national winner of top sales awards and numerous accolades. But none of her success could soothe the deep pain she experienced when her husband died after a two-year battle with Lou Gehrig's disease. As a young widow with an 11-year-old daughter, Carole had days when she literally could not get out of bed.

Loss is ageless, but the issues young widows deal with are unique. Five years after her husband's death, Carole had begun to recover financially; massive medical bills had depleted her bank account, even with a steady income. After the long journey of emotional healing she was ready to share her widow's wisdom with others who had experienced a loss. She wanted to utilize her experiences to educate women who needed a resource, and thus her writing career began. It has since become her passion and life mission to bring the message of hope, promise, and abundance to those who have been touched by the pain and challenge of widowhood, regardless of age.

The Things People Don't Tell You

Carole scoured the available grief and bereavement books looking for help to get her through the difficult times after her husband's death. What frustrated her most was the lack of information about what to do next, after the grief. She needed help getting her benefits from the government, battling with insurance companies, and dealing with the nitty-gritty details of widowhood that nobody was willing to discuss out loud.

She needed help with practical and financial transitioning back into the world of the living. Carole was a young and attractive woman but she struggled with the widow stigma and often felt guilty if she put on makeup or her signature high heels. And what about dating again? Could she ever consider romance again or was she doomed to be a lifelong widow wearing black?

The Black Widow

Carole remembers a lucid moment at her husband's funeral when she realized she was technically a widow but did not want to succumb to the stereotypical image of a widow – she wore stilettos after all!

Current research tells us that 40 percent of single mothers in the U.S. are widows. Carole was more determined than ever to build a support network for other women; she began a series of public speaking engagements and became known as the "inspiration lady." Appreciative widows came out of the woodwork to begin their healing journey with Carole and her audience grew from local presentations to national appearances like ABC's *Good Morning America* and a feature article in *Women's World* magazine.

In order to focus her new calling and tap into her longtime joy of writing, Carole penned the book *Widows Wear Stilettos: A Practical and Emotional Guide for the Young Widow.* She also authored and served as executive producer for her CD, *Widows Wear Stilettos: What Now?* Carole's goal is to effect positive change and help women deal with the realities of widowhood with answers to the tough questions nobody else was willing to address.

Widow on a Mission

In addition to her many national multimedia appearances on radio, TV, and as a motivational speaker, Carole's Widows Wear Stiletto's website is widely recognized as a leading resource in bereavement recovery. She receives between 800 and 1000 new messages from widows each week and takes pride in reading each one.

The plight of the young widow is unique and Carole's niche market approach deals with issues such as:

- Taking ownership of your personal healing journey.
- Coping with the comments, opinions, and insights that you may encounter from others.
- Fashion, beauty, diet and exercise tips including quick and easy recipes.
- Advice on how and when to re-enter the world of dating and what to do once you get there.

- Financial and practical transitioning with how-to suggestions, checklists, and guidelines.
- Helping children of all ages adapt and transition after the loss of a parent.

In addition, Carole also provides personal coaching to help widows move forward in their healing. Fully aware that some clients need the care of medical or psychiatric professionals, Carole's coaching intent is to serve as a complementary resource, as a widow who has walked in those shoes.

You'll Never Walk Alone

The journey of authoring books has indeed been a challenge as the publishing industry is inundated with new authors. For every twenty-five million writers, only five percent get publishing contracts. But Carole was determined to help others and developed a thick skin; with her resilience and tenacity she landed a contract with New Horizon Press. Her newest publication, *Widows Wear Stilettos: The Answer Book – The Ultimate Question, Answer and Reference Guide for Widows*, is forthcoming.

The most important message Carole provides is that widows have resources and a large network of fellow widows for support and encouragement. The empowerment of widows is what drives Carole on a daily basis, and above all, the message is that these women are not alone.

Life Support for Widows

Widowhood is a frightening prospect for any woman, but the reality of becoming a widow in your forties, thirties or twenties can be terrifying. Not only must one face normal grief, but also the additional painful issues that arise with the death of a young person. Because of catastrophic events such as the World Trade Center tragedy and the Gulf and Iraqi Wars, the demographic of young widows has grown suddenly and dramatically.

Carole's books, website, and motivational speeches have proven to be a form of life support for many young widows. She has been featured in many magazines, newspapers and websites, including: Psychology Today, The Houston Chronicle, More, Cosmopolitan, Military Officer, Philadelphia Daily News and Orange County Register. She was a featured contributor in the Hartford Courant and Boston Metro News and continues to write articles in national publications.

Today Carole resides in Lake Forest, California, with her daughter, three cats and over 100 pairs of shoes. Yes, this widow has begun a new life and is dedicated to helping others who have experienced a devastating loss do the same.

What's New?

When I checked in with Carole for an update, her good work has continued to grow. She originally thought, "All I was going to do was a book…" but her passion led her to even greater achievements.

Carole and Widows Wear Stilettos, Inc. (WWS) have formed a non-profit called the First Month Foundation. The Foundation raises funds to provide financial assistance focusing on three areas: bridging expenses pending receipt of a death certificate, helping with the cost of a grave marker or headstone, and providing "camperships" (the registration fee) for those who need help to attend the annual Camp Widow International Conferences, put on by the Soaring Spirits Loss Foundation (SSLF). Carole has also partnered with the SSLF in presenting at "Camp Widow" programs.

In 20+ states in the U.S., numerous WWS peer-led support groups have taken shape. Also, her second book was released, answering the most common questions that the widowed generally have, both immediately following a spouse's death, as well as months and even years thereafter. Questions are excerpted from thousands of actual letters Carole received from widows. The book is called *Happily Even After, A Guide to Getting Through (And Beyond) The Grief of Widowhood*.

Carole has reached an even greater audience as a weekly contributor to The Huffington Post. And it's in this medium that Carole has learned some lessons. She said she was "dragged kicking and screaming into social media," but now sees the power of the tools. Her advice to others is to "find someone in their 20s," who can fill in technology gaps for you.

On a personal note, Carole was happy to report that she met a wonderful man, and after a 5-year courtship, they were married. Because her spouse is English, she learned all about the "Widow's Law" which now allows eligible widows or widowers of U.S. citizens to qualify for permanent resident status regardless of how long the couple was married (there used to be a two-year requirement).

Amid all this activity, Carole sees areas of even greater need in the "overlooked and underserved" demographics – such as the "17-year-old war widows" and those in the LGBT community. WWS is proud to welcome the widowed community in its entirety, regardless of age, gender, technical marital status, sexual orientation or the circumstances that surround the loss of a spouse.

When asked what advice she has for those seeking a career change, Carole is pragmatic. She never dreamed her efforts would lead to something this big, and early on, she realized that you can't do two jobs well. Her first career with Mary Kay made it possible for her to move into her second career as an author and CEO. Regardless of what career you choose, "you have to embrace the business side of it" to be successful. Also, "surround yourself with people who believe in you," because not everyone will love you or what you're doing. If she could change one thing about her career transition, it would be "to take my own advice sooner!" Carole also had to learn not to take bad comments on the Internet to heart.

The future looks bright for Carole. She plans to continue expanding her reach into Canada, and "to be where people need us." Whether it's another book, another radio or TV interview, or a blog posting, Carole continues to help those facing loss and trying to rebuild their lives.

Carole's Advice and Action Steps:

- Not everyone is going to love what you do or the choices you make – let it roll.
- Develop a thick skin and believe in yourself.
- The motivation for me to do good things for others is stronger than seeking a job that just pays the bills.

Resources:

Widows Wear Stilettos: www.widowswearstilettos.com
Soaring Spirits Loss Foundation: www.widowsvoice-sslf.blogspot.com

> **"**Focusing on *'Why me?'* for too long does nothing to change your situation or further healing. Choosing instead to focus on *'What now?'*…will!**"**
>
> – Carole Brody Fleet

ॐ ॐ ॐ ॐ

16. CLAIRE GILLENSON: MAKING PEACE WITH GRIEF

Claire was introduced to me by a mutual friend who was so inspired by her strength and courage that she thought my readers would benefit from Claire's career transformation wisdom. I couldn't agree more and I'm delighted to introduce Claire in the second edition of my book.

At 19, Claire Gillenson went for a check-up to diagnose and treat what she thought was tennis elbow. It turned out to be Stage 4 bone cancer and her parents and doctors determined her every move for the next year and a half. Claire was in the hospital every 3 weeks for 18 months with immediate surgery, aggressive chemotherapy, and radiation. Her hair fell out and she lost the use of her right arm.

Defining Moment

At a time when most teens are feeling their way into adulthood and grappling with independence and social acceptance, Claire was battling for her life. Doctors gave her a 20% chance of survival. Once it was determined that she would survive, she felt powerless and struggled with feelings of how to exist in the world cancer-free. Claire spent the next 10 years of remission feeling numb and lost, and masking her emotions by over-achieving in every way possible.

To make up for lost time, she focused on setting and achieving goals and excelled academically and in the workplace. Claire shared that "Everything looked great on paper," but in reality she was still searching for her authentic place in life.

Claire began her career as a graphic designer and became a Director of Creative Services for a company at the end of the dot-com boom. She led a department of 30 people, and although she was successful as a leader, the role took her away from the artistic part of the industry, which she loved. When the dot-com lay-offs hit, she took the downsizing as an opportunity to open her own boutique graphic design firm.

Find Your Bliss

The new business was moving forward nicely but a defining moment came when Claire's dog Sophie died. An unconditional loving companion, confidant, and loyal friend – Sophie was always there after a long day to make things more tolerable. The relationship with Sophie was immensely comforting and the loss was so deep that Claire had never experienced grief like that before. She realized that she never allowed herself to grieve during her cancer battle so the passing of Sophie released a flood of emotions for both the loss of her dog and the loss of her young adulthood.

Claire could not stop looking at Sophie's collar and held her ID tag for comfort and to recall fond memories. This was before the Paris Hilton *bling for dogs* era and Claire came up with the idea of creating a keepsake that a person could wear in memory of their beloved pet.

She transformed the loss of Sophie into **Luxepets**, an exclusive collection of luxury keepsakes to cherish and celebrate the memory of a pet's impact on our lives. Before long, stores were calling to purchase her grief products and also seeking advice for their grieving clients.

Chance Encounter

While on a long flight from New York to California, Claire struck up a conversation with her seatmate. She explained that she designed keepsakes to celebrate the bond between people and pets. Her seat-mate was enthralled. By the end of the flight, Claire had an initial company investor at $10,000!

Claire was a novice regarding business investing; she looks back and confesses that she "gave away the farm." However, this seed money did allow her take **Luxepets** to a new level and to develop products that are still thriving today. Six months later, she re-negotiated the deal and remains the sole visionary today.

Claire talks about earning her MBA on the street by trial and error. Her advertising and branding background coupled with her design expertise was the perfect fit for the new company. The products started to become very popular and so did the calls from the store owners who were inundated with grieving customers. It was not uncommon for Claire to get a call from a store owner who needed assistance with a grief stricken pet owner who had broken down in tears in the store.

Since Claire was naturally empathetic and experienced so much loss in her own life, she was able to relate to the grieving customers and bring them comfort. And so– unexpectedly– a new career calling came.

Back to School

The epiphany came when Claire decided to answer this new career calling and delve more formally into grief counseling. She went back to school and earned a Master's in Spiritual Psychology from the University of Santa Monica and became a certified Grief Recovery Specialist. It was through this process that she was able to heal the emotional parts of her that were affected by the cancer .

Like many, Claire came from a stoic family where grief was never discussed and feelings were harbored and never expressed. Sophie's death precipitated an awakening of emotions and a wonderful catharsis that empowered Claire to come to terms with her own grief issues and use that knowledge to help others deal with their grief.

She still had her own personal battles to fight – she was told that her cancer treatments would not allow her to become pregnant. Against all odds, Claire *did* become pregnant. The same week she found out she was pregnant she also received a call that her mother had committed suicide. Through her training and amazing personal journey, Claire developed the confidence and strength to deal with the painful grief of her mother's death while also celebrating the joy of becoming pregnant.

Sweet Surrender

Early on, her newborn daughter began to have seizures, but by using the tools to navigate relationships and cope with losses in her life, Claire was able to gain the strength to handle her daughter's health problems. Three years later, she mustered the courage to leave her marriage. Even after serious relationship work, the marriage was not working for her. Knowing that the grief of divorce would be painful, Claire recalls this as another turning point in her life that has made her the woman she is today. The tools she gained in her grief therapy training have made all the difference in how she lives her life. She is on a mission to help others utilize their own personal set of tools to live better, more anxiety-free lives.

Claire's grief therapy practice is based in Los Angeles and she serves clients throughout southern California. She specializes in pet loss, miscarriage, and In Vitro Fertilization (IVF) or chemical pregnancy loss. These are the kinds of grief that are not part of mainstream conversations and Claire is there as a resource to help people work through these very real and painful losses.

Fighting for the Underdogs

Claire shared that in our mainstream American culture, we have a way of explaining away loss with phrases like: "Time will heal," and "It was God's will." But these phrases never address the real heart of the grief and rarely do they bring comfort to those in need. They are ways of dealing with grief on a superficial level.

Loss means something different to each person and Claire's practice has grown organically based on need. While her connection with **Luxepets** and veterinarians connected her to grieving pet owners, she also works with people who have lost their job or faced a major disappointment in life. Her focus remains on "the underdogs" of grief – the life events that don't get much attention or may be seen as taboo, such as suicide, miscarriage, loss associated with IVF, and pet loss.

As a certified Grief Recovery Specialist, Claire is not a therapist but her style is like that of a counselor and a coach combined. Her method is to empower people with real life tools that they can use with day-to-day coping skills to live with and work through their grief. The goal is to help people find relief from the pain of grief.

Reset Your Clock

Grieving people miss the routine of their loved one or situation. From walking your dog at a certain time of day to getting up and going to work, these routines are embedded in our psyche. Claire focuses on shifting one thing at a time to help a client function better. The process involves establishing new routines that are enjoyable and comforting. It takes 32 days to make a new habit so Claire is patient and caring with her clients along their journey. She wrote a book to help others with this process: *28 Days of Grief and Healing—Transforming the Loss of a Beloved Animal Companion.*

And Life Goes On

As she hopes to help her clients do, Claire has used all the experiences in her life to grow into a better place. Things are going well with her Grief Recovery practice, and **Luxepets** almost runs on its own. She has also established a partnership with the Morris Animal Foundation as their pet loss go-to person.

Establishing two healthy businesses was a great undertaking for Claire. True to her over-achiever DNA, she put her heart and soul into both ventures and also utilized many resources including business coaches, *Savor the Success* and *Ladies Who Launch,* which she highly recommends.

Her companies are self-funded and Claire took out a second mortgage on her LA home to ramp up the businesses after her initial experience with an investor. She likes having the control over her own finances and values the autonomy of being her own boss. While finding suppliers who can create her new products can sometimes be a challenge, Claire is up for the task since she knows that both of her businesses help others deal with their grief. Now in a new phase of growth, she is in the process of seeking venture capital to take her business to the next level.

Growth and Change

After working with many clients, Claire shares, "I've realized I'm not a fit for everyone." Claire can help clients who have work to do concerning their grief, IF they are ready to "take off the coat of grief." She can provide the tools and help with the skills necessary, but only if a client is ready to do the work.

I asked Claire what she would have done differently if she had the hindsight of her experience. "I would have created more of a business plan!" Claire said she was fueled by passion, not market data. Some of her products are needed, but that doesn't mean every pet store is ready to carry items dealing with pet loss. Market research may have changed Claire's product priorities or approach.

Looking Forward

Claire is looking forward, too. She's considering the benefits of being a non-profit in gaining funds and access for her counseling services. She has been very lucky in finding and keeping business through referrals, but says she often hears from people who need her help with processing their grief, but have no funds left after paying vet bills. Claire uses the latest technology in her practice; she is able to work with clients all over the country using teleconferencing software.

Claire is driven to change how loss is perceived. In our culture, loss is "a four-letter word." If we can learn to live with loss and death in a more holistic way, we can all live fuller lives. In this effort to change perspectives, Claire has written several books and is working to get them published. *My Heart Remembers My Pet* is written to help children understand and work through their grief. *My Heart Remembers Grandma* and *My Heart Remembers Grandpa* are also in the works.

On the wish list for the future are retreats for people who are working to transform their grief – focused on the dying *and* the living. Claire wants to help others learn to "fill up their own cup" and to shift the culture regarding loss.

From Grief, Peace

Making peace with her own grief gave Claire the ability to recognize her career calling. She is the happiest she has ever been in her life and ready to help others deal with painful loss. She has a vision map for the future and is truly living the life she wants to lead.

The happy ending is one that she envisions for all her clients in their respective situations. Now, Claire is happy and fulfilled and enjoying her vivacious daughter, surrounded by a loving community that is her new family. She loves her career and has happily remarried. In a word – she is thriving.

Claire's Advice and Action Steps:

- Think big as a woman business owner and tap into the resources around you.
- Don't play down your assets – focus on your strengths.
- Shine in your light!
- Find your calling – it's worth the journey.

Resources:

Claire's website: www.ClaireGillenson.com
Luxepets: www.luxepets.com
Savor the Success: www.savorthesuccess.com

66Be the change you want to see in the world.99

– Gandhi

 of of of of

17. Take a Step Forward

The women in this chapter changed careers because life dealt them very difficult situations to overcome. Jessi Walter Brelsford's Wall Street career was a casualty of the recession. Claire Gillenson, Christine Clifford, and Mary McManus overcame debilitating diseases against the odds. Carole Brody Fleet became a widow at a young age and her world turned upside down. But each of these women found a new beginning and they are thriving in different careers.

What inspires me most about these women is their ability to face the unknown, as well as their fears. Many people resist career change because they are afraid to take a leap into the unknown. The truth is that even without a challenging career wake-up call like each of these five women experienced, life is all about navigating the unknown.

Facing The Unknown

If you think you have carved out a career plan for your life that is set in stone – think again. There will always be constant changes beyond your control and that's okay. Life is change and if you are able to tap into your adaptability and resilience you will always land on your feet.

Likewise, if you are in a career you dislike, you have the power to change that. I encourage you to loosen the mental grip you have on your life that is preventing you from considering the change that will empower you to reinvent yourself and your career. If you find the courage to consider change, you will muster the energy to transform your career and your life. By being proactive, you can find a new career that brings you joy, or you can let life impose change on you. Reading this book is a positive step towards being proactive. Cheers to you!

REINVENTION TOOLBOX

Know Thy Self; Showcase Your Resilience; Utilize Soft Skills

After reading about the *survive-to-thrive* women in this chapter, I hope you are inspired by how they are flourishing after dealing with incredibly difficult situations that impacted their lives and careers. These four action steps will help you thrive as you begin to develop the new and reinvented you.

Action Step #1: Take the time for self-reflection to discover what is really important to you. Think about your values, interests, personality, and skills and connect these dots to find career opportunities that match the real you. Consider your career passions. What occupation(s) would you pursue if you had no obstacles in your way? Get quiet with yourself and reflect – a true self-assessment takes time and focus.

Action Step #2: Write it down! Use this book as a career journal to write down detailed thoughts about your VIPS, hopes, dreams, and goals. Store a pocket-sized notebook in your purse so that you have it with you on the go and can jot down impromptu thoughts and inspirations. Putting your wishes on paper helps you articulate things more clearly and gives you accountability for achieving your goals.

Take a close look at the next 90 days and write down what you want to accomplish. You can always change your mind and adjust your game plan, but dig deep to think about what you really want. Split your 90-day goal into smaller, attainable actions and chop it into manageable baby steps. Research tells us that you are 90 times more likely to accomplish a goal when it is written down. What are you waiting for? Grab a pen and write down your goals!

Action Step #3: Showcase your resiliency! Now more than ever employers want to see that you can bounce back and recover quickly from adversity. Resilience is a key competency that employers value because it transfers well into the workplace. One constant in every career field is change. If you can show an employer that you can deal with change you can be seen as a valuable commodity to that organization. Attitude is just as important as your skill set in a competitive marketplace.

If you were downsized out of your last job, pick yourself up and get back on that proverbial career horse. Showcase this adaptive skill to illustrate that you are scrappy, flexible, and able to recover from a setback with a positive attitude and a game plan. There is no room in this job market for a negative attitude, and badmouthing your former employer is the kiss of death. Put your game face on and forge ahead with confidence.

I have seen negative attitudes get the best of amazing job candidates because the applicants are still grieving the loss of a former position and have not let go emotionally. Take the time you need to vent, rant, and rave in the privacy of your own home – this is therapeutic and essential to establish a new and positive mindset. But when you are ready (sooner is better than later!) focus and concentrate on your goals. Put your best professional foot forward and show the job world that you are ready for a new opportunity.

Action Step #4: Utilize Your Soft Skills. Quite often people brush off the soft skills as the touchy feely people skills that serious professionals don't need. Nothing could be farther from the truth! The soft skills include abilities and traits such as self-awareness, initiative, time management, empathy, political astuteness, integrity, and many more.

Tap into your emotional intelligence and consider seriously how you perform in these four areas:

- **Self-awareness** – The ability to recognize your own emotions and how they affect your thoughts and behavior, know your strengths and weaknesses, and exhibit self-confidence.

- **Self-management** – The ability to control impulsive feelings and behaviors, manage your emotions in healthy ways, take initiative, follow through on commitments, and adapt to changing circumstances.
- **Social awareness** – The ability to understand the emotions, needs, and concerns of other people, pick up on emotional cues, feel comfortable socially, and recognize the power dynamics in a group or organization.
- **Relationship management** – The ability to develop and maintain good relationships, communicate clearly, inspire and influence others, work well on a team, and manage conflict.

Some people enjoy a self-directed assessment, and others work better utilizing a coach who can lead them through the self-discovery process. I am here as a resource for you if you prefer a customized plan. You can email me through my website www.carolinedowdhiggins.com.

BECOME A MEMBER OF THE CREATIVITY CLUB

The Creativity Club women each tapped into her experience, resourcefulness, and innovation to reinvent her career.

18. STACEY KANNENBERG: MOM-ON-A-MISSION BUILDS PUBLISHING EMPIRE

After 14 years in corporate America, Stacey made the decision, while she was pregnant with her first child, to stay home and raise her family. It was a life-changing move. This suburban Wisconsin mom was not a teacher by training, but she went on to create Kindergarten and first grade books now used in schools across the nation. Now a successful author, publisher, motivator, consultant, and mom, Stacey is nationally renowned as an education expert.

From Strollers to First Grade

So how did this all begin? When Stacey's first daughter was a toddler, Stacy walked the neighborhood with other moms and like many American women, she tuned into Oprah daily for entertainment and inspiration. Like a good mom, Stacey was eager to prepare her young daughter for the new world of kindergarten and tried to find resources they could use together to help with this transition to formal education. Alas, there were none.

A lot has changed since Stacey's days in first grade and kindergarten. There was new terminology that seemed foreign to this corporate mogul turned full-time mom. Partly to help other families of the same generation understand how to help their kids and to better prepare their little ones for this new school adventure, Stacey developed *Let's Get Ready for Kindergarten*, a resource that was a big hit with children, parents, and teachers.

The Power of the Mommy Brigade

What made these books unique was not only the content that empowered parents to bridge the proverbial generation gap with the new school language – these books were designed with durable dry erase material for every page. Ever read a book to a sticky-fingered youngster? These books were ingeniously designed to be kid friendly and mess proof.

The prototype passed muster in the neighborhood and the kids were the toughest critics helping to design the many versions before publication. But how does a first-time author publish a book? Here comes the Oprah connection! Stacey recalls the *Millionaire Mom* episode on Oprah that motivated her to make this book project a reality. She picked up additional tips from another Oprah show on self-publishing and was inspired by yet another show about Africa where youngsters asked for books to read instead of dolls to play with. Talk about tugging at your heart strings!

Stacey was a mom on a mission with a passion to get her book published and that is what she did. Along the way, she had the unconditional support of her husband and kids, who she calls her "saving grace" during this publishing journey; it was a journey which included times of frustration and challenge. Stacey is committed to paying-it-forward by helping other moms realize their entrepreneurial dreams.

How did she get published? Oprah's show on self-publishing was the first time Stacey had seriously thought about self-publishing her book. She researched self-publishing online and found many people who raved about Dan Poynter.

"To me he is the Oprah of Self-Publishing. I read Dan Poynter's *The Self-Publishing Manual* and followed the steps in his book. I found a local printer who introduced me to Two Bit Productions and they were willing to take a chance on me to do my illustrations and website. They believed in what I was trying to do and were willing to work with me to bring it to life. They believed so much in the mission that they were willing to tear up their bill if it was a flop. Having their faith gave me the courage to soar! Thinking back, they took a great risk and I would never be where I am today without them and many other people, many of whom I did NOT really know all that well, who believed in what I was trying to do and stepped up to the plate to offer words of encouragement or forged connections to get me to the next step."

Amazed by the number of people who believed in her to the point that they became brand evangelists sharing the news about her books to teachers and schools, Stacey has seen firsthand the power of networking. She decided to do a small press run of 3,000 books and did not order an ISBN number (this number needs to be coded on the back of the book in order for it to be sold by major distributors, such as Barnes & Noble and Amazon).

Stacey thought she would have the rest of her life to sell those 3,000 copies and literally drove around from school to school and bookstore to bookstore selling books out of her car. The book was featured in the local newspaper and then TMJ4 Milwaukee Television did a story, which had Paula Jones from Barnes & Noble calling and asking to carry her books. Paula helped Stacey get the all-important ISBN number and get the books into the national Barnes & Noble retailer and set up numerous book-signing opportunities.

Life on Her Terms

Was it easy? No! Stacey had to jump over her fair share of hurdles and had many a dark day, but so many people believed in what she was trying to do that she took baby steps which advanced her project to a profitable business. According to Stacey, "I bootstrapped and self-funded my business from day one!"

"I love an Oprah quote that really resonated with me from one of her shows: 'Obstacles are really just opportunities in disguise.' It is so true. Every obstacle along the way has turned out to be a blessing. I had the amazing support of my family, whom I invited to join the process. I mean, who better to help me write *Let's get Ready for Second Grade* than Megan, who just finished second grade and Heidi, who just finished fourth! My husband gave me a clear crystal clock in 2004 for the first Christmas celebrating Cedar Valley Publishing. He had the logo engraved along with a phrase he coined that has since become my mantra: *The Dream is Clear to Believe is the Reward*. I can't tell you how many times a day I look at that clock and it makes me smile and it keeps me going because the dream is crystal clear for me. This concept has become bigger than my products – it has morphed into a movement to empower parents, kids and teachers to work together to change education starting at the core – preschool and kindergarten!"

Stacey is fiercely passionate about helping others learn from her experiences. "One of my challenges was in trying to build my own Google footprint for my titles and my company. It took a long while before I realized that the one thing that ties us all together is my name – and I hadn't even thought about branding that. If I was to do it all over I would have named my book 'Kindergarten'. Had I done that I would have been using my key search word as my title without any other words to get in the way of people finding my kindergarten book."

With a powerful personal network that started with the playgroup mommies, Stacey is the Founder and CEO of two publishing companies: **Cedar Valley Publishing** and **Stacey Kannenberg Unlimited**. By the way, Cedar Valley was the street Stacey used to walk along with her young daughter in a stroller, so how fitting that she chose this name for her first business.

The Spanish/English edition of *Let's Get Ready for Kindergarten! iA Prepararse Para Kindergarten!* was released and has already sold thousands of copies. Overall, Stacey has sold more than 130,000 copies of her three titles.

This entrepreneurial mom made her mark by designing a much needed resource for parents and kids. Using her transferable skills from the corporate arena and honoring her values as a mom who wants to raise her own children, Stacey made this career move work based on her terms.

What's New?

Stacey's success and growth has continued. In promoting her books and companies, Stacey learned about and excelled in the use of social media. She became a "social media maven" and was way ahead of the curve in using the technology. But soon she learned that social media is a "double-edged sword." What was meant to be a time-saver, began to take too much time away from a balanced family life. She realized the irony of the situation; after all, she became a "Mom-entrepreneur" so she could maintain a balance between work and family life. Lesson learned, she scaled back her online time, and regained a happy balance.

She sees this challenge becoming more common. Entrepreneurs can get very wrapped up in technology time-wasters that don't necessarily lead to success. Stacey took time to "detox" from technology; she doesn't post as often or speak out as often. But she's learned that when she does have something to say, more people listen. She said entrepreneurs can get "tuned out" by the groups they are trying to reach because they "talk too much and listen too little."

Like many Mom-entrepreneurs, Stacey has had family and life challenges to deal with while trying to build and run her businesses. Those challenges help "keep her focused on the things that matter most." They also drive Stacey's goal of paying it forward – helping other entrepreneurs on their journeys.

Although life throws up obstacles along the way, Stacey realized that the skills she developed as a business person can (and do) help her manage her personal life challenges as well. Her growth has gone full-circle – from want-to-be entrepreneur, to successful Mom-entrepreneur, to being more skilled in managing life in general. She has developed "the skills to help those who don't have a voice yet – in business AND in life."

Her advice to others is clear: If you have something that you really love, it can become a career. Figure out what you love to do, then how to make it a business. Or, if you're happy in a job (not everyone has to be an entrepreneur), ask "where can I help?" to start your journey as a volunteer. Give back, and get more in life. Be sure to take baby steps. It's also good to set a timeline, but it could be as simple as "I will take a year to figure out what I want to do."

Stacey emphasizes the critical role of research. "Research is vital to success." You can learn what's trending, how to make money doing something you love, what the needs are in the market, and so on. "There's no excuse for lack of research now, because there is so much available on the Internet. Writing a book or building a product is one tiny piece" of success; research must be there to support and guide your efforts.

So what's next for Stacey? She plans to continue growing her business, possibly partnering with someone who can help the "Get Ready For" endeavor to the next level, with her focus being the improvement of education, not necessarily personal gain. Stacey feels that in some ways, her business has taken a backseat to life. If she starts to feel guilty about that, she remembers – "the goal is to build a company that can work for you, not you for it."

Stacey's Advice and Action Steps:

- If you are starting a business find a niche market. No one ever thought of a national kindergarten textbook – and it took off!
- Consider a platform based on need. What is the need of your client base – do your research.
- Tap into your personal network. The Mommy and Daddy brigade is a powerful group; learn from each other.
- Seek out mentors and supporters who share your values and mission.
- Believe that one person can make a difference!

Resources:

HARO, Help A Reporter Out: www.helpareporter.com
Media Bistro: www.mediabistro.com
Reporter Connection: www.reporterconnection.com
Cedar Valley Publishing: www.cedarvalleypublishing.com Savor the Success: www.savorthesuccess.com

"The dream is clear to believe is the reward."

– Mike Kannenberg

☞ ☞ ☞ ☞

19. CARLA FALCONE AND ROMY TAORMINA: TURNING MORNING SICKNESS INTO A BUSINESS ENTERPRISE

Romy Taormina and Carla Falcone met and became fast friends at an award-winning advertising agency on California's Central Coast many years ago. Carla has an extensive background in public relations and advertising and earned degrees in journalism and industrial arts. Romy has an in-depth knowledge of marketing and earned a business degree.

These women have extensive experience strategizing, creating, and executing multimedia campaigns for a myriad of clients in a variety of industries. But their entrepreneurial spirit blossomed after both women experienced ongoing morning sickness during their respective pregnancies. In fact, at Carla's baby shower, the two were commiserating about the drab gray acupressure wrist bands that were helping Carla keep her morning sickness at bay. She was no longer nauseous but the dull wristbands did nothing to enhance her adorable maternity outfit!

With 20+ years of collective marketing experience, Romy and Carla hit the mother lode of ideas and conceived the plan for a more fashionable and functional acupressure wrist band. Two years later **Psi Bands** (pronounced "sigh") were born.

Ancient Wisdom Meets FDA Standards

Psi Bands use acupressure, an ancient healing art supported by scientific studies, to relieve nausea when placed at the Nei-kuan acupressure points on the wrists. These drug-free wrist bands help relieve nausea in a natural way. **Psi Bands** have been used successfully to help those suffering from motion sickness, post-surgical anesthesia nausea, and chemotherapy-induced nausea. Wrist acupressure is widely used for the relief of nausea because it is noninvasive, easy to self-administer, and affordable. These FDA-cleared bands are now available in major retail stores nationwide and internationally.

Romy and Carla are on a mission to provide high quality, fashionable, comfortable, and affordable products that make a positive difference in the lives of people suffering from nausea. If that weren't impressive enough, Psi Bands donates a percentage of its profits to *Fertile Hope*, dedicated to providing reproductive information, support, and hope to cancer patients and survivors whose medical treatments present the risk of infertility.

Back-of-a-Napkin Idea to Sustainable Business

These women have a wealth of marketing and advertising experience between them, but how did they actually get this product off the ground? Romy told me that the initial product sketches were drafted on the back of a napkin! Friend and colleague Peter Schouten joined the women in the business, and his expertise in product design and development was the perfect complement to the PR and marketing expertise of Carla and Romy.

Romy and Carla knew from the get-go that they were onto something when they conceived the idea for **Psi Bands**. After extensive research, the two women decided that they had a solid business model and quit their day jobs. They admit it was a scary leap of faith, but necessary to make it a sustainable business. Since they love what they do and love that they are helping people in the process, Romy and Carla know they made the right choice.

Work/family balance is their largest challenge, but they enjoy their work and would not have it any other way. Romy reported: "We try to stay 'in' the moment – whether it is with our children or working on the business." With 20/20 hindsight, the women know now that some of their hiring choices would have been different if they had to do it over again. They would start with a focus on ensuring that their team members share the company's goals and vision.

Future goals for **Psi Bands** include continuing to build brand awareness, landing some additional large retailers nationally, and growing the international expansion. At the end of the day, Romy and Carla both believe you must love what you do. These mothers of invention are thriving!

What's New?

As noted in the original story, work/family balance is a challenge. In fact, Carla decided to leave the business to focus on her family and her young children. Undaunted, Romy is continuing to grow and manage Psi Bands.

Psi Bands can be found on the shelves of national retailers, and have international distribution in five continents. Long-term growth and sales will be sustained through a pipeline of future innovation by adding new products to the portfolio and through licensing opportunities.

Reflecting on her journey so far, Romy said, "It is good that I didn't know what I do now when I first started. If I had known all that's involved in being an entrepreneur, I might not have chosen to do it!" Yet, she loves what she does, which is to help those with a debilitating medical condition find nausea relief, and to help other entrepreneurs learn about business via her blog, "Both Sides of the Retail Table." She emphasizes to those who want to launch their own businesses, "It is not a hobby. It has to be about the bottom line. When you have an opportunity, you have to determine if it's on target with where you want to go. You have to be tenacious and passionate, and you must be *patient.*"

Romy and Carla's Advice and Action Steps:

- Be sure your partners and employees/consultants have the same goal and vision for the company as you do.
- Seek out the advice and expertise of others when you don't have the experience to make an informed decision.
- Join women entrepreneur groups to network, find inspiration, and share ideas.
- Follow your dreams, do what you love, and believe in yourself!
- Listen to your gut, do your research, and believe in your product/service 100 percent. Your passion will need to carry you through the inevitable business ups and downs.

Resources:

Psi Bands: www.psibands.com
Make Mine a Million $ Business: www.makemineamillion.org
Savor the Success: www.savorthesuccess.com
Tory Johnson's Spark & Hustle: www.sparkandhustle.com
Romy's Blog: www.retailtable.com

"There will be bumps. Savor the journey."

– Carla Falcone and Romy Taormina

♌ ♌ ♌ ♌

20. HEIDI ROIZEN: GET INTO YOUR SKINNY JEANS

Heidi Roizen is a household name for many, recognized for success as an entrepreneur, a corporate executive, a corporate director, and venture capitalist. She has also held positions of leadership within a number of industry organizations, and is a sought-after spokesperson for the technology industry and entrepreneurial community. So why did an incredibly successful career woman need a new project to add to her already full career plate?

"As they say, necessity is the mother of invention, and I can say for certain that *SkinnySongs* exists because I really, really needed it. In May of 2007, I got on the scale, and the numbers were a disaster – at 190, not only was I at an all-time high, but for the first time I weighed more than my husband, and he's not a small guy.

Cursing myself, I vowed that I would change, this time for real. My 50th birthday loomed only months away, and I promised myself that I would fit into my skinny jeans again by then – but with close to forty pounds between them and me, I had some serious work to do."

The Power of Inspiration

And so Heidi was on a mission to lose weight and get into shape, but she realized that if she was going to resist her old temptations and get mentally prepared for her lifestyle shift, she would need some inspiration. Since music had always been a powerful force in her life, she looked for songs that would inspire her to stick to the new healthy living plan and get her back into her skinny jeans; but alas – there was nothing that fit the bill. Ever the entrepreneur, Heidi set out to create a CD filled with music to inspire and empower her, and others, to get through daunting and long-term personal challenge of shedding the weight and staying healthy, for life.

> "I started penning lyrics that would inspire me to stick to my plan – songs about my relationship with food and my need to become 'the boss' of that relationship, a love song to my skinny jeans, a fantasy song about fitting into designer clothes, a song reminding me to get up and move."

Heidi is a woman of many talents but a musician she is not, so after writing the lyrics for *SkinnySongs* she set out to enlist some of the best producers and talented emerging artists in the music business and enticed them to work on her new project. Starting with the expertise of Dave Malloy and George Daly as producers, the team grew to include Tania Hancheroff, Kaleo Sallas, Larkin Gayl, Rachelle Byrne, and Susan Ashton who provided vocals for the project. Lori Sutherland was onboard as Consulting Producer and ensured that the project became a monster hit.

Heidi reports that during the actual CD recording and production process the artistic team lost weight and became determined to live healthier lives. The inspiration and results began even before the recording was available to the general public.

> "Of course, it wasn't just the music – I also made a personal commitment to take charge of my life, to stop coming up with excuses. As a lifelong yo-yo dieter, I knew that what I needed was a set of permanent lifestyle changes that I could live with, on both the 'input' and the 'output' side of the equation. I'm pleased to report that I am 40+ pounds lighter and went from

a size 14 to a size 8. And I still listen to the music EVERY DAY, especially in my car when I am heading to an event where I know I'll be tempted."

Turning a Personal Quest into a Profitable Venture

SkinnySongs served a personal mission in Heidi's life but as a savvy businesswoman, she also knew it had money-making potential. As with any new project she took on, *SkinnySongs* forced her to dive in, do the research, and run the numbers to determine if this project was viable and worth her investment. Heidi used her own money to finance the project and was committed to doing it very well; she hired the best in the music industry to realize her goal. She took an entire year off to work on this labor of love but admits that she does not want *SkinnySongs* to be the platform of her main career.

As a small business, *SkinnySongs* runs on its own today with CD and merchandise sales bringing in profits. Heidi and *SkinnySongs* have been featured widely, including appearances on *The Martha Stewart Show*, *CBS Early Morning*, *Oprah & Friends Radio* and *CNN*. *SkinnySongs* is available on Amazon and iTunes. But Heidi's physical reinvention also led her to consider some additional lifestyle changes. After many years in the heart of the corporate world, Heidi realized that at 51 she had a new set of values. She no longer defined success by a high-powered CEO career and wanted more variety and control over the time in her life.

SkinnySongs served as a catalyst for change and reinvention in Heidi's career and personal life. Not only did she shed the pounds and embrace a healthy lifestyle, she considered what was most important in her life and discovered that she wanted intellectual stimulation in her work, but also the time to spend with her family and to maintain her new healthy habits.

Reinventing Yourself Personally and Professionally

She is now embracing a new career in public governance and took this new role very seriously by attending Director's College to learn the essentials of serving on Boards of companies. Heidi wants to serve companies that are good investments and that pay Board members with equities, but she vows she must have a passion for their product. Currently, she serves on the Board of Directors for TiVo Inc. and Yellow Pages Group.

With these new opportunities in public governance, Heidi has more control over her time and can focus on her husband and teenage girls and still get in a good workout daily while pursuing a meaningful career. While *SkinnySongs* empowered Heidi with the confidence to lead a healthy life, Heidi also inspired many others to do the same. She feels proud that *SkinnySongs* is helping others and also allowed her to "...focus, deliver, and get out of my old head space and define a new head space and goals."

Careers change over time and it's empowering to know that we can all be more in control of our career destiny. We all have unique goals and aspirations for career and life so take the time to consider yours. Have you worn your skinny jeans lately?

What's New?

Heidi told me that "life should be in Beta," referring to what software companies call the test version of their products. "You should constantly be testing, checking in, and making adjustments" to your life and career plans. And Heidi has done just that. After going through a divorce, she decided to take a break for a few months and moved to Scotland. This break helped her focus on what she wanted to do. When we talked, she was serving on four Boards, and had the honor of being the first female Director in a company's 116-year history!

Looking back on the *SkinnySongs*, Heidi said she really enjoyed the creative process, but after a year, "I was done." In hindsight, she realizes that branding was an issue; she could have marketed *Skinny-Songs* as music, or as a weight-loss tool, instead of working in the gray area between the two. If she had focused on *SkinnySongs* as a music product, Heidi said she should have aligned with a specific artist and/or stayed within a single musical genre. If she had marketed *Skinny-Songs* as a weight-loss tool, she could have aligned with a weight-loss industry partner. Having "one little product" that isn't clearly defined "makes it hard to rise above the noise." After much deliberation, Heidi decided to shut down *SkinnySongs* altogether, so she can focus on her board work.

Heidi is a great example of how you can create, grow, assemble, and change your career over time. Moving through life, your values change and you gain new skills and experiences. Using these basic building blocks, you can re-design, re-create, and re-launch your career to reflect who you are becoming. Try to "live life in Beta," and see where it can take you!

Heidi's Advice and Action Steps:

- Spend some time getting to know yourself – what you like, what you don't like, strengths and interests. Don't play to your weaknesses – focus on your strengths!
- Get some distance between yourself and what you did before. Wind down to zero, be quiet and listen to your SELF. What do you want? So many of us rarely consider this.
- A woman's career is like a marathon run in segments. What is your 5-year, 10-year, 15-year plan? Chances are you will be working a long time so give yourself the liberty of changing your career course as you wish.
- To craft a career change, think about combining your skills and strengths with a current need in the economy or your community – whatever niche you want to fill.

Resources:

Heidi's Personal Website: www.heidiroizen.com

❝That which does not kill us makes us stronger.❞

– Friedrich Nietzsche

☞ ☞ ☞ ☞

21. GRACE CHON: FROM THE AD AGENCY TO PUPPY LOVE

A self-proclaimed *crazy dog lady*, Grace Chon grew up wanting to be a veterinarian. She majored in biology as an undergraduate and volunteered in animal hospitals to really test-drive the profession before committing to vet school. Her Korean immigrant parents wereauguring for medical school, so that Grace could be a physician for humans instead of animals, but in the end Grace surprised everybody and opted for art school where she earned a Masters of Fine Arts.

Little DoggieLips

She had a very successful career in a huge advertising agency in Los Angeles working on campaigns for national brands including Panda Express, Saturn cars, eBay Motors, Shutterfly and The San Francisco Giants, to name just a few. As an Art Director, she was responsible for full-scale guerilla marketing from websites to TV commercials and everything between. The work was exciting and fast paced but after many years it left her stressed out, unbalanced, and unhealthy.

As a way to relieve her stress, Grace began to take photos of homeless dogs at the local animal shelters in order to help them find loving homes. As an Art Director, she had developed a wonderful eye and worked with photographers regularly so she knew the craft even though she was not formally trained in the medium.

The hobby morphed into a sideline business and Grace began working early mornings, late nights, and weekends on her photography in addition to her ad agency job. She was clocking over 70 hours per week and received a significant raise at the agency after launching a popular national television campaign. But after nine months of the cottage industry business and the grind of the day job, Grace quit the ad agency to focus on her photography full-time. This woman, in love with organic gardening, old books, and little doggie lips recognized her calling and took the leap.

Do You Zig or Zag?

Grace's background in advertising gave her the perfect set of transferable skills to launch her new business ShinePetPhotos and make it a successful full-time venture. She designed her own website, developed her brand, and marketed the business in order to attract clients. Grace uses social media resources to spread the word about her business including a blog that has become very popular with clients.

While Grace capitalized on her self-reliance, she also knows the importance of distinguishing herself and her work. Since the time Grace launched ShinePetPhotos, over 70 new pet photographers have popped up in the Los Angeles area alone. She continues to be strategic and tap into her business sense to differentiate herself and separate her business from the pack.

At the ad agency she learned how to serve clients well and to solve problems. Advertising is not just marketing a product or a service; it involves solving real life problems. These skills have helped Grace tremendously in her new business. Grace knew it wasn't enough to just identify her passion for animals in the form of photography – she had to monetize it in order to make a livelihood out of this new venture.

A Clear Picture of Success

When I asked Grace to distill her personal brand down to a few words she responded with modern pet photography. Her images are beautifully real and capture the relationship of the animal and their human families as well as the unique personality of each furry friend. She aims to capture the pets in their natural environment, with gorgeous natural light, doing their favorite things.

The adage that time is money is even more applicable according to Grace, who now works from home. She goes on location for her photography shoots, but her days are filled with hard work managing and building the business. She does find time for gardening and cooking, which was not always possible when she worked at the ad agency.

Grace feels more balanced, healthier, and has a sense of calm in her new work that everyone around her has recognized. Working with dogs and cats as your subjects takes a lot of patience. Although

Grace considers herself impatient with most things in life, she has developed a sense of serenity and peace with the animals which makes for a successful photo shoot.

The accolades are piling up and Grace has become widely recognized in a short period of time. She is the official photographer of *The World's Ugliest Dog Contest*, has cover photos showcased in *The Bark Magazine* and her shots were in a feature story about Perez Hilton's dog, Teddy. Grace was also named LA's best pet photographer two years in a row by *Tails Magazine*.

Grace's grit and determination have helped her transfer the ad agency skills into her own business. She is committed to doing everything she can with character and integrity and has built her business on those values. She finally feels as if she is doing what is right for her and has a sense of gratification and fulfillment about the new career that she is designing.

Coming Full Circle

As a little girl, Grace knew she was passionate about animals. Little did she know then that many years later she would develop a business to celebrate her furry friends and capture their essence with photographs.

Grace's friends and colleagues thought she was crazy to quit a lucrative job in the midst of a recession but she kept her eye on the prize and never looked back. In two years, her business has grown significantly. She operated in the black her very first year and nearly tripled her intake during the second year. Working full-time while growing the business was one of the most challenging things Grace has ever done, but she earned her dream career with sweat equity, business savvy, and the wisdom to know the importance of distinguishing herself from the competition.

And needless to say, she has the most lovable furry clients to work with on a daily basis, so life is grand.

What's New?

In the time since our first conversation, the pet photography market in Los Angeles has exploded. Grace found herself in a field that was getting more crowded by the day. She realized that she needed to scale up and find other ways to monetize her passion. So Grace found ways to extend her market, and has launched a line of greeting cards, back-to-school supplies, and has her photos featured in magazines and advertising campaigns.

I asked Grace what she would have changed about her career transition given the benefit of hindsight. She was very clear in saying she wouldn't change a single thing. "Everything happens for a reason; everything is connected and leads to the next thing."

Her career transition came about because her values were no longer being met with her job in advertising. "I was a slave to work, a slave to the clients, and I had no life. Nights and weekends are mandatory in that business. It was like being on-call, but not getting to do anything important when the urgent call comes in." Grace also shared that the lack of female role models in the Creative Director field was disappointing. She struggled with the lack of balance between work and life, and shared that "it didn't make my soul happy." But now, Grace is "dealing with my calling every single day. I'm doing what I love and I happen to make money with it. I have much more balance in my life."

Because of the demands in advertising, Grace always swore she would never return to that industry, not even as a photographer. She was a little intimidated because she knew the quality of work expected for commercial photographers in advertising – she wasn't sure she could compete at that level. However, when the agency for Purina came calling for images, she couldn't resist the opportunity. Now, she shoots regularly for ad agencies, in addition to commissioned pet portraits and products.

Reflecting on the challenges she faced being a woman in advertising, Grace said she sees some of the same challenges being a woman in commercial photography. "When you're in an environment where you are the only woman, you have to be confident, assertive, and strong. It's easy to get lost in that environment, but good work speaks for itself."

Grace had some great advice to share with anyone thinking about a career change. "It's really important to focus. It's fun to brainstorm about a career change with friends at a coffee shop, but it's really hard to follow through. Focus on one thing at a time, and get really good at that one thing. Then move on. Otherwise, you will be spread too thin trying to do 5 things at once." Grace first mastered the skills to take great pet photos then she branched out from there.

"Have fun, and be nice. Remember that you're chasing your dream! There is so much to be grateful for. Don't take things too seriously." Words of wisdom to be sure!

Grace's Advice and Action Steps:

- Identify your passion – then monetize it!
- Be strategic and learn how to differentiate your personal brand to separate yourself from the competition. Identify your niche market.
- Know that if you start a new business you will have to work extremely hard and manage your time wisely. It's all up to you.
- Learn how to connect your transferable skills and experiences with a new opportunity.
- Develop a plan.

Resources:

Shine Pet Photos: www.shinepetphotos.com
Blog: www.shinepetphotos.com/blog

> **"**If you are more excited to leave your job on Friday than you are to come in to work on Monday, something is wrong.**"**

– Donny Deutsch

ശ ശ ശ ശ

22. TANA POPPINO: NEVER WANTING TO WONDER *WHAT IF?* RODEO COWGIRL GOES PRO

When word got out that I was interviewing women who had reinvented themselves, it wasn't long before I heard about this amazing woman. I knew her story would inspire others to take control of their career destinies. So enjoy reading about Tana's mission to become an award-winning Barrel Rodeo Rider – she will take you on a career ride you will never forget and I'm delighted to include her in the second edition.

Raised on a ranch in southeast Colorado, Tana Poppino has spent her entire life around horses. That love of horses and a competitive nature drew her to the world of rodeo at an early age. She participated in the amateur rodeo ranks throughout high school and college, but pursued a career at Grand River Dam Authority (GRDA) in their media and communications department.

GRDA is a state-owned public power producer. They operated two coal-fired generating plants and three hydro plants that produced electricity for about fifteen cities and towns in Oklahoma, as well as rural electric cooperatives. Tana worked for more than twenty years in the Media/Marketing Department producing corporate videos, annual reports, company brochures/media, and corporate photography. She also worked with many cities and civic organizations on their marketing efforts and, although she enjoyed her job, she never considered it her career passion.

In her spare time, Tana continued to participate in rodeo weekend competitions, but she always wanted to do more. The ultimate goal on the rodeo circuit for a Barrel Racer is to find that special horse that could compete at the top professional level. Soon, Tana thought she found him – a bay four-year-old gelding, whose official name was Perrymans Star, but she called him Amigo.

Competing with the Big Girls

Tana took her time training and seasoning him for three years, and Amigo continued to prove himself a winner. Finally, Tana took the big step and entered the winter pro rodeos, sanctioned by the Women's Professional Rodeo Association, to see how she would do against the "big girls." Although their first run wasn't good, Tana and Amigo came back and won the second round at the National Western Stock Show in Denver. For the next three years, she continued to work at her marketing job and pursued rodeo on the side, using accumulated leave, comp time, and unpaid leave.

Each year, Tana and Amigo would finish in the top thirty, but only the top fifteen qualify for the Wrangler National Finals Rodeo in Las Vegas. Finally, she was ranked in the top fifteen but she had run out of leave time. She had to make a decision: either quit her job, or quit rodeo. But dreams and reality are two different things. Tana didn't want to look back and wonder *what if?* But she didn't want to put her family in a financial bind either. After much prayer and reflection, Tana took the leap and left her job to pursue life on the road as a professional rodeo Barrel Racer. Her husband Marty and son Brodie encouraged her to go for it.

On the Road Again

After a month on the road, Tana had only won a couple of thousand dollars and, after expenses and she was broke. She told her husband that she would finish out the next week at the rodeos and then she'd go find a *real* job again.

> "I also had a long conversation with God about the whole situation, and He gave me a whole new insight. Although I didn't win a lot that week, things started clicking, and I went another week. We found our "zone" and started winning, and climbed back into the standings, winning enough to qualify for our first Wrangler National Finals Rodeo in third place!"

While the earnings picked up with additional wins, Tana says her new career is more about passion than finances. It can be feast or famine – she won $100,000 at Calgary, which carried her through two years when Amigo had to have surgery. Tana also broke her ankle, so the unexpected expenses really added up. To an outside observer, it might look like Tana is rolling in the dough of her winnings, but they don't see the expenses of travel, veterinary care, and human health care. Tana admits, she has not made it yet, but she is still going strong.

At the Top of Your Game

While the critical element is having a great horse for a partner, Tana also learned that it takes perseverance and really knowing your horse to help him stay at the top of his game. In addition to the now eighteen-year-old Amigo, Tana also has eleven-year-old Goose with whom she is partnering. It is definitely a partnership – she takes care of her guys and they take care of her.

Tana has learned the importance of financial planning since she cannot count on regular winnings. She advises others interested in pursuing a high risk career transition to never look back and never give up.

Family also plays a very important role in Tana's success; she could not continue on this path without their strong support. Tana's son Brodie kept telling her in the first few years when she wanted to quit and go home, "No Mom, you've got to keep going so we can go to the NFR!"

Her husband Marty works hard to help keep her on the road. He is the reason she can live her dream. Tana's parents hauled her to *Little Britches*, one of the oldest, continuing youth rodeo associations in the world and High School rodeos while she was growing up, and her parents still go with her on the road when they can. Marty's parents also lend a hand helping to feed the horses and assist with housework while Tana is on the road.

Road Report

Tana loves to encourage others to follow their dreams, so she speaks at church services, barrel races, rodeos, and other organizations. She has put on clinics for 4H, Girl Scouts, and church groups, and supports an equine-assisted therapeutic riding center. Tana also serves as the director of the Women's Professional Rodeo Association.

Her goal is to make the Wrangler National Finals Rodeo again. Tana would like to give both her horses a chance to compete there.

"Amigo deserves the chance to run there when he is healthy. – A gold (World Champion) buckle would be nice some time, too!" according to Tana.

A Time to Nurture

Tana and I had the chance to talk a few years after our initial discussion, and I was eager to get her update. She explained that in rodeo, the winnings are based on the horse's performance. When a horse gets hurt, the revenues decrease while the expenses increase. And this can make it tough financially.

Because of Amigo's health and expenses, Tana decided to take some time off from rodeo and focus on taking care of her horses and her family. She was able to leverage her horse-based experience in a new job in property and casualty insurance, focusing on the horse industry. The position allows her to use her exceptional knowledge about horses and her communication skills from her corporate experience, while she supplements her family's income.

Tana is also getting a lot of satisfaction from teaching clinics to other horse-lovers. "It's very hands on, and I have to be home to be able to run clinics. I really like giving back and helping people. As Zig Zigler said, if you help enough people reach their dreams, you will reach yours!"

But Tana is not giving up on rodeo. She looks forward to getting to the top of the circuit again – perhaps with a young horse she would need to train, "at least one more time." Tana has no regrets about her decision to pursue rodeo; she wouldn't do anything differently if given the chance.

Tana's Advice and Action Steps:

- Take a risk and pursue your passion.
- Plan well financially.
- Seek the support of friends, family, and your resource team.
- Do what you love and it will never seem like work.

Resources:

Tana's website: www.tanapoppino.com
Rodeo Promotions: www.rodeopromotions.com
Women's Professional Rodeo Association: www.wpra.com

> ❝Discover your God-given talents, follow your dream, work hard, and never, never, give up!❞
>
> – Tana Poppino

ᑲ ᑲ ᑲ ᑲ

23. TAKE A STEP FORWARD

The women in this chapter tapped into their creativity to launch new career opportunities. Stacey Kannenberg, Carla Falcone, Romy Taormina, Heidi Roizen, Grace Chon, and Tana Poppino all had safe and practical careers they could have stayed with, or gone back to, but they chose to pursue new ventures that spoke to their passions.

These women found their unique niche and tapped their networks and built resource teams to help them achieve new goals.

Don't Wait Until You Need a Network to Build One

Building professional relationships is not something you do only when you need a job or promotion. It's not something you can force, buy, or borrow days before you need it. Developing meaningful relationships should be a regular part of your life as a success-oriented individual. Just like friendships, the most authentic and meaningful professional relationships evolve naturally over time.

Stacey Kannenberg tapped into the mommy network, which is a powerful resource of talented women who are currently focusing on raising their children. Don't overlook the obvious; count all the people around you as members of your prospective network from the playground to the boardroom. One of the best ways to grow your network is through personal referrals from your friends and family.

Believe in Yourself

These women launched risky new businesses and career goals and went against the pack by **not** doing the safe, reasonable, and secure thing. They all had naysayers discouraging them from moving forward with their plans, but they were able to filter out the negatives and focus on the positives because they had the strength and conviction to believe in themselves.

The group mentality is often fear based but these women broke through the pack and showcased their innovation and individuality. How do you want to be seen in the world? As one who follows the crowd or as a cutting-edge thinker and leader. By honoring yourself and building a support system of people who share your vision, you can create and thrive in the new career you want, whether it is an entrepreneurial venture or a new profession.

REINVENTION TOOLBOX

Build Relationships – Not Networks; Tap into Your Resource Team

I believe that the six degrees of separation theory is being whittled down since not a day goes by that I don't make a valuable connection with a new person based on a referral from someone I already know. The women in this chapter also utilized their respective networks to move forward with their new career goals.

Having successfully reinvented my career, I am confident that I can achieve my dreams; but I have also realized that I can't do it all alone. My personal Board of Directors and mentor team has provided a valuable opportunity for me to cultivate and nurture quality relationships. I don't like to think in terms of increasing my network; instead, I build my community!

Good things happen through other good people, so I encourage you to build quality relationships and think about how you can help others in addition to getting what you need from your personal posse.

In the career world, 80 percent of jobs are unadvertised and these positions are landed through the power of networking. Whether you are seeking a new position, launching an entrepreneurial venture, or marketing your wares or services in an existing business, building and stewarding professional relationships will help you on your way. Here are some best practices to lead you to success:

1. **Ask yourself what your goals are** in developing networking relationships so that you can seek out individuals who will help you gather relevant information.

2. **Know your personal brand.** Have a clear understanding of what you do well and what makes you special or different from others doing the same thing. In order to get referrals, you must be able to articulate what your brand or *special sauce* is to others.

3. **Know what you want.** Be able to articulate what you are seeking and how others may help you – and how you can reciprocate.

4. **Stay positive**. Be prepared to speak with anyone who will listen; don't be afraid of rejection. Be friendly and put yourself out there.

5. **Search out a common denominator**. Figure out the common interests you share with those with whom you speak. Build the conversation around that topic to get the ball rolling and ease nerves.

6. **Take risks** and reach out to some *wish list* contacts or join a professional group that could lead to something significant.

7. **Become known as a powerful resource for others.** When you are known as a strong resource, people will turn to you for suggestions, ideas, and referrals. This keeps you visible to them and gives you a chance to give back.

8. **Make yourself useful.** Reach out to others in a capacity where you can actually do something good and show off your skills at the same time. Join a board of a worthy organization; offer to take notes at a conference where people in your desired career sector will be, and look for opportunities to solve problems.

9. **Be gracious and always thank the people** (in writing) who have been helpful. Stewarding relationships in your network is essential for your professional reputation and it's most appreciated.

10. **Always ask: "How Can I Help You?"** A trusted mentor taught me how make networking reciprocal by asking how I could help the other person. The best professionals generously help others grow and by doing so sharpen their skills. Paying-it-forward is part of practicing good career karma and will empower you to succeed. Focus on how you can help others achieve, grow, stretch, and develop and you will benefit.

LEARN A LESSON FROM THE RECOVERING LAWYERS

I have provided career coaching to thousands of lawyers over the years from their beginning journeys in law school to their varied career phases as minted attorneys. While some attorneys thrive in their legal careers throughout their professional lives, others utilize their transferable skills to find new careers that play to their strengths and speak to their passions. The women in this chapter have found another life after the law and are relishing their new beginnings.

24. ELLEN COVNER: FROM LAW TO LANDSCAPING

Early in her career, Ellen Covner, like many other professional women, noticed that working with men could be a very mixed experience. She also learned that group and workplace dynamics often had a style and language all their own that did not promote cooperation, creativity, and "drive." She came to realize that as important as it was to be self-supporting and have a good income, money was not a sufficient motivator to stay in a "good job." After 20+ years practicing health law in major hospitals and law firms, she was ready for new challenges. She wanted a change that would renew her creativity and bring her joy in her work. The call of the outdoors beckoned and enticed her to focus on promoting environments that nourish people and their properties.

A Circuitous Route to Career Bliss

Moving from a secure and high powered career in law to the world of an entrepreneur was no easy task. Ellen discussed the transition with friends, family, and her husband, all of whom supported her in this daring new career move. She phased into landscaping, keeping her hand in the legal world part-time at first. Ellen worked on friends' properties and eventually got referrals from them and a local nursery.

Building and stewarding client relationships is something that Ellen did regularly as an attorney and this skill transferred well into her new business. She enjoyed the immediate connection with new clients and the process of developing a landscape plan to make them happier in their home environment.

Ellen thrives on creating gardens and landscapes that capture her clients' vision – whether it's recovering the beauty of an overgrown or ailing landscape or developing the possibilities of an empty space, transforming it from a detriment to an asset with a little attention. She creates themed gardens to respond to a client's interest, such as honoring a loved one, having a serene place to sit or meditate, or having an herb garden that provides outdoor interest and fragrance as well as bringing extra delight to cooking. She is a listener who partners with her clients to give them a way of reaching their goals whether they understand the green world or not.

The Weeds in a Workplace Garden

As her own boss, Ellen is thriving in an autonomous work environment where she can set high standards of excellence and have the freedom to create new services and products for clients. As an owner of a new business she admits the lack of security and endless demands on her time can be worrisome. But recognizing that she is now responsible for her success, and that she is not held back by being an employee for someone else, has proven tremendously liberating.

She encourages other women to think about what they really like to do and to not be deterred by the fear of not being able to make a living. Ellen suggests that career changers "…try it on and figure it out. There is a wonderful opportunity for trial and error and you can always change your mind. When you have created your new career the money will come."

Growing the Business

This budding entrepreneur (pun intended!) admits that watching expenses is always a concern. Her strategy is to keep overhead down and continue to build her clientele with excellent referrals and services that distinguish her from other landscape companies. Ellen learned early on that record keeping was a necessity and utilizes a variety of tools to manage her books, foster client communications, and facilitate marketing and networking.

Since gardening in Pennsylvania, where Ellen lives and works, is seasonal, she keeps busy in the winter months by taking classes and learning new techniques that will enhance her services to clients. She enrolled in the three-year certificate in horticulture program at the Barnes Foundation. "It is always fun to learn more and discover new possibilities in landscaping." Ellen also speaks to garden clubs and other groups giving presentations and demonstrations. She likes to plan new projects with clients so that they can start in the spring and she has launched a series of winter-proof indoor themed gardens that make wonderful presents for all occasions.

Marketing is always an important part of growing the business, no matter what the season. Ellen hired a marketing expert and recently launched a website that has given her a much needed online presence. She uses business cards with her new logo to network, and posts lawn signs at job locations to capitalize on curb appeal and drive-by prospective clients who see her work. She offers a free consultation as a way for her and a potential client to get to know one another and discuss the client's goals.

In 2010 the Wynnewood Business Association launched a recognition program for Women in Excellence and Ellen was the first recipient of its Women's Excellence in Business Award. She is very grateful for this award and sees it as a sign of growth as well as an incentive to continue to move forward with her company.

Garden Rehabilitator

Ellen has been landscaping since she was a child. She started her first garden with her mom in Connecticut and carries many of those techniques with her today. Gardening has also been a therapeutic outlet for Ellen, who found that immersing herself in it was a new way to create life when her marriage died. Gardening was cathartic and a healthy way for her to rebuild and renew her life.

Likewise, Ellen enjoys bringing diseased plants back to good health or moving an ailing plant to a better location in the landscape so it may provide renewed pleasure. Almost no specimens are beyond rehabilitation and with Ellen's expert knowledge and tender loving care, most plants come back to thrive in time.

Growth Potential

2010 marks four years for Ellen's business as a Limited Liability Company (LLC). She has steadily grown her clientele and works with a foreman and a crew who reflect the values of her company. She has built a collegial team that enjoys working together and loves what they do.

Using her lawyerly skills in problem solving, contracts, and project management, Ellen has built a business she loves. Since she traded in her corporate business suits for jeans, a sun hat and waterproof boots, Ellen enjoys wearing skirts and dresses when she is not at work. But there is nothing better for this lawyer turned landscaper than digging in the earth and creating custom gardens that bring delight to the senses.

What's New?

When I reconnected with Ellen, her business was going strong. Her company has won multiple awards including Best Landscape Design, Best Growing Business of the Year, and Best Landscaping Services, just to name a few. And Ellen shares, "I've gotten better at my craft" as a landscaper and as a businesswoman.

Ellen said the growth of her company has come from growing relationships with clients, as well as referrals. She keeps her clients for many years, and has helped some evolve from small houses to larger houses with larger landscape needs. After completing her certificate of horticulture, she is getting more referrals from other professionals, such as a tree service. "It's a two-way street" with professional relationships; Ellen reciprocates referrals where it makes sense.

Part of Ellen's success comes from understanding and targeting the market she wants to work with. She doesn't use coupons or ads for services; she looks for clients from a higher-end demographic who care about their properties and have the resources to invest in them.

Ellen appreciates the quality of life this new career offers. Having the opportunity to work on her clients' properties allows her to be creative while she makes people happy. Her work is "so much fun" but it's still "scary to be out there" when you start a new business. As a business owner, "the learning never stops." Ellen has learned how to close more business, and how to communicate better with clients. For example, she emails clients with pictures of suitable plant options and examples of plants in flower so they can choose exactly what they want.

She also has learned the importance of developing strong relationships with her crew. She pays well and is quick to express appreciation for their hard work. "I would love to see them launch their own business one day!"

When we chatted about what it was like for her to go through a career change, Ellen became thoughtful. "People look at the reality of their life, and say 'I can't make a change because' and they list all these obligations. You need to think about your transferrable skills, and it can take several years to think this way. What's important is to let yourself dream. I had a really narrow view of what careers were possible."

At one time, Ellen thought the worst thing would be to start your own business. With hindsight, she says the preparation she did was not enough. She sometimes is amazed that the business lasted long enough for her to identify and take advantage of the available resources to make her business more business-like. "I would have looked into programs and resources in landscaping earlier; there's a lot of on-the-job learning, and I wasn't systematic enough in going about it." Still,

Ellen notes that she is still in business while many landscaping companies did not survive the economic downturn of the last few years.

Ellen's daughter is going through a time of career introspection and change. Ellen enjoys paying-it-forward and finds tremendous satisfaction in being a mentor to her daughter. In fact, she is thinking about helping other women as they consider career changes. After Ellen's career change, she is still GROWING strong!

Ellen's Advice and Action Steps:

- Take the time to figure out what you really love to do. Test-drive many things and know that you can always change your mind. You are not defined by your current occupation but have a diversity of talents and abilities within you.
- Never give up – what you are meant to do is out there somewhere waiting for you to discover it.
- Rally your support network (friends, family, additional resources) because you will need to lean on them during your transition.
- Don't be afraid to reinvent yourself – it can be very liberating.

Resources:

Custom Gardens, LLC: www.customgardensllc.com
Custom Gardens on Facebook: www.facebook.com/pages/Custom-Gardens-LLC
Think and Grow Rich by Napoleon Hill

"Be as you wish to seem."

– Socrates

ॐ ॐ ॐ ॐ

25. TONYA FITZPATRICK: TURNING A PASSION FOR TRAVEL INTO A CAREER

Award-winning broadcaster and author Tonya Fitzpatrick always knew "come hell or high water" she would become a lawyer. She did just that, and enjoyed an appointment as a Deputy Assistant Secretary at the U.S. Department of Education, and also served under a federal defense contract as the Senior Legal Advisor for the Office of Civil Rights at the U.S. Department of Homeland Security. But her dissatisfaction with her legal career and the political environment in Washington, DC, confirmed that she was ready for a change. Traveling has always allowed Tonya to reconnect with herself; her passion for travel and a desire to live a purposeful life led her to reinvent her avocation and make it her career.

Wanderlust Leads to a New Career

This "recovering attorney" has stellar credentials that empower her with a myriad of transferable skills. Tonya graduated from the London School of Economics, East China University of Law and Politics, and Wayne State University Law School. She is also a student of the arts and previously worked at the Old Globe Theatre in San Diego and the Globe Theatre (under the late Sam Wannamaker) in London. According to Tonya, her greatest education has come through traveling – discovering different cultures, learning about history, and meeting the beautiful citizens of the world. This is how she transitioned into her new role as a travel broadcast journalist, multimedia producer, and global citizen.

But how does one make the break from a secure legal career to making a livelihood traveling? According to Tonya, you honor your passion and the rest will follow. Tonya and her husband, Ian, also an attorney, left their law practices behind to create a unique global community through their travel radio show – *World Footprints* (formerly Travel'n On). Their decision to grow a community of fellow responsible travelers was affirmed when they were awarded First Place Travel Broadcast from the North American Travel Journalists Association. Since forming World Footprints Media, LLC, the producer of the award-winning *World Footprints Radio,* they have expanded their broadcast platform to include additional multimedia digital outlets such as Internet, TV, and multiple social media sites. This allows them to stay connected with their fellow travelers and to grow their audience, even while on the road. Additionally, Tonya and Ian have strengthened their social responsibility stance and advocacy efforts, specifically in the areas of human trafficking, conservation and global health, and poverty reduction.

In addition to her role as Executive Producer of *World Footprints* and CEO of **World Footprints Media**, LLC, Tonya is also an author and speaker. She and Ian wrote a chapter in a book with Stephen Covey entitled *Success Simplified*, a mobile travel app called *Baltimore & Beyond*, and an e-itinerary for Washington, DC. Tonya is a popular speaker at the annual FestiGals Conference in New Orleans, among other venues. She and Ian are adding exclusive travel opportunities for their new business entity World Footprints Discovery Tours and the two are constantly looking to expand the World Footprints business portfolio. Tonya also frequently covers travel-related legislation at the White House and Congress.

Planning for Change

Every move Tonya has made in life she has first carefully planned, and her exit from the legal profession was no exception. Her legal training helped her hone her research skills, and she performs due-diligence on every project she pursues. While she admits to being a risk-taker, she also knows the importance of staying afloat financially. Tonya worked with a life/career coach to help her reinvent her passion for travel and turn it into a viable career. She also saved money to support herself for a full year, since she knew it would take time to turn a profit from the show and her new company.

The radio show makes money from investors, paid sponsors, and advertisers, but securing those has been a challenge in a tough economy. Tonya and Ian are now expanding their broadcast platforms and growing their audience by tapping into new markets such as university students who travel, study, and work abroad, and providing them with resources and a venue to share their experiences.

While Tonya is always using her transferable skills in contracts, negotiations, communication, and writing for the show and her company, she found it tough at first to "sell" her ideas and thought it would be easier to market someone else's product. But she has since overcome that feeling of insecurity and embraced her humble confidence in this project and the company that she truly believes in.

Celebrity Power on the Show

Prominent personalities and celebrity interviews on the radio show have given the program extra punch and increased the listening audience. Those special guests include wildlife advocate Jack Hanna, director Ken Burns, actress Stefanie Powers, NASCAR icon Kyle Petty, philanthropist David Rockefeller, Jr., Robert Kennedy, Jr., Rajmohan Gandhi (grandson of Mahatma Gandhi), a number of Travel Channel hosts, and Iron Chef Cat Cora, among many other celebrities and newsmakers.

World Footprints was granted accreditation to cover the 2010 Winter Olympics in Vancouver. Although some sporting events were covered, such as the Luge, Bobsled and Biathlon, the broadcast focus was on the cultural stories behind the games: how the First Nations people were represented, Vancouver's sustainable/green development legacy, and animal conservation efforts of the Olympic mascots. Tonya and Ian were credentialed to cover the 2012 Summer Paralympic Games in London and covered the 2014 Winter Olympics in Sochi, Russia.

An influential commentator, journalist, and thought leader in the travel arena, Tonya has been heard or seen on *MSNBC.com, NPR, Retirement Living, AllAfrica.com*, local CBS and NBC affiliate stations, and others. Tonya is a member of the Society of American Travel Writers, the National Press Club, the North American Travel Journalist Association, and the Society of Professional Journalists. Both Tonya and Ian are members of the International Speakers Network.

The Joy of Being Your Own Boss

The reality of being an entrepreneur is that you have total control over your business, and that you are solely responsible for your success or failure. Tonya has always had a strong work ethic and she believes it is now even stronger because she has taken ownership of her career future and her business. According to Tonya, she relies on her spiritual strength, prays a lot, and has created a work environment with Ian that values integrity, work ethic, and authenticity.

While Tonya's life has included many exciting travel experiences, she has learned to take *calculated* risks and plan for them. She has lived, studied, and worked abroad in England, China, Russia, and Romania. Her travels have taken her through many regions of the world, including a five-week backpacking trip through Asia during which she returned to China and visited eight other countries in the region. As an avid scuba diver, she gravitates to coastal areas. She loves adventure and wants to trek through Nepal and climb Kilimanjaro someday. But this adventurist has made a conscious effort to grow her business wisely instead of quickly, honoring the vision she and her husband created.

From the beginning, responsible travel, culture, and heritage were values that Tonya and Ian brought to their show. *World Footprints* is unique in that its entire focus is about leaving positive footprints by raising awareness about important social issues, fostering cross-cultural understanding and friendships, encouraging positive impacts on local people and their environments, supporting local trade and fair markets, and promoting authentic travel experiences that respect cultural heritage.

Tonya is on a quest to help others respect the natural environment and eco-balance of the planet by encouraging travel choices that minimize negative environmental impacts. One trip and one radio show or media product at a time, she and Ian are spreading their message, fulfilling their purpose, and living their dream.

What's New?

I checked in with Tonya several years after my first book was written. With the benefit of hindsight, Tonya had additional pearls of wisdom to share with anyone considering a career change.

Looking back, Tonya said she felt compelled to change her career because she had "a nagging feeling that there was something more fulfilling out there. I was thrilled to serve my country using my law degree, but the work didn't feel meaningful enough. I was involved more in policy than enforcement, and the job was temporary (i.e., tied to an administration)." So she took that first critical step of understanding what really made her feel alive – travel – and designed her career around that.

Tonya says she was always a risk-taker. When she was younger, she moved to London "on a whim" with only $300 in her pocket, yet managed to get into school and to get work. Tonya "was used to having everything work out," and this gave her the confidence to launch her travel career.

Still, she increased her chances for success by planning and saving for her career change. This is advice she gives others who are thinking of making a change: plan wisely for transition, have an exit strategy, and get a mentor in your new industry to help you. Although Tonya had saved for 2 ½ years, she wishes she had sought a "low-demand" job to continue working (and having income) while she started to build **World Footprints**.

Looking forward, Tonya plans to continue to grow and evolve **World Footprints**; she wants to narrow the focus of the company and emphasize what differentiates it. She and Ian have created new World Footprints Discovery Tours to foster cultural-immersion, and have developed two travel guides (for Washington, DC, and Baltimore). They also want to make documentaries in the near future. Essentially, Tonya and Ian want to be the "go-to" organization for information, voluntourism, and travel resources relating to an area's culture and history, and they want **World Footprints** to be financially secure and solvent.

After several years in her new career, Tonya has come to appreciate the transferrable skills she brought with her from her former law career, such as working on contracts and public speaking. But she is the first to admit that she doesn't know everything. Tonya said "it really takes a village" to raise a corporation; she developed an advisory board to bring skills and knowledge to the company that she and Ian lack.

One last bit of advice she shared with us was to stay true to your brand. She and Ian were contacted by a national talk show doing an episode on what it's like to work with your spouse. After several discussions, it was clear that the show wanted stories of conflict and difficulty, not success. Tonya and Ian declined to be in the feature because World Footprints is about building positive relationships; it wouldn't support the brand to manufacture conflict that didn't exist. Although they missed out on national coverage, their integrity, and the integrity of World Footprints, remains unscathed. "When you work hard to build something, you don't want to compromise your credibility in any way."

Tonya's Advice and Action Steps:

- Honor your "red flags" and trust your gut.
- Grow your business wisely and not just quickly.
- Utilize your mentors and personal resource team.
- Be ready to pay-it-forward and help others.
- Be aware of your total skill set and tap into your strengths.

Resources:

World Footprints Media: www.WorldFootprints.com
International Speakers Network: www.bookaspeaker.net
Twitter: www.twitter.com/WorldFootprints

"Honor Your SELF and the rest will follow.**"**

– Tonya Fitzpatrick

⚘ ⚘ ⚘ ⚘

26. BETH PATTERSON: LAW AND ENLIGHTENED ORDER

Beth Patterson has always been passionate about music, so her career progression from a boutique entertainment law firm, to RCA Records, and then to Elektra Entertainment was logical for this attorney after earning her JD from Brooklyn Law School. After the merger of AOL and Time Warner, Beth was laid off from Elektra and began to think seriously about her next career move. Ageism and sexism were alive and well in the corporate arena, according to Beth, so at 40-something she was ready to take her career into her own hands and make a change.

As a New Yorker who witnessed the second plane hit the World Trade Center on 9/11, she believes that this horrific event was also a catalyst that propelled her towards a change. Beth was with her husband in Vail, Colorado, attending a jazz music festival when they both fell in love with the idea of relocating and starting anew. Quite a bold decision for a native New Yorker who was not yet sure if there was life beyond the Big Apple.

A New Life Beckons

As a practicing Buddhist, Beth suffered through sexist bosses in the corporate arena who gave her additional grief for her enlightened spiritual ways. Colorado beckoned also because it is the home of Naropa University, a fully accredited Buddhist-oriented university, where Beth earned a Masters Degree in Transpersonal Counseling Psychology in 2006. She came to the conclusion that "...law just wasn't me anymore," and started on a personal journey at Naropa that ultimately led her to develop a private practice in psychotherapy and grief counseling in Denver, as well as a position as Life Care Coordinator for a Denver hospice.

Beth's studies at Naropa in human development in the second half of life allowed Beth to dig more deeply into her personal journey, and to develop her feminine self. Her life as a product of the Feminist Revolution did not accord with the traditional developmental model of Carl Jung, who had posited in his work during the Victorian Age that women in the second half of life worked to develop their masculine energy. One of her favorite books is Maureen Murdock's *The Heroine's Journey*, which details the passage women like Beth take in their quest towards wholeness in the second half of life, rediscovering their feminine energy that had to be suppressed to "make it" in the male-oriented corporate world.

A Jill of Three Trades

Beth is now enjoying a three-tiered career as a therapist in private practice, a Hospice bereavement and volunteer coordinator, and as a some-time attorney, representing musicians and other individuals in the arts. The foundation of her private practice is built upon the premise that a safe and non-judgmental therapeutic environment can help clients discover their innate inner resources in order to navigate life's inevitable changes more successfully. Changes such as the death of a loved one or pet, divorce or separation, job loss, illness or disability, infertility, stressful caregiver trials or other life challenges.

> "My therapeutic style is informed by my spiritual practice and deep belief that we all have the inherent wisdom to use our losses and other life challenges and transitions to grow and heal. My counseling practice is client-centered, grounded in wellness not sickness, and blends solution-focused, contemplative, body-centered and cognitive behavioral approaches."

In addition to her certification as a hospice trained grief counselor, Beth also practices EMDR (Eye Movement Desensitization and Reprocessing), an effective and scientifically proven tool for alleviating trauma, negative self-beliefs, chronic pain, depression, and anxiety by enhancing performance in all fields. A certified mindfulness meditation instructor, Beth has grown her professional skill set with these additional tools to empower her in her new career.

An Authentic Career Fit

This new career path comes as "such a relief" according to Beth, who is finally able to be herself in the workplace. She is also appreciated and acknowledged for her strengths and hard work, which she finds very rewarding. It was tough for Beth to leave the high salary security of corporate law in New York, but shedding the golden handcuffs was worth it in the long run for this legal counselor turned therapist. Beth shares an office with other practitioners to cut costs.

By nature, Beth is not a risk taker so the cross country relocation and career move was a leap of faith. She and her husband love the lifestyle in Colorado and her practice is on-the-grow. The cost of living is less than in New York, but she struggles with the health care system and dealing with insurance companies. As a solo practitioner, she does not accept insurance payments directly, but clients can submit her bills for reimbursement if their plan includes mental health and wellness coverage. It's a challenge to help clients understand this process but she remains optimistic. Her goal is to have 10 steady clients a week, in addition to her 30-hour a week hospice position, and to develop a strong referral system as her practice grows.

Breathing the mountain air of Denver has cleansed her body and soul and Beth is at peace with her transition. She reinvented herself career-wise and tapped into her inner woman to release a person who is passionate about helping others and in control of her happiness.

What's New?

Beth's work has continued to develop. Her practice is growing, in part because she "had to bite the bullet" and get listed with several insurance companies. Although this creates extra paperwork, she is now able to help more clients. Beth is focusing on networking – by writing articles and being available as an "expert" – and this increases her practice also. She still faces challenges in the workplace, but the nature of those challenges has changed. In her community and her practice, Beth works to change the mindset that "therapy is a luxury."

Looking back on her career transition, Beth said it was really her values that drove her to change. She wanted to make a more meaningful difference to others. She also wanted to share her wisdom and experience, while being free to express herself fully. By shifting to counseling, Beth was able to bring her work in line with her evolving values, to live a more congruent life .

Beth has lots of advice for others looking for a new career identity: "stay with your passion; think outside the box with making yourself known; don't give up; have a support system of successful mentors in your field, and don't be afraid to call on them." Remember, "Work can be joy!" Good advice for us all.

Beth's Advice and Action Steps:

- Don't beat yourself up – you need to be your number one advocate!
- Consider sharing office space until you can afford your own unique space.
- Be truthful with yourself. Listen to your heart and know what you are passionate about.
- Don't be afraid to be a woman – tap into your femininity.

Resources:

Beth's website: www.bethspatterson.com
Maureen Murdock's *The Heroine's Journey*

> **"Be a good person and be mindful that your actions matter."**

– Beth Patterson

♐ ♐ ♐ ♐

27. LIZ WILLIAMS: LEGAL EAGLE FORGES NEW PATH WITH FOOD

The legal profession is under stress as the oversaturation of attorneys in the market has skewed the talent supply and demand making it difficult for many to find work. I have interviewed and coached thousands of lawyers throughout my career and continue to be amazed by the transferability of the legal skill set.

Liz Williams was first featured on my blog and I love her story because she took a true passion in food and made it career worthy. She uses her legal skills every day and tastes the rewards of her hard work in a newfound profession she adores. I am thrilled that she is part of the second edition.

Fascinated by the way the lure of nutmeg and peppercorns motivated the exploration of the world; Liz Williams was lucky to be born into a family of Sicilian heritage in New Orleans. She grew up eating in two great food traditions. In her sixth decade, Liz now looks back at the variety of careers she has in her repertoire and is thriving in yet another new role as Founder and Director of the **Southern Food and Beverage Museum.**

Don't Learn to Type!

Her career journey started after Liz earned an undergraduate degree with an English major at Louisiana State University. At the time, graduates went to employment agencies to find a placement in the world of work . But the woman owner of one particular agency told Liz she would never get a job unless she went back to school and earned a professional degree in law, medicine, or perhaps even architecture. She also warned Liz never to become adept at typing or she would be stuck in secretarial roles for her entire career.

While Liz's male counterparts, including her husband with an Art History degree, were landing great positions after college, she was hitting the proverbial brick wall. Although architecture seemed appealing at first, the three years of engineering pre-requisite classes made law school look all the more doable.

So Liz and her husband entered law school together and three years later took on prestigious Army JAG (Judge Advocate General) officer positions in Germany. They were young and eager to work overseas and the US Army afforded them the opportunity to grow their legal careers and fulfill a call to serve.

Paving the Way for Women in JAG

Liz quickly distinguished herself as a criminal trial specialist and, at the time, she was the only woman JAG officer in all of Europe. She was highly sought after as an attorney and defined her niche as a sex crime specialist. The JAG training and experience sharpened her skills as a lawyer and taught her a lot about how the world works. Liz was responsible for writing Army transgender policies that addressed sex change operations and honorable discharges. She also worked at the overseas division of the University of Maryland and taught Business Law during her Army tenure in Germany which led to future teaching posts in the states.

Although Liz enjoyed her JAG career, she and her husband eventually returned to the states to begin their civilian careers and to start their family. An attractive offer to teach Constitutional Law at West Point almost wooed Liz to New York but instead she began pro bono legal work with non-profit and arts organizations in the Washington, DC, area.

New Orleans beckoned and Liz returned home to serve as the Director of the Arts Administration Program at the University of New Orleans. She taught Arts Administration Law and several other courses such as Historic Preservation Law, Business Ethics, and the History of the Restaurant and was thrilled to have her family back home in Louisiana.

Coming Home

The next transition was to a position with the University of New Orleans Foundation, in which Liz served as President and CEO for seven years. During her tenure, the UNO Foundation opened the D-Day Museum, the Nims Center (a film studio with motion capture laboratory), established a 33 acre research park with over 250,000 square feet of office space, and established the Ogden Museum of Southern Art and several other projects, including the UNO Press.

It's clear that Liz's energy is limitless and her transferable skills know no bounds. What I really appreciate is that Liz is very much in tune with her passions and she has consistently pursued careers that met her values during different points in her life.

Building Something Positive

Liz began building another passion, the **Southern Food and Beverage Museum.** It is the only non-corporate food museum of its type in the USA. Liz and her team are building a new institution in New Orleans and creating ways for people to learn about culture and the world through the lens of food.

With her litigation days behind her, Liz is thrilled to be building something that is positive instead of fighting or dealing with peoples' emotional ties to a controversy. Now she can work together with people to enjoy a common goal.

What drives Liz's passion for food is the sociological and anthropological origins of food. Liz explained that food is a source of identity for cultures. Food plays an important role in hospitality and celebration and it has economic implications that go back to the time of the spice trade routes.

New Orleans Needs SoFAB

What better place to open a food and beverage museum than in New Orleans, a city of cooking with its rich and historic appreciation for food. Liz identified some of the indigenous foods that define southern cuisine including: corn, tomatoes, peanuts, and potatoes.

According to Liz:

"The Southern Food and Beverage Museum celebrates, interprets, investigates, entertains and preserves. A collaboration of many, the Museum allows food lovers of all stripes – Southerners and non-Southerners, locals and tourists, academics and food industry insiders — to pull up their chairs and dig into the food and drink of the South. And although we are based in New Orleans, we are bringing our message about the entire South to the world through exhibits, collection of oral histories and videos, and other research."

Liz has an enthusiastic team of foodies on her staff ranging from the Business Manager and Archivist to a Chef in Residence and a Director of Collections to name just a few. She also has an army of interns who are passionate about food and are learning the museum ropes at SoFAB. The staff self-identified and made their skills and passions clear to Liz so the *if you build it they will come* philosophy rings true for staff as well as museum guests.

Collection of artifacts for exhibits started back in 2004, and sadly, Hurricane Katrina devastated New Orleans in 2005. The launch of SoFAB in 2008 was part of the rebirth of the city and preserving the cultural heritage of the south. Liz believes they were the first new institution to open post-Katrina.

Eat Your Way through the Museum

While there are special events that involve eating and drinking the delicacies of southern foods, most of the museum involves exhibits that are hands-on and educational. One of the jewels in the museum crown is a 32-foot long bar, donated by the founding family of a restaurant started in 1859. The challenge was taking the massive piece of furniture apart and then reconstructing it in a space that was large enough to showcase its beauty.

Space continues to be an issue as this young 501c3 non-profit is bursting at the seams and always looking for larger accommodations. Liz has to think several steps into the future to stay ahead of the game and plan for contingencies.

The museum has multiple funding sources from some generous private donors to grant support and corporate giving. Revenue is also generated from admission fees and gift shop sales.

What Do I Really Want to Do?

Liz left her lucrative post at the UNO Foundation because she introduced the idea of creating a food museum to her Chancellor and he said no. Instead of settling for no, she left and decided to make it happen on her own. Ever tenacious, scrappy, and determined, Liz Williams and a group of like-minded food enthusiasts created SoFAB as a labor of love and a way to honor New Orleans and the greater south through food.

Liz continues her research and writing, which centers on the legal and policy issues related to food and foodways. In addition to establishing this new museum, she consults on issues of non-profit management and governance, as well as public/private partnerships, intellectual property, and publishing. Her first book, *Controversies in Law and Food* was published by ABC-CLIO.

Thomas Jefferson believed that one should always be *coming* and never *arrive* – and Liz subscribes to this mantra. One thing builds on the next, and the future is bright for this lawyer-now-museum-director living her passion with a new, food-themed career.

The next big issue Liz has on her SoFAB plate is where to house the many cookbooks donated by a famous New Orleans chef. So many people lost their cookbooks as a result of Katrina; these books are worth their weight in gold and will help to preserve the living history of the food, drink, and related culture of the South. Cheers to Liz for leading the cause!

Planning Her Next Move

When I checked back in with Liz, her projects, and her career transition, were still going strong. The SoFAB museum (soon to be renamed "SoFAB Institute") is moving into its own building on its own land. Plans include a restaurant, bar, and demo kitchen to bring Southern Food and Beverage to life.

The cookbook collection has grown to 10,000 volumes, including a lot of author notes, signed copies, a large collection of community cookbooks, and pamphlets from food manufacturers. Liz worked with the public library to develop a culinary branch and have the materials designated as a special collection. The development of this branch will bring library service to a neighborhood that had none, so the entire community will benefit.

What's really remarkable about Liz is that while she's actively engaged in her current career, she's also planning and preparing for her next career steps. To Liz, "retirement" does NOT mean stopping, but she knows she "needs a transition plan when SoFAB continues without me." Her long-term plan is to get more involved in food policy, and to use everything she's done so far to give back to others. She always wanted to write, so she's using the platform of SoFAB to become established as a writer. Then, when she leaves SoFAB, she will "already be up and running."

Liz plans to achieve these goals by increasing her exposure through interviews and television appearances related to her books. She's nurturing her career as an author, and has already published two food-related books: *A-Z Encyclopedia of Food Controversies and the Law*, with Stephanie Jane Carter, and *New Orleans: A Food Biography*. "Once an editor sees you've finished two books, they know you can meet deadlines and be relied on to deliver." Now she's being asked to submit other book proposals.

When Liz looks back on her career journey so far, she notes – "I wish I'd known that food was okay to pursue." She had a strong interest in food, but didn't want to follow "traditional" food career paths – she didn't want to be a chef or have a restaurant. Liz says she never had the sense that her career path would be a straight line, but more a meandering river. Early on, she felt she needed a job that supported her and that "reflected me – and provided identity," and law met that need.

But Liz continues to grow and change, and so her career grows and changes with her. Her advice to others is "figure out what you want to do, AND CREATE A PLAN TO GET THERE. If it doesn't exist, you may have to invent it." If you are at point A, and you want to get to point B, how will you do it? Liz provides a great example of how to stay in the moment while planning and working for a future goal. I can't wait to see what Liz does next!

Liz's Advice and Action Steps:

- Think about what you really want to do and then make it happen.
- Surround yourself with passionate people who share your goals.
- Never stop learning and be willing to serve as a mentor for others.
- Define your niche as an expert in something.

Resources:

Southern Food and Beverage Museum: www.southernfood.org

"If It Doesn't Exist, Invent It!"

– Liz Williams

ๆ ๆ ๆ ๆ

28. LISA MONTANARO: ORGANIZING GEEK LAUNCHES ONLINE UNIVERSITY

Lisa and I are kindred spirits as performers who have channeled our artistic sensibilities and talents into other careers. I really enjoyed getting to know Lisa when I featured her on my blog and I am delighted to include her in the second edition of my book. She is a lawyer with moxie that reinvented her career to play to her strengths and she is thriving.

Lisa Montanaro realized early on that she did not like the practice of law even though she had given it her all for 9 years. She loved law school, and later teaching law, but the practice of law was never an ideal fit.

Like many lawyers, Lisa spent time at a large firm learning the trade and working 90+ hour weeks. She was working in New York City law firm where the environment was competitive and intense. Lisa was able to move from that firm to an in-house counsel position that seemed to be a better fit. This was 1999 and the Y2K craze was consuming all business sectors including the legal field. Lisa started thinking seriously about finding a different career that honored her passions while still playing to her strengths.

We Plan Lives

Lisa was known for sharing her wisdom and life planning skills with friends over the years. A dear friend sent Lisa an email telling her about the National Association of Professional Organizers (NAPO) and encouraged her to learn more about this field. Lisa's friend was on target! After researching NAPO and attending an event, Lisa discovered her true professional "peeps" and found that people actually organize for a living. This association was leading the profession for organizers and Lisa's career world opened up.

The long time friend knew that Lisa was a talented organizer and encouraged her to establish her own business. Lisa's husband named the business **Montanaro, Inc**. with the slogan – We Plan Lives.

Monetizing Your Passion

Lisa's interest was piqued and she began to really consider how to make a career as a professional organizer. She attended a life coaching event with Cheryl Richardson that inspired her to make a move away from the legal profession.

As one would expect from a natural organizer, Lisa had a plan to execute her new career goals. At the time, she was working as Associate General Counsel at Pace University, her law school alma mater. During an 18-month period, she articulated a plan on paper, paid off her remaining student loans, and banked $25K to start her new business venture. She even shared her plans with her employers at Pace, knowing it would take time to conduct a search to find her replacement.

Her superiors at Pace recognized her organizational expertise and encouraged her to work part-time – with benefits – while launching her new business. That career boost was delivered on a silver platter and allowed Lisa to build her business and her brand slowly while still having the security of a steady income and benefits. She knew she was very fortunate to have such a well-cushioned exit strategy.

Understanding the importance of being credentialed in the industry, Lisa became an inaugural Certified Professional Organizer® through a rigorous and intensive training program through NAPO. This put a stamp of approval on her business, and validated her as an expert with additional learned skills that go beyond her natural organizational abilities.

Lisa's business is called **LM Organizing Solutions, LLC** (LMOS). She realized that as a multi-passionate entrepreneur, her company is an umbrella organization with many spokes that include professional organizing, business and life coaching, and motivational speaking.

Recognize Your Calling

Lisa was able to identify her calling a second time in her life. Her first calling was as a performer. She spent her childhood singing, acting, and dancing, and wanted to go professional. While she decided to pursue the law after college, she never gave up performing and turned it into a wonderful hobby that continues to this day. Lisa is also able to tap her performance skills to be an engaging, motivational speaker.

Equalize Your Work and Life

Her law background makes Lisa a sought-after business expert, mediator, and trainer for entrepreneurs. She offers business coaching to a variety of clients from solo-preneurs and non-profit organizations, to major corporations and municipalities. Lisa served as an instructor for New York State's Entrepreneurial Assistance Program.

As a coach, Lisa taps her mediation skills and guides clients to achieve results by motivating and encouraging without judgment. According to Lisa:

"During my time of career transition, I realized that I had been organizing people's lives on an amateur level my whole life, and that my organizing and coaching skills transcended my work as a lawyer, teacher, mediator, writer, speaker, and performer."

Lisa's LMOS clients rely on her for leadership, guidance, support, encouragement, and coaching.

"I took a leap of faith and created a business that allows me to meld together many different, but related callings at the same time, while helping people live better lives and run better companies and organizations. The result has been both successful and rewarding."

Break the Roof Off the Cottage

Lisa was well equipped as a lawyer to create a business plan and establish her LLC for the business. She set up her separate business bank account early on, even before she had steady clients and tracked expenses and kept meticulous records for tax purposes.

She conducted a lot of industry research and became a self-described organizing geek. She read every book on the market to study her competition and to distinguish her value-add in the industry. Lisa visited IKEA and The Container Store to learn about the latest organizing products. From the beginning, she wanted to treat her business as a real venture and pursued trademark and copyrights for her signature themes and strategies.

The messaging of a real business is powerful, and Lisa encourages her entrepreneurial clients to adopt this mindset immediately. She recalled a NAPO conference with a famous speaker telling the participants – "If you want to break the roof off your cottage industry – do it. Don't treat your business as if you are the Avon or Tupperware Lady." This was a powerful message that helped Lisa think about her endeavor as a legitimate business early on.

Are You Ready?

Lisa's target market is success-minded individuals and busy professionals. Clients must be committed to behavior modification and be ready to work. An example of an organizational project she works on with clients is de-cluttering the paper in their home or office. She helps them sift through mountainous piles of paper and develop a filing system for management. Some papers may be scanned, archived, or shredded but the goal is to develop a system so the client can manage their files (on their own) in the future.

Lisa developed and trademarked her own unique organizing process after years of noticing that disorganized people have difficulty making decisions. These decision-making road blocks in turn cause delays and stress, which translate into personal and professional frustrations.

She believes a client must decide to be organized and buy into the premise that becoming organized will empower their future. Here is Lisa's DECIDE™ plan to allow clients to take control of their lives:

- Discover what you have and want at home, at work, and in life.
- Eliminate what is unnecessary and does not further your goals.
- Categorize what remains.
- Implement a system designed to match your needs, habits, work and lifestyle.

- **D**edicate yourself to maintaining your new system and integrating it into your life.
- Enjoy the freedom and positive results that being organized brings.

Lisa feels strongly that – "DECIDE™ is an empowering process that leads to change. It will assist you in achieving results at home, at work, and in life in general. While the process guides a person or organization in making decisions that lead to a more organized state, it is itself a decision; a decision to take control."

The Solutions Expert

In addition to a multi-tiered business model that honors her work values and allows her to play to her strengths, Lisa maintains a blog that delivers organizational strategies we can all use. A national publisher recognized her blog and she was asked to write a book about organizing.

The *Ultimate Life Organizer: An Interactive Guide to a Simpler, Less Stressful & More Organized Life,* was published by Peter Pauper Press. The target audience for the book is women, and Lisa has incorporated two pages of journal space at the end of each chapter so readers can make plans and take notes directly in the book. She calls the book a best friend to help you get organized and purposefully made it an easy and enjoyable read to demystify organization. Organizing is a learned skill and Lisa believes anyone can do it if they are taught how.

Rent Her Brain

Lisa shared that often she feels like clients are "renting her brain" during a session, and there is a lot of truth in that description. Lisa is the brand of her own business and has built her success by earning the trust of her clients and obtaining referrals.

She is using social media and a fabulous website to market the business, and her national public speaking engagements certainly get her noticed out in the field. Lisa knows that working for yourself can be the hardest endeavor since you can only hold yourself accountable.

But LMOS is built upon integrity and loyalty to her customers and Lisa has earned her many accolades and positive testimonials.

As for work/life balance – it's easy to want to do it all, especially for a professional organizer who manages her time so well. Lisa has learned to say no to clients if they are not a good fit or if they don't work into her schedule. Every good organizer knows that you must schedule time for yourself and your priorities first.

Lisa is thrilled with her career reinvention and even though it's not her official slogan – she is helping to plan lives and loving every minute of it.

The Era of Virtual Business

Lisa's energy, passion, and drive helped her grow and re-define her successful business. When we talked about the update to her story, there was much to share.

Lisa is still a successful entrepreneur, but she has changed her focus, in part because of changes in her personal life. Lisa's spouse decided to advance his veterinary career, which required a cross-country relocation. This meant that Lisa needed to redefine her approach so she could be non-location specific; she developed and launched her global / virtual business model.

Now, Lisa still coaches and consults on organizing, but she's not doing the hands-on work with the clients. "It's less about the brawn, and more about the behavioral change. After my first few years as an organizer, I realized it's not really about the stuff – it's about the relationship to and the behaviors with the stuff. You can't be successful by just treating the symptoms; you have to treat the underlying problem." Lisa pursued additional training in how to help clients make changes in their behaviors.

The book Lisa wrote was published as planned, but she wasn't satisfied with the results. She's looking at other options for a new book – perhaps using self-publishing or creating an e-book. Meanwhile, she recently launched LMG University, also known as LMGU or Lisa Montanaro Global University. LMGU is interdisciplinary in scope and will provide courses and programs for business, career, and life through the LMGU Business School, Enrichment Center and Career Services Office. In the future, she plans to roll out a full expanse of LMGU offerings, which will include semester-long courses, one-day intensives, live retreats – even study abroad programs.

LMGU has been key in helping Lisa return to her love of teaching and helping others with personal and professional development. These are favorite skills for Lisa, and are perfectly transferable into her new career.

Performance has always been a passion for Lisa, and she's found ways to keep that passion going. Professionally, she's focusing more on speaking engagements and has opportunities to speak at universities and at professional association conferences. Personally, she's very active with community and regional theater. The week we spoke, she was performing several parts in a production of *Les Miserables*. As an entrepreneur, she can work her theater engagements in and around her busy speaking seasons.

Although Lisa's passions are being met, that doesn't mean her life is without challenge. "Being an entrepreneur whose spouse is in a residency program means that I'm running both of our lives." At the moment, Lisa is the primary breadwinner of the family, and this adds some pressure. "I'm very lucky to have the freedom and the flexibility to do this, but it's an enormous logistical challenge to move and build a new network." Since Lisa is multi-passionate and multi-talented, she has to "keep it in check" so she doesn't spread herself too thin. "I want to be a master of a few things, instead of doing lots of things half-way. And I still want time to enjoy life, and ride a bike now and then." Lisa confesses: "There is so much I want to do!"

Reflecting on her career journey, Lisa shares that she would have done a couple of things differently. One lesson she learned has to do with her previous career. "I was so ready to leave the field of law that I was almost rebelling against it. I didn't mention my law career in my bio or in any aspect of the business. I learned that I could have used it to my advantage much earlier. My background in law gives me a unique selling proposition. I've learned to be proud of my history, and use it to help me in my new career."

One of the biggest lessons Lisa learned is about being an entrepreneur. "I would have taken the business more seriously from the start. I liked the short-term transformations that came with organizing, and focused there. I was self-employed, but I was not yet a CEO of a company. I run a company! You are a business owner right from the start."

Lisa's advice to others who want to start a business is still to "figure out what you love and what you're good at and do it – BUT know that it's not always easy. AND you must make sure there's a market for the product or service you want to provide. Lisa continues: "Follow your passion, but learn how to run a business and to think like a CEO. You have to be objective. You have to see the business as a separate entity from you. And you must realize from the beginning that you will need help." This is wonderful advice, and it really hit home for me.

Lisa's Advice and Action Steps:

- Figure out what you love and what you are good at and do it!
- Focus on skill sets not job titles or industries.
- It's ok to be multi-passionate but pick one to focus on for your reinvention. Add other passions incrementally.
- Dump your brain on paper and create an action plan. Seek the help and wisdom of others to achieve your goals.

Resources:

Lisa's website: www.LMOrganizingSolutions.com
Lisa's Blog: www.DecideToBeOrganized.com
LMO on Facebook: www.Facebook.com/LMOrganizingSolutions
Lisa on Twitter: www.Twitter.com/LisaMontanaro

66What you do makes a difference, and you have to decide what kind of difference you want to make.99

– Jane Goodall

ↂ ↂ ↂ ↂ

29. TAKE A STEP FORWARD

Many people study law because they are interested in a profession. Throughout the ages, lawyers have enjoyed careers that focus on a call to serve, intellectual challenge, and growth opportunity that comes with financial gain. There are diverse practice areas, dynamic work environments, and prestige, to name just a few of the rewards of a legal career. Ellen Covner, Tonya Fitzpatrick, Beth Patterson, Liz Williams and Lisa Montanaro needed more than these rewards to be gratified in their careers.

You Can Change Your Mind

For many who have spent a number of years in a given profession, it can be hard to let go and move on to new opportunities that better suit their passions and their values right now. I want you to erase the notion that you are *throwing away* one career for another when you make a change. Instead, think of yourself as a newly hatched butterfly ready for a fresh career journey. Giving yourself the freedom to understand that you can enjoy multiple careers in very different job sectors during your lifetime will liberate you to spend your time at work happy and fulfilled.

Often ego can get in the way of a career change. Our culture can ingrain in us the need to achieve a powerful rank or position that equates with career success. Some career changers don't want to let go of their elite position even if it makes them miserable because they worked so hard to get to where they are.

If your achievements don't echo what your heart and soul are feeling, then you are letting your ego get the better of you. Muster the courage to reinvent your professional identity and seek out help to explore new options. Dig deep to find a career that makes you joyful every day at work. Tap into the strengths that give you energy and satisfaction. You must define success on your own terms in order to thrive.

Can I Afford to Change Careers?

The reality is that we all need money to survive. But how much do you need to meet your needs, to make you happy, and to enjoy your life? Every person will have a unique answer to that question. Consider your relationship to money. Is it healthy and well balanced or do you have an addiction to acquiring things you *want* versus things you *need*?

It all comes back to values and how money plays a role in your life. If you prioritize financial wealth then you can certainly pursue a career that honors that value. But if you are transitioning to a new field or launching a new entrepreneurial venture, you may want to ease into the new opportunity so you can be prepared for the financial changes that may be ahead. Some of the women with whom I spoke kept a day job or worked at it part-time until their new business was financially solvent.

Have a plan and calculate what you really need to survive financially and how you want to utilize your savings (or not!) as you pursue a career change or new business. A career reinvention does not mean you have to move backwards financially, but you do need a plan so that you can make wise financial decisions.

REINVENTION TOOLBOX

Own Your Passion; Take Calculated Risks; Be Authentic

Earning a law degree takes an intense commitment, a large sum of money, and in most cases, three years of study. I applaud the self-described recovering lawyers in this chapter for taking a risk, owning their passion, and making authentic choices about why the legal profession was no longer for them.

Authenticity is the ability to be genuine and sincere with your intentions. All too often we make career decisions based on what others want us to do, or what we think they want us to do. Many of my clients and students over the years have shared that they pursued *practical* professions because their families encouraged them to do so. While I believe families and support systems are important, ultimately the decision about career pursuits should be yours alone.

As the self-assessment process reveals, getting in touch with your values, interests, personality, and skills can help you discover career opportunities that truly match your authentic self. The realities of this job economy often force us to take stop-gap jobs in order to make ends meet, but never lose focus of your career dreams and continue to work towards those goals.

- How do you want to show up in the world?
- How do you want others to see you?

Most often, our personal and professional values are closely aligned. Have the courage to be true to yourself and trust your gut. The lawyers in this chapter took a risk leaving their solvent professions as attorneys by taking an opportunity to pursue more authentic careers that honored their values.

The philosophical movement of existentialism has studied authenticity for centuries and helps us understand more about what authenticity is, along with its relationship to the concept of meaning. Existentialists assert that if an individual is not living authentically in their life, then they lose meaning and can fall into chronic anxiety, boredom, and despair. You spend a large portion of your waking hours on the job so you deserve to be happy in your career. Muster the courage to make authentic career choices that are meaningful to you. If you can align your values, talents, and vision, you can unleash a powerful trifecta that will lead you towards career satisfaction.

- Are you willing to take risks?
- Reflect on how you can move forward in your career by expanding your comfort zone and taking a risk.

When we meet successful people, we often mistakenly envy them for their great luck. Of course, their success has nothing to do with luck at all. Good fortune doesn't come to us; we go to it by taking risks. Life is all about taking risks. And we willingly take chances every day. What separates achievers from ordinary folks is their willingness to take optional, as well as necessary, risks.

Without question, each of the 150 women I interviewed for this book took some form of risk and stepped outside their comfort zone as part of their career reinvention. Was it scary? Yes, but they grew and developed in ways that helped them succeed in the long run.

"Security is mostly a superstition. It does not exist in nature, nor do the children of men as a whole experience it. Avoiding danger is no safer in the long run than outright exposure. Life is either a daring adventure or nothing."

— Helen Keller

ↂ ↂ ↂ ↂ

6

MAKE WAY FOR THE ARTISTS

A career transition doesn't always come from a place of unhappiness. Many of the artists in this chapter found new challenges to engage their passion or discovered new strengths by taking a career risk. Research shows that those with an artistic temperament are endowed with high levels of energy, self-confidence, sharp thinking, and humor, and often they assume leadership positions in their professions. That certainly describes these amazing women!

30. ANGELA JIA KIM: UNDERSTAND THE POWER OF AN ITCH

An accomplished concert pianist, Angela Jia Kim was about to step on stage when she developed an allergic reaction to a body lotion she had applied just before her performance. A consummate professional, she played the concert with her game face on and later discovered that the culprit lotion contained no less than 55 ingredients, most of which were chemicals. Most people would have simply searched for a new lotion, but Angela is not most people. Determined to create chemical- and preservative-free skin care made from organic ingredients, Angela set up shop in her New York City kitchen and experimented with all natural elements. She created a skin cream so delicious it was like food for your skin.

One Thousand Tries

Angela said it took over a thousand tries to perfect her skin cream before she was satisfied enough to give it to friends and family as gifts. The luxurious cream was an instant hit, but it was never meant to be a business (she meant only to create creams for herself and her loved ones); however, the passion developed organically as did the company. Friends were enthusiastic and shared samples with their friends, and Angela's skin cream took off!

Angela began working with a team of holistic formulators, aroma therapists, and skin care experts, and **Om Aroma** was born. This line of skin care products is free of parabens, formaldehyde, mineral oil, and synthetic fragrances.

Soon after the company launch, **Om Aroma** won four gold medals at the annual Beauty Olympics, beating out some recognizable industry brands. All products are made in the USA and embody the fusion of luxury and organic. Angela's company is eco-friendly, with products packaged by hand, using sustainable materials.

Angela is also committed to social responsibility, using fair-trade ingredients. Her *Dollars and Scents* program provides opportunities for women who are re-entering the work force and need a flexible work schedule due to having children, health issues, or a desire for a career change. Om Aroma products are never tested on animals.

Turning Problems into Opportunities

While growing her skin care business, Angela needed to also grow her professional network. Without any formal business training, she was in need of some "...nuts-and-bolts guidance, from launching to making millions," as she comments on her website. If a concert pianist, turned natural skin care guru is not amazing enough, you'll be pleased to know that Angela and her husband Marc also created **SavortheSuccess.com** – a boutique social network and PR Co-Op for female entrepreneurs and professionals.

SavortheSuccess.com is a tremendous resource that brings women together to share knowledge, expertise, resources, and enthusiasm.

Transform Yourself

Angela is proof that women can transfer skills and switch career sectors. She turned a hobby into a thriving business and her passion, persistence, diligence, and strong work ethic transferred seamlessly into her new entrepreneurial venture.

Since hindsight is 20/20, Angela shared that if she had to do it all again, she would be more careful about choosing the people she hired. At first, she hired anyone who would work for her because she didn't know any better. But she soon learned the importance of being very selective so that you can surround yourself with an A-team that can propel the company to the next level.

As self-proclaimed skin care product junkie, I was eager to try **Om Aroma** and I can say that I am hooked. Not only do I use the products but I have also found **SavortheSuccess.com** to be a tremendous resource, which actually connected me to many of the fabulous women I have interviewed for this book.

What's New?

There are all kinds of entrepreneurs in the world; some go to business school and put in years working for others before they start their own companies, others are "naturals" and just jump right in. Angela Jia Kim is a great example of a natural entrepreneur.

Since my first story about Angela was published, **Om Aroma & Co.™** has continued to grow and develop. The organic spa collection can now be found in five-star luxury resorts, upscale spas, salons, and exclusive inns.

And from that success, she launched a new business – Savor Spa + Boutique located in the West Village in New York City. **Savor Spa™** is a boutique spa that offers organic facials, deep tissue holistic massages, organic waxing, and eco-manicures and pedicures. The spa features the Om Aroma product line in the eco-chic lifestyle gift boutique, along with favorite things that are green, good, and gorgeous. Everyone from high-profile clients to neighborhood locals enjoy the privacy of this hidden hot spot while the discreet staff provides the highest quality service in the industry.

SavorTheSuccess.com has also grown and improved with the launch of *Savor Success Circles*, an accountability group for women. Each member is placed into a circle of four women based on group chemistry. Together, they take a 9-month journey to hold each other accountable to accomplish one massive, life-changing goal. The philosophy of the club is similar to a tennis club: to improve your game, you must play with teammates who can hit the ball back as hard as you (if not harder) so that you can grow.

At the root of Angela's success is *The Manifest Method* an approach Angela says she's been working on since age three! It's a five-step method to help women who want to develop and put something great in the world. It teaches participants how to increase cash flow, save time, get more organized, and simplify both business and life. By clarifying a five year vision and tapping into their creativity, workshop participants learn to have more fun, which means they will stay motivated and on track in the work to manifest their goals. Customers can purchase an All-In Kit to use at home, and instruction is also available online through the Manifest Method School.

As an accidental entrepreneur who launched without an MBA, money, or connections, Angela has become passionate about using her "other hand" to help entrepreneurs with a "we're in it together" philosophy. It's this Give, Give, Get spirit that has created a national movement.

She launched the 7-Figure Club for successful businesswomen who use the power of business to do massive good in the world. She saw the need for CEOs who were lonely at the top and craved a sisterhood of trailblazers who understand the crushing demands, responsibility, and privilege of leadership. Give, Give, Get has never been more powerful among the nation's top leaders.

Angela has become the go-to connector for the national press, America's top entrepreneurs, and the movers and shakers of the world. "I love making the connection between people when I know it will create electricity on both sides. Whether it's connecting the Wall Street Journal to the best national expert for a story, or connecting an investor to a passionate entrepreneur with chops and a brilliant idea, I love bringing together the power of people for the greater good."

Major corporations have partnered with Angela to help women entrepreneurs rock the world. She hosts an annual Rock the World conference in NYC for 500 women leaders.

What makes Angela different? "I take at least ten steps a day to reach my goals. Others take ten a month. Some take ten a year… [Success] isn't for the dreamer – it's for the doer!" And I can't wait to see what Angela does next!

Angela's Advice and Action Steps:

- Get rid of toxic people in your life – it drains your energy.
- Always try and recognize (from good and bad experiences) what works best for you.
- Identify what makes you, your service, or product special or unique. I call this the Chanel No. 5 factor. What is your Chanel No. 5 factor?
- Don't be afraid to ask for help. Surround yourself with supportive people and utilize resources. Follow your passion.
- Don't give up too soon. Try something multiple times before you throw in the towel. It took 100+ attempts to perfect my first batch of face cream.

Resources:

Om Aroma: www.omaroma.com
Savor the Success: www.savorthesuccess.com
Manifest Method: www.manifestmethod.com

> **"**It's all about how you play your game.
> Are you ready to *Savor the Success?***"**

– Angela Jia Kim

⚘ ⚘ ⚘ ⚘

31. Danielle Bobish: Making the Most of Your Curtain Call

A Broadway actress, Danielle was tired of being a struggling artist and knew she wanted more out of life and her career. But what – and how? Dissecting her career on the stage helped Danielle quickly realize that her professional theater background was the perfect training for planning large events.

> "With any big event like a wedding, you'll find the same key elements: costumes, lighting, set decoration, production and timing, and lots of details to coordinate. I thought– why not bring that same excitement and theatrical sensibility to non-Broadway events?"

She is now the Owner and Creative Director of Curtain Up Events (CUE) and an excellent example of a woman who combined her passions, skills, and experiences and used them to transition into a new career.

Danielle has planned both intimate and large scale weddings and corporate events, including events for some of New York City's largest and most notable businesses. Located in the Big Apple, Curtain Up Events serves the greater New York area but Danielle also travels out-of-state for destination events.

Use Self-Discovery for Career Transformation

Danielle shared that she hit the wall as a performer; she wanted self-validation as a person and not just as an actress. She felt vulnerable as she moved through a self-discovery process, but soon realized that she was ready to leave the arts. This was a very emotional decision for Danielle. After many tears and a lot of deliberation about this major life and career change, Danielle was ready to reinvent herself and she moved forward with confidence and conviction.

As an actress, she had worked many a catering gig when not performing and since her Mom was a professional caterer, she grew up surrounded by people in the special events industry. After leaving show biz, Danielle developed phenomenal vendor contacts from a 2 ½ year stint at another event-planning firm where she worked prior to launching **CUE**. She received excellent reviews from colleagues and customers who encouraged her to set out her own shingle. Danielle combined her creative flair and business acumen to plan innovative and chic events under her new business name and thus, **Curtain Up Events** was born.

By the way, Madeline, Danielle's daughter was also born in 2009, and this working mom was producing events up until a week before she gave birth. She returned to work shortly after Madeline was born, and now does the logistical event planning from home to be closer to her daughter.

You Can't Move Forward Without Taking a Risk

Launching her own business was quite a risk, but Danielle is experiencing a validation that she finds very empowering. Her feedback from clients and vendors has been amazing and being her own boss has given her the freedom to make her own business decisions and to design her work schedule around raising a daughter.

As a proverbial Stage Manager, Danielle calls all the shots in her business and enjoys having the opportunity to work with fabulous people designing special events that make people joyful.

"If you've ever been backstage during a performance, there are so many things going on which keep the show running that the audience never sees. The same is true for a wedding. I'm calling a million different cues, but the guests just enjoy a seamless event. My musical-theater background also enables me to have a long list of theatrical vendors such as Tony-nominated lighting designers and Broadway performers that can make the day a little more spectacular.

Overall, I think the most unique thing I employ is my ability to connect with people. A wedding is a very personal event and all the special touches should reflect the couple and not me. Those special touches will make people say "that wedding was so THEM.""

Her work and creative ideas appear on Brides.com, where she consults for numerous wedding planning stories. She was also a key producer on a team that planned an episode of "My Celebrity Wedding," which aired on The Style Network.

Balancing Act

The challenge for this working mom is balancing work with raising a daughter. Danielle wants to be an inspiration and a role model for her daughter but admits, "…sometimes you just have to budget to have someone watch the baby."

> "My biggest challenge is balancing work and personal life. My daughter is very important to me and I constantly feel guilty about not spending enough time with her. I know that I really do give her everything she needs and then some. But you're always second guessing yourself and I'm always working at odd hours. There's always work to be done when you own your own company. Even if the clients are completely taken care of, you still have to tend to the company itself.
>
> You really have to have an amazing support system. I have wonderful friends and family who are all hands on deck because they love me and believe in my company. I also have an AMAZING group of women who work with me. I couldn't do it without them and I tell them every chance I get. If you think you can do everything yourself, you'll just be running yourself ragged. It's so important to let others help you!!"

The curtain will rise and fall many times throughout our career lives. Danielle found her passion a second time and serves as an inspiration for others who are looking for that next career opportunity. She deserves a standing ovation!

What's New?

When I checked in with Danielle, her business, and her career, were still going strong. Curtain Up Events has won numerous awards for event planning, including Bride's Choice award from Wedding-Wire, and Best of Weddings from The Knot. Danielle is co-chair of the New York City Event Planners Association, and received BizBash

Reader's Choice Award for Social Event Planner of the Year. And she has hired her first full-time employee!

Danielle enjoys helping others get started in the industry. She brings interns into the firm, and is hiring one for a full time position. Her short-term business goal is to have two fulltime employees, and an assistant for each.

Generously, Danielle shared lessons learned after a few years in business. The most important thing she's learned is the value of relationships. When Danielle started her career by working for another event planning company, she was dedicated to building very strong relationships with every vendor. Later, those relationships helped her successfully launch her own company, and kept it growing even through tough economic times. She attributes her great first year to the referrals that came from those relationships. And as Curtain Up Events began to deliver fantastic events, the referrals started coming in from customers, too. Another key relationship was with her best friend, who helped get the business off the ground by working as an assistant. Because of their strong relationship, "there was not one conflict."

Danielle also has learned the value of interpersonal communication skills, and the ability to remain calm in crisis. When things go sideways, "yelling doesn't help. We all work together as a team; we all want the same end result." When a team is working as one, success can follow. And customers feel much better in the hands of an event planner that leads – calmly – though a crisis.

Ever vigilant about work-life balance, Danielle shared, "My clients and my vendors get to know and love my daughter." She balances her work with the school schedule, and she works with other Moms who are trying to do the same thing.

Danielle's success is a great example of what can happen when you learn about your values, consider your skills, and take a risk on a new path. May her example be a great lesson for us all!

Danielle's Advice and Action Steps:

- Do what you love! I found something else I love, beyond my original career plan. I'm good at it and it makes me happy. Give yourself the opportunity to explore new things and find what you love.

- Take a risk – it could take you someplace wonderful.
- Be open to many things – you just might find something you never thought you would.
- Women can be competitive in the workplace so learn to work together and support each other and everybody wins.
- Always treat people with respect – sometimes it's contagious and that's a good thing.

Resources:

CUE: www.curtainupevents.com
Savor the Success: www.savorthesuccess.com

> ❝I believe in the power of giving back and I have realized that you can't please everybody all the time.❞
>
> – Danielle Bobish

৶ ৶ ৶ ৶

32. GINGER HODGE: WHEN DONKEYS FLY

Born the youngest of five children in the small town of Sumter, South Carolina, Ginger Hodge was a bit shy as a child. With the love and support of her third-grade teacher, Ginger found the confidence to embrace her imagination and create unique ways to entertain herself and those around her. Those who know her best love that she always seems to have a new song, game, joke, or story to share.

Ginger landed her first job performing singing-balloon-a-grams while attending the College of Charleston. After graduation, she struggled to find her own way by dabbling with a few restaurant, real estate, and ad agency jobs. When she finally found her niche, in the movie industry, she was able to use her unique passion for entertaining others to market family-friendly films. But Ginger's true passion for living wasn't fully ignited until she published her first children's book: *When Donkeys Fly.*

What Will Your Epithet Say?

Looking back at how it all began, Ginger recalls waking up one morning after attending her uncle's funeral, worried that even if she were the very best at her job in the film industry, her epithet would read: "Best B Movie Buyer in the Business" – and that just wasn't enough. As a senior "blurbologist" (her own unique term), she wrote the copy on the back of DVDs/videos, scouted new producers, and licensed family films to be sold at retail.

After learning of all the wonderful ways her uncle gave back to the community during his lifetime, Ginger decided then and there that she wanted to make a difference in the world and began indulging her true passion – writing. She wrote When Donkeys Fly, left her six-figure career in what she called the "gloom and doom entertainment industry," and embarked on a mission to lead an extraordinary life, and encourage others to do the same.

When Donkeys Fly is an inspirational book for all ages that encourages people to believe in themselves despite any obstacles. *When Donkeys Fly* won the Mom's Choice Award® for "Most Inspirational/ Motivational" new book, and this is the message she is on a quest to share with anyone who will listen.

Ginger and her faithful flying donkey travel to schools, churches, colleges, and women's groups all over the country to read the book, sing a song, and encourage other donkeys to fly.

Flying without a Net

In the spirit of the book, Ginger and a friend started a band called "Cosmo and the Flying Donkeys" to encourage other music lovers to follow their own passions. But how does one walk away from a financially secure job and start a new career as a first-time author or musician and make ends meet?

This new author took advantage of the growing self-publishing movement and borrowed against the equity in her home to finance the book and launch her new career.

This leap of faith was incredibly scary but also invigorating for Ginger who, for the first time, was flying without the proverbial safety net. The ability to shed corporate policy for personal satisfaction was very liberating for Ginger, who is now relieved to be able to speak her own truth.

She recalls being on pins and needles in the film industry – much of the time, working in a stress-based environment. Now, as her own boss, she can spend the afternoon playing with her niece, walking the beach, or taking her dad to the doctor because she is in charge of her own time.

Quality of Life

Even though she can't count on a regular paycheck every Friday, Ginger believes that her lifestyle has changed for the better. For the first time in years, she can literally taste and enjoy the food she eats and not have to wolf down meals to make the next meeting or deadline. Ginger has embraced a life of "living in the moment" and appreciates the simple pleasures more than ever.

> "I knew that I made the right decision when I had my first massage after leaving the entertainment industry. After a few minutes of massage, my magical masseuse was surprised to find that the 'stress knots' she routinely battled in my back were gone. Who knows how many years I have added to my life by choosing to follow my heart instead of my wallet."

Ginger reports that financially things are going well and although she is not making what she did in the film industry (yet!), she is happy because she is living her values and following her passion, and you can't put a price tag on that. She encourages others to follow their hearts and that is the premise of her book.

In addition to the book, donkeys are flying through classrooms with the help of Ginger's techno-savvy sister who developed a series of activities and resources for collaborative technology and literacy integration projects. Using Skype and Voicethread, kids can instantly connect with the characters and the events in the story. Students enjoy the rhythm of the text and the captivating illustrations and can even connect with Ginger directly through www.skypeanauthor.com. Ginger is thrilled to be able to find new ways to share the positive message of the book with children all over the world and maintains a blog – Friends of the Flying Donkey – where she shares moving stories of her adventures in the classroom and beyond.

Here is a letter that was forwarded from a first-grade teacher after one of Ginger's school presentations:

"I think Ms. Hodge did a wonderful job! One child in my class had struggled drawing a picture of herself yesterday so I asked her to finish it today. She did a wonderful job and as I bragged on her, she stated, 'I just let my donkey fly.'"

The Mission

Ginger is on a personal mission to improve self-esteem and literacy in schools. For younger students, she reads her book, sings her song, and walks kids through the publishing process with a message that will boost self-confidence and creativity. For high school students, she adapts the message to focus on career development with practical tips to follow their dreams to the job market.

Ginger's Flying Donkey team also has plans to further promote literacy by recruiting college and semi-pro athletes to go to schools, read the book to the students, and share stories of how their own donkeys learned to fly.

According to Ginger:

"It has been statistically shown that students whose reading scores are below the national average in third grade rarely ever catch back up, so our goal is to share the positive message of *When Donkeys Fly* with every third-grade student. And South Carolina is only the beginning....

For students to learn to read, they first have to believe it is possible, right? Our goal is to take literacy to a higher level by encouraging kids to believe that they can do anything, including excel at reading despite their own circumstances or previous test rankings.

To date, we have a commitment from The Carolina Gamecocks, interest from The Citadel Bulldogs, The Charleston River Dogs, The Florence Red Wolves, and yes, even a few Roller Derby teams... and this is only the beginning!"

Donkey Power

The charming book assures girls and boys everywhere that their dreams can come true. Several scenarios describe how people scoff at the heroine's hopes to play baseball, to own a big boat, to be President of the United States, etc., by saying "You'll do that...when donkeys fly." Then one day she spots a flying donkey and realizes that all things are possible.

The book has an added challenge of hunting for the hidden donkey in the illustration on each page. And the "Note from the Author" in the back of the book reveals the deeper, more spiritual, message of the hidden donkey for those who wish to find it.

Although *When Donkeys Fly* is a child-friendly book, it can also be the perfect gift for graduation, birthday, or any holiday for the special people in your circle of friends and family.

After growing up in the direct-to-retail world of the film industry, Ginger's transferable skills and experience were very applicable when the time came to market her book. She attends national conferences and speaks to groups from kindergarten classes to national professional organizations.

In fact, *When Donkeys Fly* was chosen by Executive Women International (EWI) as the book featured at their National Reading Rally. When asked about her finest hour as an author, Ginger recalls the looks on the faces of the students chosen from Louisville, Kentucky, to be honored guests of EWI. As they entered the convention center, pages of the book were blown up bigger than life, animated donkeys flew across 30-foot screens, and over 600 executives gave a rousing standing ovation as the music played from a special rendition of "I Believe I Can Fly." Anyone could tell, simply from their expressions, that these students from one of the most poverty-stricken schools in the state believed that anything was possible...when donkeys fly.

Everything Happens for a Reason

Ginger doesn't take full credit for writing the book and believes that the book was simply a gift that was meant to be shared. The day the ideas came to her, Ginger literally pulled her car over to the side of the road and remembers the words coming to her faster than she could write. She wrote the entire book in less than seven minutes, but feels that the ideas for it must have been "baking" in her mind for years.

Once written, Ginger sent an email to all of her college friends who now have children, to get their reactions to the story. Soon after the email, her friend C.B. Markham answered and said "I love the story so much I am going to illustrate this book... just for me." Long story short, Ginger loved her illustrations and the power of *seek and you will find* was confirmed.

Ginger has plans in the works for her own publishing company, Donkey Fly Press and has two other books in the pipeline: *When I Get a Dog* and *When Pigs Fly*. She has taken stock of what is important in her life and made sacrifices to follow her passion. After the initial shock of job separation, she is now at peace with her decision and has made it her mission to help children and adults overcome obstacles, achieve empowerment, embrace their self-confidence and follow their own flying donkeys.

Ginger still lives in South Carolina with her faithful Labrador, Sadie, and her boat "Mr. Right."

What's New?

When I caught up with Ginger a few years later, I was amazed at how her career continued to develop in creative and unique ways! Ginger's newest adventure involves frozen yogurt, a used meter-maid cart, and an island. Initially, Ginger described her new endeavor as "getting distracted by other things," but there is consistency in her story.

One day, Ginger wandered into a self-serve frozen yogurt shop. She loved the product and was intrigued by the concept. She soon "became obsessed with it" and decided to open a little frozen yogurt shop inside a friend's gourmet food to go restaurant. It didn't take much to get started; she provided the machines and the product, and the customers served themselves. Once the concept caught on and big-name frozen yogurt chains started popping up on every corner, she decided to try selling her frozen treats on the street.

Oddly enough, Ginger found a used NY City meter-maid cart that had been recently restored by a small vehicle enthusiast in Texas and it was just the right size! She had the teeny truck shipped to South Carolina, then "found a local guy who was good at tricking things out," who up-fitted it with a freezer and other necessities. Ginger saw this "ice cream truck" as the perfect marketing vehicle for her book, customized it with images of the Flying Donkey, and the Story and a Snack concept was born.

The finished cart brings waves and smiles from everyone, even if they are stuck behind it in traffic. And so, it was named "The HAPPIE Truck."

Of course, no ice cream truck is complete without the music that draws children (and adults) from far and wide. Ginger knew she would go crazy if she had to listen to the same song over and over, so she picked one song (Turkey in the Straw) and recorded ten versions in different musical genres. Again, she found friends with the skills, such as composing and recording, to help her bring this dream to life.

Ginger lived in South Carolina, and often vacationed on a small island off the coast. Just for fun, Ginger decided to try selling frozen goodies from her HAPPIE Truck on the island's beaches. Once she figured out that prime time to sell was from 3:00 p.m. to sundown, "it was a ridiculous success!" There is so much business during the summer months that Ginger can make enough during peak season to sustain the simple life she loves all year. Following her dream and her instinct, she moved to the island full time.

Marketing and creativity have always been strengths for Ginger. In the off-season, she rents The HAPPIE Truck for special occasions, and decorates it accordingly. The HAPPIE Truck made its wedding debut this past fall fully decked out with a bridal veil, white lights, and long eye lashes over the headlights and delighted reception guests with frozen dessert treats. The HAPPIE Truck was also a huge hit selling boiled peanuts at festivals in the fall; this may be another business line Ginger will pursue.

Meanwhile, spreading the message of The Flying Donkey is still a focus. Ginger most recently served as the keynote speaker at a Young Writer's Conference with 200 aspiring authors in grades 1-5. She will participate in a weekly program this summer at a local resort, sharing the "you can do anything" message of her book as young visitors learn how to make their own stuffed animals… and teach them to fly… as they learn to fly themselves!

Reflecting on her career path, Ginger said "all my careers have led me to the here and now." She's a master at using her transferrable skills in each endeavor she pursues.

Given her success with the ice cream business, I asked about plans for growth and whether she was thinking of franchising. She is not. Ginger "is a minimalist by nature" and likes the life she has now. "Getting bigger goes against what I want. I don't want to turn into a corporation and end up back where I started. I like the life I have now. I don't need 'more'. I'm happier now, and that's the point!"

Ginger advises those who want to make a change: "If you stop worrying about pleasing others and focus on pleasing yourself – as in 'healthy selfishness' – you can pursue your own dreams without worrying about judgment from others. That's where happiness starts."

What an inspiration!

Ginger's Advice and Action Steps

- Set your intentions.
- Follow your passions.
- Savor every moment.
- Don't let money drive your decisions.
- Strive to be peaceful and productive.
- Help those who help others.
- Remember that everything happens in divine time.

Resources:

When Donkeys Fly: www.whendonkeysflybook.com

> "Take a moral inventory of what success means to you – really think about it! Everyone can sing – you've just got to find your song."

– Ginger Hodge

🎵 🎵 🎵 🎵

33. JO LAURIE: DO YOU LIVE TO WORK OR WORK TO LIVE?

A quintessential Jill-of-all-trades, Jo Laurie has experienced many career changes in her life. As a young student in her native England, Jo was pushed into the empirical sciences in school and specialized early on in chemistry, physics, and math. She is dyslexic and these disciplines were meant to help her focus on her strengths with numbers and equations.

Jo was successful in the sciences and in the British system under Margaret Thatcher; she was paid to attend university (free tuition plus a stipend) and earned a BSc (Hons), a degree with honors in Psychology. While Jo was stimulated intellectually, she yearned for a more creative outlet. So she left England and headed to New York City to reinvent herself and test-drive a new world.

Millinery Mania

For two years she explored her artistic side, working a total of 17 different jobs from modeling to jewelry making to restaurant work. She taught herself how to cook and sew and she discovered a passion for making hats. Her millinery creations took off and Jo hit the big time when her hats were picked up by the exclusive three Bs department stores in New York City: Barney's, Bergdorf Goodman and Henri Bendel, and soon after, 70 stores worldwide.

While the hat business was successful for a good while, Jo's artistic wanderlust led her to try additional opportunities, including styling props and creating environments for photographers. In her bones she knew that she did not enjoy working for other people in a corporate or structured environment. She longed to be her own boss and match her creative talents with her scientific skill set. Friends asked her to consider designing a bar for them back in London and that was the beginning of **Jo Laurie Interior Design**.

Values of a Dual Citizen

Jo enjoys the best of her American and English worlds as a dual citizen and her design firm is home based in the USA to capitalize on the significance of New York City on the global stage. She shared with me her frustration about the American system of a typical two-week vacation allotment for most employees in an organization and thus, she really values being in control of her own time as her own boss.

This globetrotter doesn't live to work but works to live. She subscribes to the continental work philosophy of enjoying six-plus weeks of vacation annually. This is the norm in Europe, Australia and Canada but it saddens Jo that most American companies offer only a paltry two weeks of vacation. There has been significant research that indicates European executives are more industrious per hour, as they are more rested mentally and physically. This translates into better productivity on the job. Jo is in touch with what she values and has made priorities in her life accordingly to live these principles.

The Reality of Being Your Own Boss

Jo has come a long way from her millinery days and established a multi-discipline design company, with projects ranging from corporate and hospitality to high-end residential. Located in downtown Manhattan, she has been operating internationally for over 15 years, and has developed an extensive portfolio of award-winning projects. As an interior designer, she has developed an understanding of the specialized needs of her clients worldwide by creating visually stimulating surroundings that produce unique, flexible, and functional environments.

But success does not come easily and even though Jo prioritizes multiple-week vacations each year, she works around the clock to keep her business thriving. Ninety-five percent of her business comes from referrals and satisfied customers. Her website is a powerful marketing tool and offers an impressive look at the types of interiors Jo has created.

Her personal Board of Directors includes an old friend who has a very successful architecture firm who helps Jo navigate the business side of interior design. This mentorship has helped Jo identify and market her strengths in the design arena. Another friend developed her website, brand, and identity. Her team is rounded out by an accountant, a marketing specialist, and another friend who has achieved great success in the financial industry. Jo has assembled a great resource team.

Dollars and Sense

While Jo is flexing her artistic muscles, she must always be concerned about the nuts and bolts of the business. Like many creative individuals, her first passion is the creative process, which in itself was not initiated by the desire to make money. With the help of some good mentors, Jo has seen a steady increase in clients as the businesses continue to grow – even in the recession. Cultivating new business is a constant need, so she also adheres to a realistic budget and a business framework that keeps her in the black.

The recession has hit the design industry as a whole, and for Jo, it has made cultivating new business more important than ever. She is always prepared to take a risk and try new things to make her business viable. Inspired by her grandmother, who always told Jo to go for it, she believes that taking a risk forces you to go to the next level. According to Jo, "You must continue to take risks to build your business and your dream. When you fail, you pick yourself up and start again because that's what it's all about."

The Belle of the Bar

While Jo has achieved international recognition for her pub and bar interior designs from Sydney to London and beyond, she remains grounded in what is important to her. Personal life situations have helped Jo put it all in perspective, keep her focus on what is important in life, and to truly live what she values.

Jo continues to travel internationally to build her clientele and her inspiration for new designs. This straight-talking modern Englishwoman, whose formal education is steeped in the empirical sciences, has found a way to blend form, function, and art to build a business that meets her values and her passion. I have every confidence that Jo will continue to grow her career in different directions because blended within her inner scientist is the true temperament of an artist.

What's New?

When I checked in with Jo, she was excited to report that she survived the recession. Many interior design firms did not survive because people were using much smaller budgets, or weren't renovating at all. But Jo's creativity and international successes have kept her going strong.

In fact, Jo is growing her business to reach a new, specific market – newly divorced men. She has found that members of this demographic group want a pad in New York City, but they have no idea how to complete an apartment. They need someone who has the time and the experience, to help them set up their new life. Many know what they want, but need Jo to make it happen. Jo relishes the opportunity to be on their side as they start fresh in life.

Quality is what sets Jo Laurie Design apart from her competition. There are many designers who work via the Internet, so problems can arise when an item doesn't have the proper color, finish, or quality that was expected. Jo still works in 3D; she will not recommend an item, a finish, or a piece of furniture unless she has physically examined it in person. She takes the time to really know her vendors' strengths and weaknesses, and uses that knowledge to benefit her clients.

Jo continues to travel internationally. Her travels have shown her that women in the United States "are incredibly lucky to have education, and to have control over our bodies." This realization drives Jo to give back and help other women improve their lives.

Future goals for Jo Laurie Design include developing an ecommerce site and providing some "flat fee" services. She also hopes to develop a homeware line that could fund healthcare for women in third-world countries.

Looking back on her career, Jo wouldn't have done anything differently – except maybe work a few more years in a company so she could have gained more business acumen. Her advice for others reflects this: "Listen to what other business people tell you if you don't have the expertise. Get the basics of your industry as soon as you can. If you get angel investors, take them, but know what you want to do with the investment. It's not a bad thing to get experience with a company!" And finally, Jo advises, "Don't worry about being broke." Spoken like a true artist!

Jo's Advice and Action Steps:

- Unorthodox is good – don't be afraid to be different.
- Get other people to do what you can't so you can concentrate on what you love and what you do well.
- Develop a resource team of experts to rely on when you need assistance. It's a worthy investment.

Resources:

Jo Laurie Design: www.jolauriedesign.com
Savor the Success: www.savorthesuccess.com/member/jo_laurie
Jo on Twitter: www.twitter.com/JoLaurieDesign
Jo on Pinterest: www.pinterest.com/jolauriedesign/
Jo on Facebook: www.facebook.com/JoLaurieDesignLLC
Jo on Tumblr: www.jolauriedesign.tumblr.com/

> 66Your generation of women should do
> because you can!99

> – Jo's Grandmother

❧ ❧ ❧ ❧

34. MELANI LUST: RENAISSANCE WOMAN SEES LIFE THROUGH A CREATIVE LENS

I was introduced to Melani by a mutual friend who is also her client. The power of the women's network is alive and well and it's always exciting to see women promoting other women. Melani certainly had an interesting career reinvention that has put her in control of her own career destiny. Her story really resonates with those who share an artistic sensibility and I'm pleased to include her reinvention in the second edition of my book.

From her first darkroom class at the age of 13, Melani knew her life's work would be about creating imagery. A native of San Diego, she left California to move to Manhattan where she earned a BA in Art History and an MA in Fine Arts from New York University on full scholarship with magna cum laude distinction.

This Renaissance woman has a sophisticated understanding of aesthetics and composition and her earlier career pursuits explain her profound ability to create moving works of art in her photography.

Melani enjoyed a career as a professional dancer while earning her undergraduate degree at NYU. Dancing with the world renowned Alvin Ailey American Dance Theatre, she also danced in numerous off Broadway productions and as a featured commercial dancer during the birth of MTV when dancers were highly sought after for the emerging music video genre.

The Show Must Go On

While working as a dancer fed her artistic soul, Melani was routinely frustrated with how women were treated in that artistic world. Sexism and inflated egos were rampant and even though she stayed with it for a while, Melani knew this was not a long-term career for her. She started her Master's program at NYU while still dancing on the side, but an injury precipitated a permanent change, which launched her in a new career direction.

On full scholarship – plus a stipend, which was extremely hard to come by at a private school like NYU, Melani began her graduate studies in the Art History division of the Institute of Fine Arts. Her focus was on two subjects: 17th century Dutch and Flemish artists and Ancient Roman sculpture groups. At the time she thought she would advance directly into the PhD program and pursue a career in academia but the birth of her first child changed her mind.

Objets d'Art

While at the Art Institute she studied photography and would archive works of art with photos as a way to catalog and study individual pieces. Melani worked with a studio in the basement of the Institute to photograph these historical artifacts from Ancient Roman sculpture to fine paintings and antiquities.

Through her NYU program she also studied photography at the famous Parsons School of Design in New York and learned the nuances of lighting, composition, and photographic technique. She further enhanced her study with a year at the International Center for Photography in New York and fell in love with the art form, especially the lighting, which remains a favorite part of the photographic process for her today.

Open for Business

Friends started asking Melani to take their photos and before she knew it she had clients before she had an official photography studio. By this time she had three kids and it was a great way to earn money, go on location for a shoot, and then spend quality time at home with her kids. For 15 years including her school days, she enjoyed city life in the Big Apple before moving to Connecticut, where she built a photography studio in her garage.

In the middle of her emerging photography business she got divorced which changed how she could spend her time growing the business while also caring for her three children. Her former father-in-law was extremely generous in sharing his entrepreneurial and business acumen to help Melani establish her business in Connecticut where she is now thriving.

With a full studio in her garage, Melani learned the essentials of tax ID, business insurance, trademarks, etc., and the necessity of beautiful brochures and printed samples showcasing her photos to share with prospective clients. In her line of work, customers expect something tactile, not just a website image, when considering whether to hire Melani for a shoot.

The showroom space was a big expense and Melani is at a point where she can say that she is now earning her living as a professional photographer. Initially she would reinvest a lot of her earnings into the business to upgrade equipment and keep products in stock. She recalls the importance of having a strong line of credit since in the early days she relied on that to get her business up and running.

Cutting Edge

Melani went digital with her photography which gave customers more immediate gratification and the ability to see their photos faster. For example, Melani will upload highlights of a full wedding shoot to an iPad or smart device so a newly married couple can enjoy a sampling of wedding day memories on their honeymoon. The trend is to share these highlight photos on Facebook and Melani is able to use social media to her advantage in this digital age, which makes her customers very happy.

Melani wants budding entrepreneurs to understand how intense running your own business will be. She advises others to be prepared to work harder than they ever imagined and be ready to lose sleep. Her former father-in-law was very helpful in coaching her on how to deal with clients. In addition to old adage that *the client is always right*, he encouraged Melani to become an active listener and to validate her customers, since building a trusting relationship was essential for her kind of business.

Always prepared to keep things professional, Melani learned to check her emotions at the studio door when she was ready to meet with a client. They deserved 100% of her time and focus and she learned that the referral was the key to her business growth. She currently forms 95% of her business clientele from referrals.

Poetry in Motion

The bread and butter of Melani's business is wedding photography, but she also does commercial, editorial and architectural photography, as well as custom portraiture, engagement and special occasion sessions. Melani's images define a moment in time. With grace and playfulness she captures the poetry of the ordinary and her work clearly celebrates life. Blending journalistic truth with artistic vision, Melani captures moments in time that delight her clients.

Her studio offers complete post-production services including archival printing on museum quality cotton rag papers, cutting-edge printing on Plexiglas and large scale framed prints on canvas. All of the albums and books are hand printed and Melani's art history expertise is evident in every inch of the finished product.

Fluent in Spanish and French, this multi-faceted artist also travels the world to pursue photojournalistic and editorial assignments in addition to on-location weddings, and portraits beyond her studio walls.

Melani looks forward to future projects where she will photograph cancer survivors and exhibit these photos in museums and art shows. Her exhibition "CarHavana" showcasing pre-embargo autos in Cuba has earned international acclaim and will be exhibited in Vienna. A sought after authority on wedding photography, future plans for Melani also include offering best practice tips for wedding photography on TV and in an online blog. She has won "Best Wedding Photographer" for two years in Fairfield County and is a member of the esteemed WPJA . Her work is regularly featured in magazines including Connecticut Brides, atHome Magazine, Architectural Digest, Greenwich Magazine and The Knot.

While growth can be good for a business, Melani has a desire to keep a boutique-y feel for her studio so customers feel special and honored in the process. A true artist with multiple layers, Melani Lust is living her passion as a professional photographer. Her roots as a dancer are evident in the movement of her photos and she is living the life she designed.

Quality Over Quantity

When I spoke with Melani recently, she was still growing in her photography business. Her quality work and her outstanding customer service means that she is highly sought after, and busy year-round. She's been named *Best Wedding Photographer* for five years in a row, and her jobs are booked more than a year in advance.

With this success, Melani has been able to shift away from the family portraits to take more editorial work and high-end weddings. And as her business grew, she needed help. In addition to the photography work, Melani now oversees a full-time office manager, a part-time bookkeeper, and two additional photographers. Friends who see her success have urged her to create a franchise and open locations in multiple states. But that's not for Melani. She is so successful because of her talent – and she fears the quality would suffer if she had multiple locations.

This is the classic entrepreneurial challenge of scalability. If you do something wonderfully, and you are the only person who can do it, then you're limited by the number of hours in a day. Melani's approach is to focus on the very high-end weddings she's becoming known for. She has had to turn away business, and that's when she decided to add staff. But many of the previous customers insist that Melani be their photographer, so it's a constant challenge.

As the weddings have become bigger and bigger, her time spent per wedding has increased. There are shot lists and formal portrait lists to prepare, time to spend with the bride before the wedding, and time scouting locations. If the wedding photos will be submitted to a magazine, there are even more demands.

One change in her business is that customers want photo albums again. When we spoke, Melani had 13 albums underway. "It's exciting to have this challenge – I love thinking about the layouts and pulling everything together."

If given the chance to go through her career change again, the one thing Melani would change is her knowledge of business in general. "I would learn more about business first, and not spend time attending workshops on the craft, but on how to run a business. I would also find a mentor, and figure out sooner how to hire the best people." Hiring has been a challenge, but Melani has learned to look for the passion – for photography AND for customer service. "Passion isn't teachable, but the rest is."

Cash flow is one of the lessons she learned the hard way. "In the beginning, I thought 'I have a lot of money coming in!' – I was focused on those big payments that came with each wedding. But I didn't realize how much money was going out – for bills, equipment, everything. So I didn't understand the big picture – 'where's the profit??'" The best advice that Melani offers new business owners is to make sure you have "a stash of cash and be prepared to not make money for the first couple of years."

She also reinforces the importance of referrals in building new business. Word of mouth works both positively and negatively. "You have to think about your pricing, too. You don't want to be known as the budget option – it's important that you don't undervalue your services. Volunteer to gain experience if necessary, just don't low-ball yourself."

Also critical to successful entrepreneurs is a support system. "A lot of photographers quit the business because of the time demands – we work every weekend, and if you're leaving kids behind, it can be rough. You need to have good support going in, and you have to be okay with the demands for your time."

Melani shared another unexpected tip: Be careful with your public appearance! "You represent your business at all times. You don't want to be caught in the grocery in sweat pants, or post politically charged items on your Facebook page."

So what's next? Melani longs to do more destination weddings, especially those that allow her to speak French. And she is still working toward her goal of appearing on television, perhaps to give tips to brides. Melani has landed several magazine covers, and has more in her sights as she works on weddings of increasing prestige.

This is just a "snapshot" of Melani's career – what can you take from her story to improve your own career?

Melani's Advice and Action Steps:

- Be willing to take a risk to grow your business.
- As an entrepreneur be ready to work your ass off.
- 95% of any business is referral so stay current and be ready to change and adapt your business as the market dictates.
- The customer is always right!
- Believe in what you love.

Resources:

Melani's website: www.melanilustphotography.com

"Play the game for more than you can afford to lose. For only then will you learn the game."

– Winston Churchill

❧ ❧ ❧ ❧

35. TAKE A STEP FORWARD

Throughout the journey of interviewing hundreds women for my book project, I have met people with infectious positive attitudes. Angela Jia Kim, Danielle Bobish, Ginger Hodge, Jo Laurie, and Melani Lust are great examples of women who have created careers they can live with positive energy. Not only are they flourishing in their professions, they are paying-it-forward to help others, and savoring each moment.

Be Accountable

The truth is that you alone are responsible for your personal and professional growth. No company, boss, or mentor is on a mission to create your perfect work environment. The buck stops with you and you owe it to yourself to take control of your future. It begins with a critical self-assessment of your values, interests, personality and skills and moves forward with your motivation and ability to devise an action plan.

If you don't like the way you are feeling, the quickest and most effective way to change is to adjust your thinking. Do everything in your power to achieve a positive and optimistic attitude. Employers have confirmed that attitude is more important than education and skills. You can learn new skills but if you don't bring a positive attitude to the table, you are selling yourself short.

Positive attitude affects your day-to-day performance and plays a role in every aspect of your life. The way you envision your career and your life is the way you will live it. Remove toxic people from your daily life and surround yourself with people who share your positive and buoyant outlook. Positivity is infectious and you will reach your goals faster if you are living and working in a constructive environment with a support system that is cheering you on to achieve your goals.

Savor Each Moment

Angela Jia Kim has built her business, SavortheSuccess.com on the philosophy that you should relish every moment of success as you work towards your goals. Our education system is predicated on helping students improve by showing them what they did wrong. Do you remember the big red X on your childhood tests indicating an incorrect answer? How sad that we were not commended for the questions we answered correctly; the focus was always on what we needed to improve.

I urge you to focus on the positive and learn to showcase what you do well. You are not broken; if you take the time to play to your strengths instead of always trying to fix your weaknesses, you will be much happier. Savor what you do well and relish the small things each day that make you smile. Literally stop to smell the roses and focus on what you really need to bring you satisfaction.

Often we are so busy working that we don't enjoy living. Take a tip from Jo Laurie and work to live as opposed to living to work, so you can enjoy your life in addition to your profession and have more time to do what you really love outside of work. My new mantra is: **Enjoy Your Career. Love Your Life!**

REINVENTION TOOLBOX

Recognize Your Transferable Skills; Develop Your Professional Poise; Give-Give-Get

As a fellow artist, I can truly relate to the women in this chapter. My colleagues refer to me as the *Queen of Transferable Skills* because I have learned the broad spectrum of skills I possess and I now know how to tell others what I do well.

Ideally, I want you to tap into the skills that give you strength. I happen to clean my house very well – that is a skill. But it's not a skill that gives me strength or one that I choose to utilize in my career pursuits.

- *What are the skills in your repertoire that give you strength?* Write down at least three.
- **What tasks energize you and leave you wanting to do more?** Add to the list as you discover new tasks.

I want you to think about the kinds of things you enjoy doing so much that you can actually lose track of time while doing them. These are the skills that you probably enjoy using the most. They are transferable because you can use them in any career field that you choose which needs that skill set.

Start your career reinvention research focusing on the skills that bring you strength. Don't think about job titles or industries yet. First, identify what you really enjoy doing and then research ways that you can employ these skills in a career.

Don't confuse transferable skills with traits like: *dependable*, *works well under pressure*, and *has a great work ethic*. These are traits and, though important, it is the skills that you are first selling to a prospective employer. Be ready to tell your skills story as you network and pursue research about new career opportunities. Eventually, you will share your skills story in a job interview.

A client of mine identified her top skill as *organizing* but her story fell flat because she did not flesh out exactly what she liked to organize. After some coaching, and a full-scale reflection about her organizing experiences, she developed a more effective narrative. She was able to articulate that she organized people, ideas, and events and was able to take brainstorming sessions from the boardroom to full-scale implementation working with vendors, staff, donors, and volunteers. She landed a position as an Events Coordinator in a nonprofit organization and is happily playing to her organizational strengths.

Do You Have Stage Presence?

As an opera singer, I know from experience that stage presence speaks volumes about how you are perceived. The audience forms an impression of you before you even open your mouth, and the same rings true in the world-of-work. You have control over the way you carry and comport yourself and these traits can help you own your self-confidence.

Here are some quick strategies to ramp up your professional poise:

- **Stand tall and use good posture** when sitting in a board meeting, making a presentation, or even grabbing coffee in the company break room. Good posture is healthy, conveys confidence, and can make you look five pounds thinner (that's my kind of diet!).

- **Analyze your speaking voice**. Be sure to speak slowly, clearly, and keep your volume constant throughout your statements. Use proper grammar and work towards eliminating filler phrases such as: *like, um, you know,* and *you guys.*

- **Dress the part**. Take stock of your professional wardrobe and make sure you are neatly groomed and wearing clothing that reflects the culture (and decade!) of your work environment. Ill-fitting and sloppy clothing sends an immediate negative message to your clients and colleagues.

- **Have a positive attitude and avoid workplace gossip and politics**. Positivity is infectious and can impact how you perform on the job. Pay-it-forward with an upbeat mindset and watch your colleagues follow suit.

- **Be mindful of the rules of etiquette** whether you are hosting a client for a business lunch or a guest at your boss's holiday party. Retool your etiquette know-how so that you can be comfortable eating and socializing in a professional environment.

Giving Back

I formed my singing group *The Grateful Divas* so I could use my musical talent to give back to nonprofit and charitable organizations and because I still love to perform. By helping these groups raise money and awareness, I am making a contribution to institutions I believe in.

So many of the women profiled in this book have incorporated ways to give back in their businesses and private lives. Whether it is volunteering your time and expertise or donating a percentage of targeted proceeds towards a worthy cause, generosity and the spirit of community are being celebrated on a grand scale.

In an era when business ethics have been questionable in our world, what better way to teach the children of the next generation that philanthropy matters than by paying-it-forward?

- **How will you share your time, talents or treasure in your community?**
- **Give yourself a 90-day window to do your research and implement your give-back plan.**

Considering how you can help others will increase your personal capital. Careers are a lifelong journey and we've all had people that were instrumental in helping us along the way in good times and in bad. Make an effort to be conscious about how you are helping others because what goes around really does come around.

7

LET'S HEAR IT FOR THE WAHMS: WORK-AT-HOME MOMS

Work-at-home moms, or WAHMs, are on the job 24/7. While working from home may seem like a luxury, it is also the definition of multitasking and adaptability. These amazing moms are nurturing their careers and families, as well as themselves.

36. VIANESA VARGAS: FIRST, TAKE CARE OF YOURSELF

With ten years of active duty service under her belt, Vianesa Vargas was on track to be a commander in the military. But after the birth of her second son, she was given orders to serve in Iraq for another year plus three additional months of training. That's when she decided to leave the Air Force and pursue her other call-to-serve, to help women be the best moms they can be and to lead confident, fulfilling lives.

Vianesa (or V, as her friends call her) spoke to many military career women who were also struggling with the question of whether to serve themselves and their families first, or their careers. With four deployments to the Middle East already under her belt, Vianesa knew her personal decision to leave the military was one that she could pursue without regrets. She does admit that leaving was not without guilt, but when she finally came to terms with the fact that her guilt was self-imposed, she was able to move on and embrace her new career dreams and goals.

Living a Guilt Free Life

Her new mission is to show other busy moms how they can make time for their families, work, passions, and most important, themselves. Vianesa founded the **Take Care Project**, an online health and wellness resource for busy moms. She is also a wellness coach and the author of an exercise and nutrition journal, written expressly for women who are struggling to juggle motherhood and their diet and exercise goals.

> "The products I launched are tailored to a mom's wellness. I listen to my market and create products to fulfill their needs. Casual t-shirts and the exercise journal are also available now. We're planning to launch a toolkit for moms who are struggling with the transition to motherhood as well as an exercise book for new moms."

Although Vianesa is proud of her country and her military career accomplishments, her most rewarding experiences are becoming a wife to a loving husband, and a mother to two wonderful boys.

> "I know all too well how much of an experience it is to bring a child into this world and then to watch this *experiment* grow into what you shape it. The demands of motherhood on your body and mind can be intense, but the **Take Care Project** will be with you along the way. My purpose is to give mothers the resources needed to take care of themselves FIRST!"

Honoring Your Body

Long before her military career, Vianesa learned how to get into tip-top physical shape and she enjoys maintaining this healthy lifestyle even now as a civilian. With degrees in biology and nutrition studies, Vianesa has developed simple and easy-to-remember strategies that mothers can use to improve their own health and wellness.

While she was ready to transition to a new career post-military, Vianesa says the Air Force provided her with some excellent transferable skills. She is flexible, able to adapt quickly to change, and knows how to prioritize tasks. Vianesa's Air Force career also afforded her financial stability, and with her dedicated savings plan, she was able to sock away money over the years that gave her the nest egg she needed to finance her new business venture.

But how do you transition from the military to launch a national online business for moms? Vianesa was a faithful reader of Entrepreneur Magazine and also used SCORE (Counselors to America's Small Business) advisors in her community. She hired a web designer and built her business with the support and enthusiasm of her husband who shares in her vision to help others. The goal is to build a wellness s company that empowers working moms with resources, products, and inspiration. Long-term, Vianesa plans to open a wellness center. After talking with her, I am confident that she will make this goal a reality. But every career has challenges and Vianesa was candid while sharing hers.

> "A challenge is finding the time to effectively manage a business start-up. It is extremely important for women to continue to exercise, eat right and rest, as I can attest to. I have made several mistakes by working all day, raising children, and then having to work on my business. You are more effective when healthy and well-rested."

Look to Your Communities

The military taught Vianesa how to be resourceful and the Take Care Project shows women how to do the same. Vianesa encourages moms to find a support system in their communities. Look for mentors and seek out shared services like childcare and carpooling to simplify your challenges. The messages of the Take Care Project focus on health, spirit, fun, fitness, rest, and green living. Vianesa's site features thoughtful and inspiring articles as well as a blog to help mothers achieve their personal goals, at their own pace.

While Vianesa was on her way to breaking through the glass ceiling in the military, she values her new career even more because it feeds her passion. Look for Vianesa on the national circuit as a motivational speaker and writer in publications such as Essence, Working Mother, Heart & Soul, and Family magazines.

What's New?

Like many career changers, Vianesa used skills she learned in one setting to be successful in another. Her transferable skills of flexibility and adaptability came into play again, as she shifted her focus from moms' health and fitness to helping all types of people make better food choices.

When I caught up with Vianesa several years after our first conversation, she was excited to tell me about her new direction. Instead of focusing just on moms, Vianesa wants to help all kinds of people make better choices when it comes to food and health. Her new business, Capital Food Coaching, does just that. Capital Food Coaching provides weight loss coaching for those who've had no success with traditional dieting. Customers can work with a personal chef to design menus, shop for the freshest ingredients, and prepare meals the entire family will enjoy.

In our conversation, Vianesa explained that her first business (the Take Care Project) was set up as a social networking model, which was eventually eclipsed by Facebook. Looking back on her career change, she said she should have focused on developing a product instead of on the social networking route. This, plus the fact that the business plan wasn't as strong as it could be, led Vianesa to shift her focus to food coaching. She is still focused on health, but her audience is broader now. She is turning her passion into dollars by selling information and products via her website www.capitalfoodcoaching.com.

Food coaching clients typically call with some issue – most often this is obesity, having to work with a picky eater, or having low energy. Vianesa gathers detailed information from each client, and then tailors her approach based on the client's need. She visits clients' homes to go through the refrigerator with them, identifies foods that are impeding their goals, and talks about better options. Sometimes, she provides meal planning by the week, and checks in with clients every couple of weeks.

Vianesa wants to be known as an expert in food and health, specifically concerning the obesity and stress interaction. Her longterm goal for Capital Food Coaching is to offer food products for those who miss lunch. (We laughed about the fact that I was eating a meal-replacement bar while we talked!) Her husband Pedro is a trained chef, and together they're developing product ideas. She also hopes to have her first book published soon, and is busy speaking in the Washington D.C. area about being healthy at work.

This new venture satisfies one of Vianesa's key work values. "I was born to help people be healthy. I feel out of place if I'm not in a position to do that!" Through her information, her website, and her coaching, she does just that.

Looking back on her career transitions, Vianesa has learned not to give up. "The biggest lesson has been that to succeed, you have to give it your all. You are all in, or you're not in. Running a business can't be a side venture; it has to be your focus."

She admits that finding the balance between life and work is still a challenge, and she's quick to give enormous credit to her husband. "He's been a major force in my success. I've learned that as a mom/entrepreneur, having a supportive spouse is the greatest factor for success in life and in achieving balance. It takes a special man to support a strong woman as her career grows. I can't emphasize enough how important this is!"

The passion that Vianesa has for helping others is engaging. With her desire, her direction, and her effort, she is creating a whole new food-coaching approach. The world will be a better place because of her.

Vianesa's Advice and Action Steps:

- Get clear and focused about why you want to start a business.
- Get mentored and listen to those who have already done what you're trying to do. Become a student of the trade so to speak, and read, read, read!
- Make it happen by getting a business plan written and decide if it is a worthwhile venture. If not, go back to the drawing board.

Resources:

Entrepreneur Magazine
SCORE: www.score.org
Capital Food Coaching: www.capitalfoodcoaching.com

“Excellence is what we repeatedly do. Excellence is not an act but a habit.”

– Aristotle

∽ ∽ ∽ ∽

37. PAM BEATTIE: FRIENDLY FUR LEADS TO A BUSINESS WITH REPURPOSE

When Pam Beattie, a stay-at-home mom, married for 20 years, had a yearning for something more, she focused on her passion for French furniture to launch a new business. **Venetian Décor** is her boutique upholstery and design house that specializes in creating down duvets, custom filled seat cushions and reproduction French furniture, to name just a few of her offerings. Pam is the ultimate recycler using vintage fur coats to bring a new life to these heirlooms and repurpose them for something new and unique.

Pam designs custom pieces that act as windows in time and reflect old world craftsmanship, dedication, and attention to detail. **Venetian Décor** does not promote the trapping and killing of animals, but works exclusively with vintage fur coats to ensure that these historic resources are refashioned into useful and appreciated products.

According to Pam:

"Our mission is to imbue a little corner of your life with some old-world magic and elegance by repurposing vintage items and giving them a modern twist. My love of beautiful vintage fur coats and French furniture inspired me to create this line of products for you to enjoy for many years to come."

A Little Bit of History Preserved

Her signature pieces are beautiful one-of-a-kind furnishings and throws made from vintage fur coats and buttons just like your great-grandmother owned. "We are based in the Coast Mountains of British Columbia, where the pioneer spirit of early fur trappers and adventurers still whispers through the spruce and fir at night, and the hopes of gold-seekers echo down the wild rivers." For Pam, working with repurposed fur coats and vintage rhinestone buttons and jewelry is a chance to imagine a moment in time in a world of horse-drawn buggies and mink capes that bring a touch of old-world elegance into the busy modern world.

Pam came up with the prototypes for **Venetian Décor** in her home studio, an 800-square-foot space where she also sells her creations. She uses Italian-made and imported French furniture as well as antique French furniture for her pieces. The soft Italian-made leathers, natural silk fabrics and ribbons, plus natural down cushions and wool are the ultimate in eco friendly materials.

Her first big break came from an Interior Design Show in Vancouver, British Columbia, where she showcased her wares. A writer profiled her business and featured a two-page article in the *Vancouver Sun* newspaper with photos, and the official buzz began. The writer tackled the animal rights issue and deftly wrote that repurposed fur means that no animals have died today. It also means that no faux fur, with its own environmental issues including pollution and petroleum-based synthetics are being manufactured for these artistic creations.

Pam has her own philosophy about using vintage fur:

"I truly believe that I have found a final resting place for these animals. It's a way to say that we appreciate you and respect you."

Whether you believe in Pam's vintage fur credo or not, kudos are due to this *mompreneur* who has created a viable business she is passionate about.

Venetian Décor was featured in a high-profile article in the *Beverly Hills Times* magazine. Pam hopes this will introduce her brand to celebrity clientele who could really put her on the map. The Venetian Décor signature style is a blending of shabby-chic, eco-chic, French, Boho, and refined but relaxed glamour styles, blended together for a one-of-a kind design.

The Challenges of a Working Mother

Inspired by her own creative mother who was a ceramics artist, Pam feels a great sense of accomplishment with her new business venture. She still loves being a mother but finds this new work fulfilling, and it gives her a sense of purpose so that she can now put herself first. Her husband and family have been very supportive and enthusiastic and her daughters even lend a hand with her pieces.

With a new beginning in her 40s as her kids are about to leave the nest, Pam is ready to succeed in her new business but admits there are challenges. She is a one-woman show and shared that her responsibilities as a wife and mother don't change with her new business, so now she has two full-time jobs!

Without financial backing or business loans available to her, Pam used her savings to purchase the start-up materials including reproduction furniture from Italy. She reinvests her profit into the business and keeps her overhead low by working from her home studio. Her husband is a professional in the building industry so he has been helpful as a resource for some basic business fundamentals, but Pam has been on her own to learn the trade of the interior design industry. She advises other budding entrepreneurs to do their research about trademark, company name and logo first, and then focus on your product.

Waste Not, Want Not

Inspired by *shabby chic* queen, Rachel Ashwell, Pam is building her brand on the historic preservation of vintage furs as a way to honor the history of each piece with a new life. Repurposing has become vogue in the art, interior design, and fashion worlds so Pam is capitalizing on the "waste not, want not" approach. Since vintage fur can last up to 100 years, her creations make sustainable sense economically, environmentally, and socially.

Pam was featured on the Canadian TV show *Urban Rush* and she was recently approached by a jewelry designer to sell her pieces in their store. These baubles are a favorite of celebrities Tori Spelling and Anne Heche, so Pam hopes that the women might also consider buying one of her pieces. If you have an heirloom fur coat that you want repurposed, consider commissioning Pam to make you a custom piece that will live on for years to come.

While Pam is living a new dream with her own business, she is also establishing a practice of repurposing and recycling items to create new furnishings. This businesswoman with a conscience feels like a butterfly that has just begun to spread her new wings.

What's New?

The passion Pam has for her art and her business is stronger than ever. When we spoke a few years after our initial conversation, there were many exciting updates.

Pam has extended her product line to include smaller items such as "bling-on-the-go" bags, eye masks, and bracelets. These new creations allow her to use smaller pieces of fur and leather to eliminate waste.

The furniture line is still going strong. Pam has grown that line to the point where she is contracting with manufacturers to meet demand. "To grow the business, it has to be scalable. I must have the ability to produce 2,500 units *before* I get an order that large!"

In the process of contracting with manufacturers, Pam learned to trust her intuition. "I think most people have a little voice inside that guides them. Listen to that little voice more times than not; it will guide you to the right answer." She shared that she had a "funny feeling" about a manufacturing company she'd contacted to make her furniture line. "I didn't listen to my inner voice and my gut feeling, and it ended up costing me an enormous amount of money, for a product that was of very poor quality and not usable or sellable." She has since found a reliable, quality manufacturer to produce her furniture lines.

Like many **mompreneurs**, Pam has learned to appreciate the value of hiring select professionals. "Public relations and marketing is the biggest challenge. I used to do it all myself, but you can't do it all *and* make the product. So I hired a PR professional who is getting me great magazine and blog coverage. It really pays to have experienced PR help."

Pam has several goals for her business. Eventually, she would like to add a line of fabric designs, rugs, wallpaper, and more furniture options.

Still, Pam is quick to explain that being a stay at home mother and wife is one of the most important jobs in the world. When we talked about her move into business, she explained that as a creative person, she needed a creative outlet, interaction with creative, like-minded people, and a challenge. These "missing pieces" created the space in which her business was born.

I asked Pam what she would change about her initial career transition if she could. Not surprisingly, the issue of work/life integration came up. "If I could do things over, I would try to use my time better. I would have more division between family time and work time. There were lots of very late nights spent finishing products. I would set clear start and stop times for work, but that's not always easy when you're an entrepreneur!"

Even with all the challenges, Pam emphasized that you can't second-guess yourself if you're going to be successful. For those who are thinking about a career change, Pam says, "You only live once, so fulfill your dreams in life. Don't hesitate to seize the moment; there's no reason you can't have it all! My new motto is 'life is an open book with chapters that haven't been written yet' – so write the best book of your life, inspirations, and goals for the world to see!"

Pam's Advice and Action Steps:

- Don't overwhelm yourself with a new business, take baby steps and preserve your inner peace.
- Follow your heart and do something you are passionate about.
- Be sure you have a good resource team (family, mentors, etc.) to back you up.
- Go for it because you have nothing to lose by trying.
- Do your homework setting up in your trademark, company name and logo.

Resources:

Venetian Décor: www.venentiandecor.com
Fur Council: www.furcouncil.com

❝You will never know if you don't try.❞

– Pam Beattie

❦ ❦ ❦ ❦

38. Candace Alper: Name Your Tune

It all began for Candace Alper when she was on maternity leave. In Canada, new moms are able to take up to a year off, which has led to a growing number of *mompreneurs* in the country. Having a year to herself and her new baby, Candace was able to take the time to think about her life and her career. With an infant daughter, she started singing the songs all moms know and love, but she would incorporate Hannah's name to personalize the tunes.

Before long, "If You're Happy and You Know It" became "If You're Hannah and You Know It," and the idea of **Name Your Tune** was born. Candace's husband, Eric, works in the music industry and he supported the idea of the new business venture and also brought significant skills and expertise to the table. From the beginning, the focus has been on making music fun for children and parents alike. By customizing songs with a child's name, this wife and husband team has been able to take classic children's songs to a new place.

Sing a New Song

Candace admittedly has no experience in the music industry, but her background in liberal arts and education has provided her with a cadre of transferable skills that help her run the business. Directly after college, Candace hoped to pursue teaching but the lack of opportunities in the education field led her to a position in the retail industry. She was working her way up the management ladder when she became pregnant with Hannah. The plan was to go back right after her maternity leave, but **Name Your Tune** happily took her life in a different direction.

Candace has been active with children and youth in her community through social programs, summer camps, and trips abroad, so creating a new business about kids was an ideal fit. They started with nine songs and eight hundred recorded names. Candace and Eric invented the technology to personalize the songs with a child's name in the recording process.

Eric's music background came in very handy with this new business venture. As the company cofounder, he has been active in the

Canadian music scene for 15+ years and has experience with media relations and acquisitions for Koch Entertainment, which proved extremely valuable for **Name Your Tune**.

Bringing Home the Bacon and Cooking It

In the beginning, Candace admits she was useless around computers as technology was not her forte. But she is now the company's one-woman IT department and coordinates the efforts of four amazing singers, producers, and a West Coast office, handling most of the day-to-day tasks herself.

Being a *mompreneur* and a WAHM (work-at-home mom) means that Candace can be her own boss. She sets her own hours, which lends itself to a flexible schedule so that she can balance her varying roles as a mom, wife, daughter, sister, and business owner. While Candace admits to accepting a certain amount of imbalance as a reality to her day, she feels fortunate to be able to work from home and enjoy the little things that she couldn't do if she worked off-site.

While juggling **Name Your Tune** responsibilities she usually does a few loads of laundry and gets her daughter to and from school daily. She has become the queen of multitasking. On an ambitious day this might also include cooking a batch of homemade spaghetti sauce because these are things that she is able to fit into her work day now.

A Hard Day's Night

While the work day might sound idyllic, prioritizing her family during the day means that Candace often works at the computer well into the night. Eric is often at her side since this business is truly a joint venture and a family affair. She has his total support and kid coverage when the job requires her to work weekends away for promotional events to brand their product. They have developed a partnership and have each other's backs to cover things on the work and home front.

Since the company launch, **Name Your Tune** has become the leading personalized CD in the world. Children will hear their name more than 80 times throughout 14 treasured songs and they now have over 4500 names to choose from!

People Magazine called Name Your Tune CDs, "This year's most coveted item," in 2009. NBC's *The Today Show* calls the CD, "Must have baby gear – now that's something to sing about!" Celebrity parents sporting customized CDs include Patrick Dempsey, Brad Pitt and Angelina Jolie, Matt Damon, Debra Messing, Tori Spelling, Denise Richards, and many more.

Reality Check

The business is thriving now and going better than Candace and Eric ever expected. However, the start-up costs were significant. Family support played a key role. Candace's father is an accountant who shared both his financial wisdom and financial backing for the new company.

With four performers and a full studio assembled to record the customized songs, **Name Your Tune** cost $25,000 to become functional in the very beginning. Candace and Eric also have West Coast partners that manage and grow the business in the States. They see it as a four-way partnership and each person has a specific job that makes the engine run.

Candace warns other aspiring entrepreneurs to protect themselves legally early on and to seek out expert advice from a lawyer. She and Eric sought out the counsel of many specialists to provide skills they did not possess. Defining their unique brand in the marketplace has been incredibly important as has the research required to figure out the nuance of supply and demand in the kids' music industry.

At the end of the day, Candace is happy as a WAHM but warns other moms to be realistic about what you can commit to while raising your family. "Sometimes you have to learn to live with the fact that the beds aren't made and there are dirty dishes in the sink because you are working and growing your business while raising your kids. And that's okay!" Candace is still figuring out the delicate balancing act and no two days are alike. She wants her daughter to know that there is more to life than work even though as a WAHM she is never off duty.

Play it Forward

A portion of the company proceeds are donated to *Hear Here*, the nonprofit, charitable organization that purchases hearing aids for children through the Hospital for Sick Children. In 2007, Candace also launched a campaign called *Play it Forward*, a new initiative to support the Canadian Music Therapy Trust Fund. This effort collects new and pre-loved CDs to be distributed across Canada in support of Music Therapy. With the support and generosity of her customers, friends and colleagues, over twenty thousand CDs were collected and distributed last year.

The accolades keep rolling in. **Name Your Tune** CDs have won an iParenting Award as well as the Parent to Parent Award. The CDs have also been nominated for a Nickolodeon Parent Pick Award. Candace herself was nominated for an RBC Entrepreneur Award.

Out of a great idea, a song or two, and a lot of hard work and enthusiasm, Candace Alper changed her tune and reinvented her career from retail management-in-waiting to record label entrepreneur.

What's New?

When I caught up with Candace several years later, her business was still going strong. "Business is good! Thriving, actually. The product is loved all over the world and has been going strong for more than 10 years."

Recent achievements include releasing Name Your Tune 2 with a whole new set of songs to choose from, and entry into the group-buying arena. The catalogue continues to grow, and now includes more than 4,500 names.

A big milestone for the company is the ability to deliver the songs via digital download. "We had to recognize the way that people buy music now," said Candace. Having a physical CD is not as important these days; people listen to their music on their phones and other digital devices.

A big part of the company's growth stems from Candace's creative marketing and her growing skills in social media. She realized that she could get great publicity for **Name Your Tune** if she became a "baby name expert." She follows the trends in baby names, and is sought after for her insights and updates. She is also being recognized for her clever use of social media, and has spoken at conferences about this growing industry.

When I asked Candace what's next for her, she became thoughtful. "**Name Your Tune** was started in the circumstance of my maternity leave – not because I had a desire to run a company, but more from my mad desire to be present for Hannah. I never intended the company to be as big as it is! It took on a life of its own, and I've worked to keep in under control."

Candace reflected that she'd always been creative and really enjoyed collaborating. One challenge of running the company has been that she's alone for the most part, working in her home office. "I'm ready for a change – to get back out among people." **Name Your Tune** will still be going strong, but Candace wants to be less involved in the day-to-day management.

Candace's daughter played a pivotal role in her first career change, and she is a key player in her next career change, too. Hannah is now 10, "which is a wonder to me!" Both Candace and Hannah have been exposed to lots of digital content, especially social media. "We are truly a 'digital family.'" After attending a recent digital family summit, Hannah was moved to start a blog focused on the environment. "It is wildly successful, and has re-ignited my fire. I want to make a difference in people's lives!" Candace is looking for ways to return to her first career plans of working with high school kids and non-profits, dealing with social media, teaching, and entrepreneurial skills.

Candace asked herself the key question: How can I get filled up and help fill others up? Also, she knows that the time demands of working at home no longer suit her needs. Candace told me her favorite part of the day is picking up Hannah from school. With this crucial self-reflection, she will make sure her values are met in her next career iteration, wherever that may lead her.

When I asked if she had any new advice for career-changers, Candace shared the perspective of her 10-year journey. "You have to be all-in to be a successful entrepreneur. You really have to lean in. But nothing is forever. You can try it and see, then decide if it's for you."

Candace's story is a great example of how you can shape your work life to fit your values and your life circumstances. And it's a great reminder that change is constant and expected; what fits your life to-day may need to be adjusted over time.

Candace's Advice and Action Steps:

- To the WAHMs – don't underestimate how hard it is to work at home.
- Empower yourself with information and seek help from others who do what you can't.
- Don't take things personally, business is business.
- Research the market you want to enter and find out what the needs are. Plan your transition according to what you love and what is needed.

Resources:

Name Your Tune: www.nameyourtune.com

> 66It's only a good idea if you do it – so do it fully!99

> – Candace Alper

ↄ ↄ ↄ ↄ

39. LARA GALLOWAY: BE PROUD TO MAKE YOUR FAMILY THE #1 PRIORITY

Even though she was a self-proclaimed, fiercely independent, ambitious, and very satisfied IBM executive, Lara Galloway experienced a values shift that led to a new career. As half of a successful, double income, no kids couple, Lara never envisioned herself with children. She had all the accoutrements of a corporate position plus the freedom to travel, and led a jet-set existence – then life changed. She began to consider what she wanted her life to look like at age 50, 60, and beyond. It was then that she and her husband made the choice to have kids and she says, "…it was the best thing that ever happened to me."

Prioritizing What You Value

Lara now knows from experience how hard it is to create harmony in a mother's life. She also knows that moms often sacrifice their own needs and desires for the sake of their children, putting their own lives on hold for the future. So this mom-on-a-mission dedicated a new chapter in her career life to helping mom entrepreneurs earn more money doing what they love, while taking care of their number one priority – their families!

She became a certified life coach and combined her business acumen with her new coaching skills to create a community and a tremendous resource for women. Dedicated to helping others succeed, Lara knows that she is not alone as a mompreneur. She tapped into a powerful and growing network of women and created her business: MomBizCoach.

When I spoke to Lara, her energy and enthusiasm were infectious. She is truly passionate about supporting moms who choose to be in business as a lifestyle choice. Now a successful consultant, blogger and radio show host, Lara's network has a wide-reaching territory including the USA and Canada.

Clarify Goals and Create Harmony

Her coaching and consulting services are geared toward creating harmony for moms who also want to be successful in their business. Lara helps her clients clarify goals, develop a plan of action, and then she provides them with accountability and support. She customizes a personal development strategy that plays to each client's strengths, attitudes, and habits to work toward personalized success.

Lara's coaching approach is comprehensive and includes:

- Taking your business idea from concept to reality
- Personal branding, marketing, and networking
- Making the most of Social Media resources
- Creating a wealth plan and budgeting for it
- Teaching you to "get out of your own way" and sell yourself
- Setting fees and accepting them

Lara tapped into her transferable skills and understood the importance of using her former career experiences to propel her forward in
her new business venture. One of the best skills she learned from her
days at IBM was providing excellent customer service. She knows the
value of returning calls and emails in a timely manner, and how to
set – then meet or exceed – customer expectations.

Just Figure it Out!

Lara learned that she can learn how to do just about anything.
She started her career with IBM working in Public Relations; then she
moved into a consulting role in Education and Training; and finished
her career there in an executive-level sales and project management
role, providing e-business services for the automotive industry. Lara
admits she didn't know much about her last position before she got
the promotion, but within a few months, she was amazed at the new
techno-language she was speaking and the e-commerce concepts she
now understood.

"So I don't get hung up anymore on not knowing how to do something. I just go figure it out by doing it. I apply this skill almost daily
in my role as mom, entrepreneur, business coach, life coach, and marketing mentor to my clients."

But what about the steps that lie between launching a business
and achieving success and financial stability? When she first started
out as a coach, she was all about coaching and had no real interest in,
or knowledge of, how to run a business. She struggled to find new
clients, coached only one or two clients at a time and made hardly any
money, which was mostly fine since she didn't define her goals around
making money. It was clear to her that she needed the stimulation,
challenge, connections with inspiring people, and the opportunity to
"shine her light" and share her gifts more than she needed the money.
Her work fulfilled her ambition, passion, talents, purpose, and was an
outlet for her creativity that she needed to balance her role as a mom.
Then, Lara had an epiphany:

"About a year and a half ago, I made some big changes and got
serious about running a business. I realized, to my surprise, that I
was an entrepreneur, and I started studying everything I could about

entrepreneurship, small businesses, marketing, being a *solopreneur*, etc. I created my new brand/identity as the MomBizCoach, targeting a narrower niche of mom entrepreneurs. This focus has completely changed my ability to attract clients (rather than me having to go out and find them like I did before), and as a result, I've made more this year in six months than I did in the last three years put together. I have an automated sales/marketing process that keeps my pipeline full of clients and has me considering alternative methods of delivering what I do so that I can manage all the people who are ready to work with me. It's so awesome!!!"

You Can Have It All...Once You Know What You Want

In retrospect, if she had known then what she knows now, Lara would have worked with a business coach to figure out her niche, her ideal clients, and how to craft her services as solutions to her clients' problems. Lara shared:

> "...I wasted three solid years trying to explain to people what coaching is, and then tried to sell them coaching. I had no real understanding of how I was pushing myself, my thoughts, and my great ideas onto other people. It was a sales model that just didn't work. I wish someone had told me back then how to focus on my clients. I also wasted a lot of time not setting the proper boundaries around my work time, my family time, and me. I felt guilty about wanting to work and therefore only fit work in when no body else needed me (e.g., when the kids were napping, playing outside, etc.). I also built up a lot of resentment because I wasn't making my needs and wants a priority, so I blamed my husband and my kids (mostly only in my mind) for my unhappiness back then."

Starting a new career is a journey, and Lara's experience shows us some common growing pains and pitfalls. In time, she figured it out and is now thriving in her own business and able to help other moms with entrepreneurial aspirations. For those who think you can't have it all – a great career plus the opportunity to prioritize your family – you have never met Lara Galloway. Explore the possibilities with this mompreneur and design your customized world!

What's New?

It comes as no surprise that Lara and her business have continued to grow and evolve in the years since our first conversation. When we caught up, Lara was happy to talk about the new things she's learned along the way.

Work-life balance is always a challenge for a mompreneur, even for Lara. She's learned to meet this challenge head-on by adopting strict business hours from which she will not vary. "I work only from 9 am to 4 pm (when the kids are in school); this has become part of my brand." She's learned that by creating these work hours, she is much more productive with her time.

Another challenge in a coaching or consulting business is scalability. There are only so many hours that Lara has to offer her clients. To increase her income, she could either work more hours or increase her rate per hour. Neither option was attractive, so Lara created a third solution by partnering with a former client. With this additional resource, Lara could design and deliver the first live, weekend MomBiz Retreat, and has held several since then. In the future, Lara hopes to partner with women's organizations to create custom trainings and in-house retreats.

The business is also benefitting from exposure in Social Media. MomBizCoach has attracted interest and income from brands that target mompreneurs. Lara and MomBizCoach have thousands of Twitter followers and Facebook, and companies want to be a part of that. In fact, all the live retreats are funded by sponsors, not by the attendees.

I asked Lara what she would change, given the benefit of hindsight. "One thing I would definitely change is to create more passive revenue streams. I've created amazing content, but without organizational skills and time, it's just been languishing in the computer."

When I asked Lara what the biggest surprise has been so far in her motherhood and career journey, she said it was the length of time required to get a business really running. "If you compare yourself to someone online, someone who is already up and running (so you see their "highlight" reel), it's easy to ask 'why is it taking me so long'? Now I know why – the family commitment plus the sheer volume of things to know and do is enormous. When I started, I devoured any information online about Internet marketing, social media, how to write sales copy, and so on. I also had my own coaches. Once everything made sense and I had space in my life, I put that learning into action."

All of this has taught Lara an extremely valuable skill – knowing when to ask for help. Several years ago, she hired her first virtual assistant, and she continues to use them for website work; copy writing, social media management, documentation, presentations, newsletters and database work. This skill of asking for help is something she helps her clients develop. "Stop trying to do it all yourself, whatever "it" is. We get caught up in our struggle alone, but 'help' can take many forms."

When Lara looks back to the time when she decided to become a life coach, she understands how well it fit her. "I've been a teacher or mentor my whole life. Staying home with the baby just about killed me, because I am an extrovert and I missed the connections with people. Becoming a life coach was the PERFECT next step for me!"

Lara's Advice and Action Steps:

- Notice your definition of success – does it fit you? Create your own definition of success and work toward achieving that unique reality.
- Check in regularly with a coach or mentor who can keep you grounded and give you honest and supportive feedback and inspiration.
- Whatever you believe is true, so choose what you believe carefully. No matter what, believe in yourself!
- Be clear that this is your life and you are in control.
- Find a job you love and you'll never work a day in your life.

Resources:

MomBizCoach: www.mombizcoach.com
Five minute coaching MOMents on video:
 www.youtube.com/mombizcoach
Talk Radio: www.blogtalkradio.com/MomBizCoach
Savor the Success: www.savorthesuccess.com

❝Whatever women do they must do twice as well as men to be thought half as good. Luckily, this is not difficult.❞

– Charlotte Whitton

ↆ ↆ ↆ ↆ

40. MONICA CASTRO: SPANGLISH AND THE HEALING POWER OF BEES

Monica's reinvention was first featured on my blog. I was fascinated by her story and how it resonated with so many women stuck in cubicles work. I'm so pleased to include her in the second edition of my book and I'm confident you'll appreciate her ability to celebrate change.

Colombian by birth, Monica Castro recognized the value of her bilingual abilities in English and Spanish early on. She established a solid career with a major insurance company doing translations in the health care industry. But the beehive cubicle set-up in her company and the hour plus commute each way to work left her wanting more.

For a full year, Monica started saving money to prepare for her departure and plan her next move. The decision to leave was risky, but the day her young son became sick at school and Monica was trapped in hours of traffic before she was able to reach him was the tipping point that made her believe she was doing the right thing.

Find Your Bliss

Monica's parents in Colombia had always been self-employed so entrepreneurship was in her blood. With an interest in starting her own translations business, Monica read everything she could get her hands on to learn about the self employment business culture and realities. She worked with the Small Business Administration and established **Translations Wave** to play to her translations strengths, and to have more quality time with her family.

Monica is a bilingual industrial and interactive media designer with broad experience in translations, web design, and project management. She is on a mission to promote the value of translations and reduce the cost by reaching new markets and delivering quality service.

Translations Wave serves a niche market of healthcare, legal, and cosmetic industry customers and provides general translations in a myriad of languages including Spanish, French, Portuguese, and German. Her business offers desktop publishing services (among other PC and Mac programs) to help her clients solve market communication barriers.

What makes Monica's business unique is her focus on helping clients open unexplored markets by removing language barriers. She embraces different cultures and people from a variety of backgrounds and native tongues to facilitate the translations. **Translations Wave** is based on Monica's values of knowledge, talent, expertise, creativity, and hard work. The best part is that it enables her to work from home.

Spanglish

Since Spanish is Monica's native language, she knew the industry standard for translations in this market were of very poor quality. She would often be hired to clean up bad "Spanglish" translations, and this helped her understand the serious market need for quality Spanish translations.

Focusing on this niche gave Monica the ability to brand her business and market herself effectively to distinguish herself from her competitors. She is determined to provide quality, not just quantity, since subtle language details can make or break the meaning of a translation.

Monica works with consultant translators in Argentina. In the future, she hopes to grow the business by adding more team members as contract employees in different locations. She is marketing through social media and her website and the satisfied customer referrals are really driving the business forward.

Make it Happen

Monica believes strongly that *what you give, you receive,* and she has put her heart and soul into the new business. She provides her customers with personal attention and quality service that keeps them coming back for repeat projects.

In the spirit of good networking, she remained close to her contacts from the insurance company and has garnered new business from these connections. While Monica enjoys being in charge of her own career destiny, now she also knows that she is fully responsible for the success or failure of her business.

She has come to realize that she can't blame others for any business problems and she's determined not to let money drive the equation. Part of establishing a new business on her terms was to build **Translations Wave** on her professional values.

What If?

Monica is so appreciative that she gave herself the time to really consider what was important for her in a new career. She will never wonder "what if" she did not start her own business. She is thriving with the daily challenges of growing her business because it is her own company.

By researching the industry, Monica is able to stay on top of market trends and fill needs that other businesses don't – which plays to her strengths. Monica is playing to her passions and utilizing the entrepreneurial DNA that is part of her family.

The Bee's Knees

More than three years had passed when I reconnected with Monica to learn what's new. And boy, had things changed.

In the midst of running her own translations company, Monica began having health challenges. Soon, she realized that health insurance benefits were essential, and she chose to return to a traditional employer relationship. But the entrepreneur in her wasn't done yet!

In exploring natural health, Monica learned about bee-sting therapy. Soon she fell in love with all-things-bees, and today she is a beekeeper. She keeps bees while her husband keeps the translations company running. She's eager to share what she's learned about bees, and this gives her a chance to teach others.

Yoga was another natural-healing tool that Monica learned about, and fell in love with. She recently completed her training to become a yoga instructor, and will teach yoga in addition to keeping bees.

Monica takes a whole-life view of herself and her skills. To take the health businesses to the next level, she recently acquired three acres of land. The land came with a house, which needed *lots* of work – there were no windows left, and "the house looked like it had been eaten by plants!" After six months of hard work, the formerly abandoned house looks gorgeous! The beautiful deck can hold 20-30 yoga students at once, and Monica's dream of an outdoor yoga studio is becoming a reality. In addition to yoga instruction, Monica will offer teas, natural juices, honey, and other products.

When I asked Monica what she would change about her first business venture if she could, her answer came easily. "I would market it in a different way. I was always rushing everything, but I've learned there's no need to rush and be stressed – everything happens for a reason. I was wasting a lot of time on email marketing; I've learned I don't have to do it all myself!"

Monica confided in me that when she decided to return to a traditional job, she felt a sense of relief. "I was wearing too many hats, and didn't have any balance. My priorities were all over the place." Now, Monica is doing more projects, but has much more balance in her life. "I've learned to take my time."

I asked Monica to talk about how her personal values have been supported through her work. "My values were not a fit with my previous employers. One company was all about selling, and was completely money-driven – that's not me. Another employer claimed to have strong ethics, but didn't behave according to those ethics." Despite the disconnects, Monica was able to keep a positive attitude at work – "I didn't let people ruin my day." She realized that work is not her life, and she "leaves work at work."

When she got called back to work this time, "I was a different person. I was healed, and could pass that good energy along." According to Monica, your attitude matters. "Whatever you think, will be." This sentiment is reflected in her yoga practice; "Prana (the Sanskit word for life force) goes where the mind goes."

So for those who are on the brink of change, Monica has some advice. "Find or make balance in everyday. You have to prioritize! Write down everything you do in a day and week to see how much time you're spending on which project. This will help you get organized. Then, build a schedule, and respect the timeline – do what you say you will."

Monica is happy to be living a life that aligns with her personal goals of helping people and staying healthy. By making sure her work mirrors her priorities, Monica is helping herself to a happy career!

Monica's Advice and Action Steps:

- Money doesn't buy it all.
- Analyze yourself and do what you really want.
- When you give – you receive!
- Don't listen to the naysayers.
- Trust your heart.

Resources:

Translations Wave: www.translationswave.com
Small Business Administration: www.sba.gov

66 You are responsible for whatever happens
in your life – good or bad! 99

– Monica Castro

ↂ ↂ ↂ ↂ

41. Take a Step Forward

Motherhood is a calling and I have tremendous respect for all the moms who work at home, at an off-site workplace, or as stay home moms. Being a mom is the toughest profession in the world and comes with unique challenges in the career world that are very different for mothers than for fathers. I have coached many new moms who have faced discrimination from employers when trying to re-enter the workforce because they chose to take extended time off to raise their children. For one of my clients, even a six-month work leave was met with the question, "How can you explain your employment gap?" from a prospective employer.

Working moms have the power to change that culture and negative mindset by taking their time away without guilt and re-entering the workplace with confidence and a sense of purpose when they are ready. It's a tall order indeed, but we must stick together and support each other since as women, we are all in this together. It's imperative to find organizations that will support your family-raising values. Here are some terrific resources to get you started:

- National Organization for Women: www.now.org/issues/wfw/
- Catalyst: www.catalyst.org
- Working Mother www.workingmother.com

Vianesa Vargas, Pam Beattie, Candace Alper, and Lara Galloway are all WAHMs, the trendy new term for work-at-home moms. They have dedicated their lives to their families and their jobs and working from the home creates distinctive trials for them every day. But they have chosen this path because it gives them the freedom and the flexibility to call their own shots and prioritize things accordingly on a given day.

Invest in Yourself

Vianesa and Lara have created careers to serve as resources for mothers. By providing coaching, products, and other services, they are on a mission to help other mothers dealing with the realities of raising a family and growing a career. I strongly encourage you to find a career coach that can provide you with valuable insight, objectivity and resources to help you set and achieve your career goals. You need a plan, and a professional can help you formulate one that speaks to what you really want.

You would not build a house without blueprints, so don't underestimate what it takes to plan and build your career. Consider that coaching is an investment in your future, whether you are an entry-level professional or a seasoned, senior level executive.

Resources in Your Community

There are many additional resources available so check out your community to see what appeals to you. Adult continuing education classes at community colleges and local universities are great resources if you need to ramp up your skills in the workplace. The SCORE organization – counselors to America's small business (www.score.org) – has chapters across the country and targeted resources for women. Their services are free. The Chamber of Commerce in your respective city has networking events and training classes available that may suit your needs.

Look to your alma mater to see if they have alumni career coaching services available and a networking list serve or mentor pairing. Career coaches are a wise investment since they can be the conduit for all these resources and help you develop a plan that suits you uniquely.

The Joys of a Home Office

Many women enjoy the proximity of home offices. Working from home can be financially beneficial since you can write-off a portion of your utilities and office expenses on your taxes, if eligible. See an accountant for the specifics. This can be a wise money-saving option as opposed to renting office space and incurring additional overhead costs.

Your home office may save you valuable commute time and enable you to multitask while working effectively on your professional tasks. Sometimes the home office gives you the variety and flexibility that will make you happier at work. Others need the stimulation of coworkers to be content. As you are envisioning your reignited career future, think about your ideal work environment and consider whether the home office is a good fit for you.

REINVENTION TOOLBOX

Earning Versus Getting; Employing Effective Communication

The work-at-home moms, or WAHMs, have the difficult task of always being "on" in their 24/7 work/life environment. They have *earned* my respect and admiration for their intense work ethic and ability to multitask.

Let's take a look at "earning versus getting." One of my pet peeves is the client or student of mine who talks about *getting* their degree from a particular university or college. This nomenclature is everywhere from professional bios to all forms of the media. The last time I checked, schools were not giving out degrees to just anyone. Degrees are earned with hard work, diligence, and years of effort.

I encourage you to rearrange your mental furniture when it comes to earning versus getting in the professional world as well. You are in control of how people perceive you in the workplace or job search arena based on your professional behavior. Change your mindset and be clear about the accomplishments you have earned. Become the professional who can talk about your successes with humble confidence, and inspire others with your ability to self-promote in an appealing way.

Own Your Accolades

This technique of telling your story will come in very handy at a job interview or performance evaluation and it can be extremely helpful when you are making a proposal or enticing a new client to utilize your services. After all, you want to hear about how a business is successful before you buy their product or hire their services.

As customers, we expect references, referrals, and professional bragging about relevant successes before we buy into a pitch or a sale. We can learn the same lessons as individuals in the job-search arena or as experienced professionals looking to move up in an organization. It's time to own your accomplishments and help others understand how you achieved your successes. Telling these authentic stories helps others see your transferable skills and competencies and gives you credibility in the world-of-work.

Take credit for what you have earned and project your humble confidence. You work very hard to accomplish great things, so own these accolades!

Add "earn" to your vocabulary!

Practice (in the privacy of your home) talking out loud about your accomplishments so that you can prepare for networking opportunities and interviews. If you develop your success story and have it at-the-ready, you will be comfortable sharing it with others when the time comes.

Communication 101

I had the great pleasure of hearing Kathleen Oliver, COO of Oliver Winery (www.oliverwinery.com), speak at a professional development workshop. In her position at the winery, Kathleen manages the retail operation of the business, oversees the activities of the tasting room, special events, and human resources, so she communicates with a very large staff daily.

Kathleen offered these five tips for effective communication that I believe are universal to us all.

1. **Get to the point.** Communicating your point effectively and efficiently is essential in a professional setting. In a business where time is money, getting to the point

can make or break a deal. Be sure to stay on track and avoid tangents and rambling. Stay focused, and relay your message with clarity and confidence.

2. **Get to know others.** With a large staff it's easy to lose faces in the crowd and not address people by name. Make a point to get to know people within your department and beyond in your organization. Try to address people personally and learn about others so you can have meaningful interactions. Develop a system to remember names. Kathleen places photos of her employees on a bulletin board in her office, providing a means of matching names to faces, so that she can call each employee by name.

3. **Get along.** Follow the *Golden Rule* and treat others as you wish to be treated. It's that simple and applies to everybody at all levels within an organization.

4. **Get off the computer and get on the phone.** In this technology driven era it's easy to rely on email as the only way to communicate. Especially in a client-driven business, pick up the phone and make a personal connection. You may remember the old AT&T slogan "Reach out and touch someone." It's important to make that call when you can, and whenever possible, an in-person meeting is best.

5. **Get out of the office.** Be involved in your community and become an ambassador for your organization. Kathleen encourages her staff to volunteer and build their personal and professional relationships beyond the workplace. It's good for the individuals and ultimately, it's good for the company.

CONNECT WITH WISE WOMEN

Age knows no boundary in career reinvention. From a young Millennial professional to an 80+ year old, the women in this chapter will inspire you with transitions that empower and engage. These ladies are playing to their strengths at every age.

42. ALMA BOND: FORGET EVERYTHING YOU LEARNED ABOUT RETIREMENT

Dr. Alma Bond had a 5th Avenue Manhattan psychoanalysis practice that she enjoyed for 37 years before she became a full-time writer at age 68. Her career transition came as result of a tragedy that inspired her to pursue the one thing she had not made time in her life to do – write full-time.

A very serious car accident, in which she almost lost her life, left Alma in a coma with seven broken bones and a concussion. Her recovery was slow but sure, and Alma knew that with a new lease on life she would pursue her passion and become a full-time writer.

Alma moved to Key West so that she could be anonymous and write, which was also a part of her recovery process. While Alma thought of Key West as the most creative place on earth, she missed her beloved Manhattan where she had led a writing group and gave presentations about her books. She decided to return to The Big Apple and pursue her writing there where she lived for many years.

Power Point, Blogging, and Marketing for this Golden Girl

Now living in Carlisle Pennsylvania, Alma is enjoying what she describes as some of the best years of her life. In her 80s she is thriving and has had no fewer than 21 books published. *Margaret Mahler, a Biography of the Psychoanalyst*, was awarded a Finalist in the Biography category of the National Best Books awards, sponsored by USA Book News, and Finalist Book of the Year by Foreword Magazine. Her book, *The Autobiography of Maria Callas, A Novel* was First Runner-Up in the Hemingway Days First Novel Contest. Alma's most recent books include, *Michelle Obama: A Biography*; *Jackie O: On the Couch*; *Lady Macbeth: On the Couch*, and *Marilyn Monroe: On the Couch* – all part of her On the Couch series.

When we spoke on the phone, Alma was busy preparing a Power Point presentation for her next speaking engagement. She maintains her personal website and knows how to market herself and her books. In fact, she responded to my HARO press inquiry for my book and blog project!

Alma developed a career as a successful writer on her own, securing agents and publishers through grit and determination. Her writing abilities were evident early in her life, and Alma recounted that at the age of 11 she composed a poem entitled "Ambition"; as she matured, her career goals shifted from those of writer to those of psychoanalyst. As such, she had over 20 scholarly articles published in prestigious psychoanalytical journals. Her passion for writing remained constant even though her subject matter varied.

Find out What's in Your DNA

Her scholarly writing certainly provided technique and a foundation for her biographies and novels. Alma says that writing is in her DNA and the only thing that gets her tired is not writing. While writer's block has never been an issue, Alma does miss the financial gain of a thriving psychoanalysis practice. The books are a labor of love, but they do not generate the same kind of income. Her goal is to hit the best seller list and earn a Pulitzer Prize some day, and I have every confidence that she will do so.

Alma is a woman who thrives on intellectual challenge and stimulation. She belongs to the International Psychoanalytic Association, the American Psychological Association, and is a fellow and former faculty member of the Institute for Psychoanalytic Training and Research. She also is a member of the Dramatists Guild, American Society of Journalists and Authors, Florida Freelance Writers Association, and the Writers Guild.

All in the Family

Alma also has a gifted and prestigious family, all of whom have published books. She is the widow of the late stage, screen, and TV actor, Rudy Bond, who appeared in, among other productions, the original Broadway production and the films *A Streetcar Named Desire* and *The Godfather*. His book, *I Rode a Streetcar Named Desire*, was published posthumously.

Alma is the mother of Zane Bond, Jonathan Bond, and Janet Bond Brill. Jonathan's book, *Under the Radar,* was published last year by John Wiley and Sons. Zane's book, *A Prophet Operating at a Loss*, was published several years ago by Writers Club Press. Janet's book *Cholesterol Down* was published recently by Random House and is a best seller.

Alma Bond is an inspiration for women considering a career change. Her advice: "Find what you love and do it!" rings true for all of us.

> "I can't stop. I get up in the morning, sit down at the computer and I am reluctant to break away even to meet friends. It doesn't take discipline to write, it takes discipline to stop writing. It is like having a love affair."

Dr. Alma Bond is evidence that life is what you make of it and that retirement is overrated. As an opera singer, I am eager to read Alma's book, *The Autobiography of Maria Callas: A Novel*, the story of the famous American-born Greek soprano. You can find Alma's books in retail stores and on Amazon.com.

What's New?

When I followed up with Alma a few years later, she was still going strong despite suffering the tragedy of losing her 56 year-old son, Zane to kidney disease. She honored his memory by dedicating a book to him.

Reflecting on her transition from psychoanalyst to writer, Alma talked about how her values were more completely met as a writer. She has always valued creativity, and uses it every day when she sits down to write. Alma also enjoys the freedom of being able to set her own schedule. When she was seeing patients, her day was not her own.

Alma's empathic skills have served her well in both careers. Having the "ability to get inside peoples' heads" was required in her work as a psychoanalyst; it also allows her to empathize with and create her characters as she writes.

When asked what she would have done differently if given the chance, Alma was quick to answer. "I would have retired earlier. I'm not as in touch with the early years of young love and so on…" This is an important realization to consider… are you putting off doing what you really love.

Alma's Advice and Action Steps:

- Write every day and the word flow will come.
- Trust yourself and be your own best advocate.
- Anything you love is therapeutic – find what you love.

References:

Alma's personal website: www.alma_bond.tripod.com/
HARO – Help A Reporter Out: www.helpareporter.com/

> "Do it, do it, do it and enjoy a whole new life!"

– Dr. Alma Bond

ℐ ℐ ℐ ℐ

43. Beverly Solomon: Object d'Art Model to Marketing Maven

Beverly Solomon began her career as a model and earned her way through the executive ranks of the cosmetics and fashion industry. At the peak of her career she made the decision to use her techniques in sales and marketing to promote the art of her husband, renowned artist Pablo Solomon. Operating out of their historic ranch in the Texas Hill Country, Beverly was starstruck not sure that she could thrive without the action of the corporate fashion world but this wife/husband business is flourishing and proves that change can be good.

When I spoke to Beverly by phone we connected like longtime girlfriends who never missed a beat, even though it was the first time we'd met. She has a mellifluous Texan lilt to her voice that completes the package of this sophisticated and elegant professional woman. I was entranced by her career story that began at age 16 when she was drawn to the cosmetics counters in the Houston department stores.

How Fan Mail Turned into a Career Opportunity

Beverly grew up at the Estée Lauder counter and was mentored by the grand dames of the industry who showed her the ropes. But Beverly knew there was more than just the makeup counter in store for her career-wise, and she boldly sent a fan mail letter to Diane Von Furstenberg admiring her new fashion line. To her surprise, she received a telegram from Von Furstenberg asking for a meeting at an elegant Houston hotel. Needless to say, Beverly was starstruck, but was also offered a job covering the entire Houston territory, modeling at trunk shows, setting up marketing and sales, and serving as a makeup artist. This was a pivotal time for the Von Furstenberg line with the launch of the now legendary *Tatiana* fragrance and the classic wrap dress that inspired Beverly's fan mail letter. This is the stuff that movie scripts are made of and Beverly was enchanted with her new opportunity.

After two years at Von Furstenberg, Beverly moved to a position with Revlon, which she calls the boot camp of the industry. This is where she developed her business acumen in sales and marketing. She worked incredibly hard and developed key relationships with professionals in the business and eventually moved on to a position with Ralph Lauren. She felt privileged to be a top level executive at a time when other women were just entering the workforce. Life was close to perfect before the recession hit and the fashion and cosmetic world changed. On a personal level, Beverly's life was also in turmoil. Her father passed away suddenly which affected her greatly. It was time to reassess and take stock of what was really important.

Working at Home with Your Husband

Longtime city dwellers, Beverly and Pablo came upon an 1856 historic ranch for sale in the Texas Hill Country north of Austin that would begin their life transition. They bought this beautiful property which became their home, Pablo's art studio, and also the new work space for Beverly, who is now serving as Pablo's Business Manager in addition to his full-time Muse.

What better way to capitalize on her skills in sales and marketing than to promote her husband's art? An ever-savvy businesswoman, Beverly never lost her friends in the industry and frequently took trips to Houston and Dallas to be seen, in addition to promoting Pablo and his work.

But it was when a photographer friend took Beverly and Pablo under her wing that their art business developed a brand that made the difference in their bottom line. Pablo embraced a new Halston-inspired look with the requisite black sweater and jeans and Beverly was able to market his new personal image as well as the pieces he produced.

Ever the relationship builder, Beverly was able to connect with a fabulous network of art collectors, and from that network, cultivated clientele for Pablo's work. In these tough economic times, selling art is indeed a challenge. But Beverly has learned how to listen to her clients' needs and knows that selling a piece of art takes time and determination.

Don't Give In To the "Devil Boys"

Working with her husband comes with its own unique set of challenges, admits Beverly. They have set boundaries within the house – "He has his work space and I have mine" – so their work and life partnership can remain harmonious.

Beverly is a detail-oriented planner, with a vision of the future that she has depicted in storyboards and portfolios. Her goal, in addition to growing Pablo's art-buying clientele, is to develop and market art for homes and businesses. She talks about the movie in her mind that helps her visualize how she wants her life to play out.

> "It's easy to give in to the devil boys – the voices that tell you when you can't do something, but I never want to live my life with regrets. I don't want to look back and say – I never did that. It's worth reaching out of your comfort zone to achieve your goals."

While the economy is not ideal for discretionary purchases such as art, Beverly and Pablo remain positive and are enjoying the journey of their business together. With the rise of social media, Beverly has embraced technology as a way of promoting Pablo and his art. She is developing a database to track customers and prospective clients since relationship building and stewardship is the bread and butter of the business.Beverly has indeed made Pablo a recognized international artist who has been featured in books, magazines, newspapers, TV, radio and even a film. This elegant lady has forged a new career utilizing her skills and experiences from the fashion and cosmetics arena. She sums it up perfectly in her quote: "Don't fear beauty." And so, Beverly Solomon's career reinvention is indeed a beautiful thing.

What's New?

Beverly Solomon continues her work to market Pablo's art, and her public relations efforts have really paid off. Among other achievements, Beverly secured coverage in the book and blog *Affordable Couture* by Armstrong, in a college textbook about marketing, in *Investor's*

Business Daily, and in an article about the Pantone color of the year. Through her consistent and persistent marketing efforts, she and Pablo have weathered the economic storm in recent years. Beverly said that in times like these "it's easy to panic, but we didn't. I doubled down on the public relations efforts and worked on strengthening client relationships," and that has carried them through.

I asked Beverly to tell me more about her career growth and transitions, and the resources she used during that time. "I used every contact I had! My enthusiasm carried me, and I was too naïve not to know I shouldn't be bothering all these important people." Beverly also shared that in hindsight, she would have been more careful about staying in touch with people. A network of contacts is only good if you nurture it. Also, she wishes she had taken photos along the way to document special moments and to record pieces of art that were sold.

Beverly shared some interesting stories about her work in the fashion world. As with any industry, there were some not-so-nice players with whom she had to work. Her experiences taught her that she values working independently *and* with a team. If there are tough personalities or difficult situations, Beverly advises taking a wait-and-see attitude and not jumping ship right away. "It's important to listen to your inner voice. Stick to your principles, and think it through. If you're unhappy, don't have a knee-jerk reaction, but really think it through. Clear your mind. Things usually aren't as big a deal as you think."

Beverly is still relying on her vision board to keep her on track with her goals. "I look at it every morning and evening. I'm such a visual person, this really works for me." And when I asked her for her advice for women who are considering a career change, she was enthusiastic. "You're not getting any younger – go for it! If you fail, SO WHAT. Don't give up." This great advice is always in style!

Beverly's Advice and Action Steps:

- Never stop working on your dream and always be prepared.
- Use a storyboard or portfolio to illustrate your dreams and to give yourself focus and goals.

- If you work at home, set boundaries so that you can establish your own space and your own time.

References:

Beverly's website: www.beverlysolomon.com
Pablo's website: www.pablosolomon.com
HARO, Help a Reporter Out: www.helpareporterout.com

66 When my life looked like it was falling apart, it was actually falling into place. 99

– Beverly Solomon

ℒ ℒ ℒ ℒ

44. MEG NOLLEN: NAVIGATING THE CORPORATE LABYRINTH

In the spirit of good networking, Meg first reached out to me when she heard about my career transition blog for women. It was a friend of a friend who referred her to me so I was thrilled to learn about her unique career transitions - and she's had several. So many of the women I have featured on the blog changed careers dramatically from one field to another unrelated career path and others pursued entre-preneurial ventures.

I was drawn to Meg's story because she has reinvented herself many times within the walls of corporate America, albeit in differ-ent companies. And she is part of the vibrant but small percentage of women in the C-Suite in the corporate world paving the way for the future generations of women in the executive ranks. Meg shares valuable career lessons for us all and I am delighted to have her in the second edition of my book.

A Circuitous Route

Meg's amazing work ethic started in college where she graduated in 3 years and worked 35 hours/week on the side to pay for tuition and living expenses. She said you want it and appreciate it more when you are earning your way through college. Her undergraduate degree was minted in 1984 when the economy was awful and jobs were hard to come by. In her home state of Texas the bottom dropped out of the oil market, including her father's business. But she was scrappy and landed a job in a bank in Houston and developed her own path, which vacillated between marketing and heavy quantitative and analytical work.

Her family valued higher education and all of her relatives had a Masters degree. Meg set her sights on law school but was discouraged by her family and instead pursued an MBA. She drove 75 miles each way to attend night school to earn the MBA. Some of her classmates were driving 200 miles to get to class and the novel concept of going to school at night was truly appreciated by this first generation of working professionals seeking advanced degrees.

Growing up in the energy driven Texas career world, Meg thought this might be a good fit for her. But instead she bounced around working jobs she knew were not right but hoping to find something that was a better fit. Progressive for her day, Meg shared that "It was not cool to manage your own career at that time." People were loyal to a company and worked there for life – happy or not. But Meg needed variety and intellectual stimulation to make her career sing.

Lesson of a Change Agent

One of her career highlights includes serving essentially as the CFO of the Houston Symphony. Working for the symphony Board of Directors she was well positioned to network with the movers and shakers of Texas energy and oil. From the symphony, Meg was recruited to work at Enron, which at the time was a blue chip company at the pinnacle of its success.

Meg learned how to link all of her transferable skills into the corporate package in the form of Investor Relations. This new IR work was very comprehensive and allowed her to serve as a liaison to all departments and to Wall Street. Meg talks about the broad spectrum of a change agent from the bull in a china shop whose job is to fix and repair damage to the immersion specialist who gets into an organization, absorbs the culture and slowly begins a ripple effect of change that later turns into a wave.

The bull in the china shop gets in and gets out while the immersion change agent is there for the long haul. As much as she wanted to be around for the long haul, Meg's tenure at many of her companies was short term, and this time was no different.

Pre-Enron, Meg landed all her jobs through ads in the newspapers. The world has changed quite a bit in the last 20 years since it's rare to see job ads in print for executive positions. The day she accepted the Enron position, her Dad was diagnosed with Stage IV cancer and this news prevented her from diving in emotionally to the new position. Despite the lack of emotional connection, Meg distinguished herself as a workhorse and learned how to, and how not to do business, from this industry leader.

The Enron culture began to change quickly and Meg experienced the "war for talent hire" when Enron recruited the *best of the best* not necessarily knowing what to do with them until they arrived. The philosophy was if you find great people, you can figure out how to utilize them once they are inside the company. Things changed dramatically with new leaders at Enron and true to form, Meg left soon after, recruited by Dynegy.

Ride the Wave until it Crashes

Meg rode the wave at Dynegy as the company was hailed on Wall Street until, of course, Enron crashed bringing Dynegy down with it in flames. Working 22 hour days, 7 days a week was not enough to keep her career there alive. She saw the stock go from its highest price in history to a paltry 50 cents a share.

Once reveled and suddenly shunned, Meg found herself in a position of having to fight for her personal reputation and the right to her career. The other option was for her to tuck her tail and give up but Meg was a fighter and knew she still had something to offer. Meg began to work with headhunters to try and resurrect her career and one interviewer actually stated that she simply couldn't trust anyone who had worked for Enron. The blue chip company that raised her clout in the corporate arena was now an anathema preventing her from moving on.

While the Enron and Dynegy waves crashed mightily, Meg remained focused and determined to power on. Working with a coach and transition specialist, Cecilia Rose, Meg was able to separate the crash of her company from herself and re-focus on her strengths and abilities. She still maintained strong relationships and references on Wall Street and in the corporate world, which when finally sought after, were accepted and honored.

Meg did let some time pass to heal her psyche and get healthy again. It was as if her power suit was embroidered with a scarlet "E" for Enron and "D" for Dynegy in the eyes of recruiters and headhunters who could not see the individual but only focused on the companies for which she worked.

The fallout of the mid stream subsector was palpable in Texas, and Houston as a city was sad, embarrassed, and in desperate need of recovery. The hard recognition came for Meg when she realized that there were no jobs at her level to be had in Houston so she had to look elsewhere to reinvent herself and her career.

One Step Back Equals Two Steps Forward

According to Meg, "Crisis is an outstanding education, once you survive it." With the realities of her family's new financial future, Meg and her husband made the difficult decision for him to stay home with the kids. Meg wore the guilt on her sleeve of not seeing the kids as much as she would have liked – she mourned the fact that she did not have time to nurture. But, studies show that most C-level working women have husbands at home who watch the kids.

Meg's husband has always been supportive of her career and she knows how lucky she is in that regard. It took 9 months for Meg to get back on the proverbial career horse. Finally, headhunters and hiring managers were willing to look at the body of her career work and get past the Enron/Dynegy fiasco. Checking references (finally!) they began to see what Meg Nollen really had to offer.

One step back was actually a huge opportunity to move forward and past the crisis that consumed Meg's life for almost a year. Georgia Pacific offered her a position in Investor Relations and afforded her the opportunity to reinvent her professional persona and play to her strengths once again.

The hiring manager at Georgia Pacific believed that Meg was fire tested and survived with credibility, which has become a mantra that has served her well. Meg has always been a facilitator and at GP, she relocated her family to Georgia and facilitated a change that led to another new beginning.

Prove the Naysayers Wrong

Meg did her job so well at GP that in 30 months after she started, the company was sold. She marketed the company "too" successfully and attracted a buyer for the whole company. Serving on the Board of GP was the leader of H.J. Heinz and so Meg landed her position there as Senior Vice President of Investor Relations in the corporate headquarters in Pittsburgh, Pennsylvania.

Far away from her Texas roots, Meg's navigation of the corporate career labyrinth did not come easily, or without sacrifice for her and her family. Meg has regained her reputation and is successful driving similar results and relationships at H.J. Heinz. She is happy to have family and good friends and her boys are well-adjusted young men now starting their professional lives.

Meg is at a stage in her life that she strives to be happy regardless of her environment. Literally having worked in cities all across the country, she is happiest when she is with her family now – no matter where that may be.

While her future is bright at H.J. Heinz, Meg does aspire to become an adjunct faculty member at a university some day and retire in Texas where she can pay-it-forward to the next generation of aspiring C-level women.

Meg's Moxie Is Paving the Way for Other Women

When I looked at the H.J. Heinz website to see the Executive Management team of the company, 32 profiles were listed and Meg was only one of two women in the elite group. Cheers to H.J. Heinz for being so progressive since many of their corporate counterparts do not have any women in the upper echelons of their organizations. Meg is really a pioneer in the workforce and continues to pave the way for future generations of women executives. While the corporate arena is not for everybody, and certainly not for the faint of heart, Meg has endured laborious hours and earned the respect and credibility of her male co-workers with grit, determination, and measurable results.

Meg talked about the intense times on her executive career path when she would get only a few hours of sleep after a 20 hour work day, take a quick shower and go back into the trenches to solve problems for her companies. Her work energized her and with the support of her husband, she was able to create the financial freedom her family has grown to appreciate.

I asked Meg about diversity and if during her career she felt we, as a country had taken significant steps forward in that regard. Meg shared that we still have a long way to go to achieve true diversity and inclusion for women and other minority groups but we were making progress. She believes that the needle is indeed moving and points to the fact that a generation of seasoned executives now has daughters in the workforce. This awareness is helping to instigate change. When it hits home on that level, progress will start to be made on a grand scale.

Today, Meg believes that C-Suite women have to work harder than their male counterparts to prove themselves, but will achieve recognition and reward for their efforts. So whether you are in the corporate world or pursuing another sector of the work world, the blood, sweat, and tears that Meg has shed at work will indeed help all women in many different careers for generations to come.

Choose to Be Well

When I reconnected with Meg we chatted by phone and she responded to my "How have you been?" question with the fabulous answer – "I choose to be well!" That describes Meg so perfectly and I continue to appreciate her palpable energy and enthusiasm.

Meg's corporate path continued to evolve as she progressed at H.J. Heinz into a Global Program Management role assisting the Chairman by keeping the organization humming. She described herself as the resident cheerleader at Heinz encouraging everyone to succeed. She was savvy enough to sometimes facilitate the communications on behalf of the Chairman and worked to draw the global leadership team together.

Her former boss, the Chairman at Heinz, once said about Meg: "I love the way you think, the way you push back – your courage and convictions – don't ever stop doing that!"

Once again, Meg worked her way out of a job and was wooed to take on a new role at Wendy's as the Senior Vice President of Investor Relations and Strategy. Meg also shared that this is her last move in the corporate world. As a woman starting her 5th decade of life, she has a lot to give back and has defined success on her own terms. While earning a great living for her hard work is a wonderful financial reward, the money is not what drives Meg. She strives to find ease, strength, and balance as she navigates this next chapter of her career life. She takes pride in having a career where she can be influential; earn trust and credibility amongst her colleagues; and bring honesty, integrity and candor to her work every day.

After six months of commuting to her new position in Dublin, Ohio, from Pittsburgh, Pennsylvania, Meg and her husband made the difficult decision that she simply wasn't having enough fun to justify such a big move. "Leaving Wendy's was one of the hardest things I've ever done. At first I felt like a failure, but I soon realized that I would be failing myself if I didn't leave."

Serving as an advisor and mentor to others is also important to Meg. She has benefitted from an executive coach, Deb Weiler – a former Olympic swimmer who helps her navigate the realities of career and life. Meg has chosen to retire from the corporate world and is now contemplating "paying it forward" by coaching others through the corporate labyrinth and dealing with Wall Street.

We talked about the book Meg is preparing to write sharing her "Pearls of Wisdom" that she learned on her career path. She is embarking on a public speaking journey and recently won an award as one of the Most Powerful and Influential Woman from the National

Diversity Council.

Meg's positive attitude is contagious. Her advice for women is to be known by those who are influential – "it's not what you know, or who you know, it's who knows you." With the imminent arrival of the new talent wars, emerging leaders are in demand. Meg encourages us all to be in control and to manage our careers so they don't happen by default.

Meg's Advice and Action Steps:

- The C-suite demands a 24/7 commitment – if you want it, you have to work for it. Take advantage of opportunities when they present themselves.
- My mantra is to always perform but the bar I set for myself is my own. You should consider setting your own bar as well.
- The needle is moving regarding equality for women and there is a now a generation of executives with daughters in the workplace. This is becoming an empathetic catalyst for change.
- Don't let anyone fault you for being ambitious and don't ever let others perceptions of you impact your performance.
- Your life and career values will change over time so be aware of what is important to you at every moment.

❝You are in control. Too often women sit back and act like a victim. Don't wait for someone to do something for you. Do it yourself!❞

– Meg Nollen

☙ ☙ ☙ ☙

45. SUSAN VERNICEK: IDENTITY CHECK

A twenty-something, native New Jersey girl, Susan Vernicek put her Fine Arts degree with a dual focus in Graphic Design and Photography to use working in the graphics department of a medical company. While she enjoyed that job, she still had a percolating entrepreneurial spirit within her that needed to be released. The two driving forces in her life from a young age have been to run her own business and to have a positive influence on others. The end result of sticking with that focus and owning her passion was the creation of **S&J Identity, Inc**. – a unique and empowering online magazine created to help women accept, appreciate, and achieve.

> "Being a woman with many interests, and all the same concerns as my female counterparts, I relied on the media for information that could help improve and inspire my life. Through my own discontentment with all the in-your-face ads and useless information about diet fads, fashion trends, and celebrity gossip found in other magazines – *Identity* was born. I believe our role models should be in our everyday lives; not photo-touched fashion plates on a page. *Identity* is my gift to every woman, for being who she is, and the best that she can be."

Day to Day and Breath by Breath

Susan is indeed an enlightened young woman, ahead of her time in many ways, who already understands the female mind is often full of doubts, questions, and insecurities. Her magazine is a positive resource and a safe place to turn for information, sharing, and permission to just be who we are. *Identity* is not a fad site with quick-fix diet tips and fashion fads or beauty cream miracles. It celebrates real women with everyday issues by providing practical resources. Susan's mission is to encourage readers to embrace their inner confidence and to achieve their potential without comparing themselves, their ideas, and their bodies to others. Targeted at the 21 and older demographic, *Identity* features articles by guest writers who share their expertise on a variety of timely topics.

Working "day by day and breath by breath" (Susan's mantra), she says her goal is to make *Identity* her full time occupation so that she can leave her day job altogether. In this tough economy she finds it scary to leave the financial security of her graphics position, but also understands the struggle and the need to move forward so that *Identity* can have her full attention and time.

Susan recognizes the freedom of being her own boss at *Identity* and can play to her strengths and her passions by helping women with her online publication. She believes we have a responsibility to pay-it-forward to younger women and help them understand their gifts and the ability to embrace their self-confidence early. Her ultimate goal is to reverse the pervasive negativity trend and help women think more positively about themselves.

With an artistic background it's easy to see how Susan uses her graphic design skills for *Identity*, but she admits that without a business background she looked to mentors and established resources to help her launch the magazine. Her dad and brother both own businesses and proved to be terrific resources for her new venture. An avid researcher, Susan also did her homework and asked a million questions to learn the best practices for online magazines. As a New Jersey resident, she also tapped into a Garden State resource designed to help young entrepreneurs – New Jersey Young Entrepreneurs.

The challenge continues to be balancing the day job with the growing demands of the magazine. Her financial strategy is to pay for new things as she can and increase incrementally. The goal is to continue to reach all 50 states and grow her sponsors and advertisers.

Just Do it Already!

The main framework of *Identity* was designed by ImpressM, LLC, but with Susan's expertise and knowledge of HTML she can manage most of the site herself and provide graphics for clients who need it. She reports that although she seeks out some contributors, many actually come to her. A future goal is for Susan to work with universities to develop workshops for women featuring the expert contributors from *Identity*. She is planning a Friday morning radio show to go along with her Identity FACT Friday!™ on the site and eventually, a book!

Susan has a go-for-it attitude that has helped her achieve success with *Identity*. Starting with no expectations and an open mind she was determined not to hold back and to stay true to herself during the entire process. Always eager to learn new things and to set new goals, Susan has learned to trust her instincts and push the envelope to grow her business.

"I am strong, positive, and extremely ambitious and these qualities have gotten me where I am today. My advice is to JUST DO IT ALREADY! Pick a starting point and go. Then give yourself homework each day. Ask yourself a question then find the answer and move on to the next. There isn't always positive feedback, support, or an answer, but you have to work around that. Get rid of the negative in your life. You can't move forward if you associate yourself with negative vibes. I know it's easier said than done, but you CAN do anything you put your mind to. Take it day by day, breath by breath. Accept. Appreciate. Achieve™"

Words of wisdom from an insightful young woman on a mission to help us celebrate our unique identities.

What's New?

Since Susan's story was published in my first book, she achieved one of her very important goals by working on *Identity* magazine full time. She finds it fits her value of authenticity much better than her corporate position did. "I was creating fake graphics to help others make money. There were also lots of unhappy employees who were working only for the money, and there was no teamwork." Now she follows her instincts and her passions to help young women grow into confident women, and it fits her values perfectly.

Another goal she achieved came with the publication of her first book, which compiles the first three years of advice columns in a single, handy volume. Susan is also enjoying speaking at events across the country, and has a goal of speaking in each of the 48 contiguous states. So far, she's spoken in eight states.

Identity Magazine has more than 40,000 unique visitors and is generating revenue. Susan has created lots of partnerships to drive revenue, so she can keep her website free to users. She's also built a strong team of goal-oriented contractors who help her provide what her readers need and want.

As Susan grows and changes in her personal life, so does Identity Magazine. Susan was married and gave birth to twins – a son and a daughter, and now has to think about how her business affects her family. The demographic she targets has moved from 21+ to the "sweet spot" of 30-45 year-old women.

Like almost everyone, Susan has to work to maintain balance in her life. She educates herself where she can, and readily seeks help where necessary. For example, Susan worked with a coach on improving her time management. "I'm very lucky in having a good balance for work and family. We schedule regular times for certain activities" to make sure everyone's needs are met.

The future looks bright for Susan. She hopes to create a series of books, which will provide quotes and advice to help readers Accept, Appreciate, and Achieve™. The books will be from and for women in similar situations, for example, one book will contain advice from college students written for college students. Business owners, divorcees, and single moms may also be the targets for future books.

Looking back, Susan tells me she would not do anything differently if given the chance. She's learned a lot as she went, and says that pacing was critical to her success. It was important that she not push too fast, too soon. For women thinking about striking out on their own, Susan shares this advice: "Instead of just talking about it, ACT. Continue to work in your current job, but start researching and networking. There are lots of baby steps you can take. You have to start somewhere, and you have to position yourself for change."

I can't wait to see how Susan and Identity Magazine continue to grow and achieve. What a great role model for women with dreams!

Susan's Advice and Action Steps:

- Set goals so that you have benchmarks for achievement; give yourself homework every day.
- Embrace the strengths you have and use them.
- You have to be willing to take the plunge if you are unhappy in

your current career. If you never try something new, you won't ignite your passion.

- Find your circle of trust (family, friends, mentors) and bounce ideas off them to flesh out your mental plans.

She has also trademarked these phrases for *Identity*:

- Feel Beautiful Everyday!™
- Accept. Appreciate. Achieve.™

Resources:

Identity: www.identitymagazine.net
National Association of Women Business Owners NAWBO:
  www.nawbo.org/
Ladies Who Launch: www.ladieswholaunch.com/
Savor the Success: www.savorthesuccess.com
New Jersey Young Entrepreneurs: www.njye.webnode.com/

66Day by day, breath by breath.99

– Susan's mantra!

ợ ợ ợ ợ

46. KAREN KIBLER: EARNING A PHD AT FORTY-SOMETHING

Karen Kibler was raised in a small farming community in Iowa, and as a result, can weld and operate heavy equipment. She earned her Bachelor's degree in science from the University of Iowa in 1977, and decided to relocate to Arizona to work in the business sector. She held several jobs, from receptionist to owning her own business. At the age of 40 she chose to refocus on her love of science and pursue a PhD in Microbiology from Arizona State University. She now serves as an Assistant Research Professor at ASU, with a focus on HIV vaccines and treatments.

A Turning Point at Age 40

When Karen turned 40 she found herself in an accounting job with a very low ceiling and no room for advancement due to her lack of a business degree. Her undergraduate degree was in science, so she decided to pursue work in that field. After applying for a few positions, she got incredulous responses because it had been 15 years since she graduated, with no science-related work since then. Since science had always been a passion, she decided to apply for the graduate program in Microbiology at Arizona State University. Much to her surprise, she was accepted and left her accounting job in January of 1993 to start graduate school – one month before her 41st birthday.

Karen was a non-traditional student starting a PhD in her forties, but her maturity, passion, and discipline served her well. She developed a strong interest in working on HIV and set her sights for a post-doctoral position at the National Institute of Health (NIH) in Bethesda, Maryland, and landed a very competitive position in one of the NIH research labs.

The Rewards of an Authentic Career Fit

After two post-doc positions, Karen took a faculty position at her alma mater, ASU, where she taught classes in addition to working on an HIV vaccine and novel HIV treatments. As a Research Scientist, Karen works on the cutting edge of new treatments for HIV. She admits that it takes a lot of patience and perseverance to make advances in research that will solve health problems.

A research project can take years to yield any results, so Karen acknowledged that her current work values are different than those of being an accountant – not better, just different. One of the HIV vaccine projects is scheduled for phase one clinical trials, which brings the long years of development and planning closer to an exciting new level.

Channel Your Energy

Pursuing a PhD in her forties was challenging for many reasons. Re-acclimating to the academic regimen was tricky enough for an older student, but mustering the energy to deal with the round-the-clock schedule was indeed a trial. Karen now counsels young people who want to pursue graduate degrees to do so as soon as they finish an undergraduate program so they can capitalize on the momentum.

For Karen, in the life sciences, earning a PhD involved about 20 hours of teaching per week, 10-15 hours in class and then all the rest of her time to study and pursue research. Financially, graduate school was challenging, too. With the intense research, teaching and study requirements, there was no way to have an outside job, and the academic stipends were not enough to make a living wage. Karen graduated with significant educational debts, but viewed the degree as an investment in herself and her career future.

The career landscape in the life sciences has changed dramatically in recent years. With fewer tenure-track university faculty positions, many PhDs leave academia for the private sector biotech/pharmaceutical companies or government positions. Others pursue law or MD programs, but career scientists have to think broadly about how they want to apply their skills after they earn a PhD.

Change is Constant

One thing that Karen has learned in her lifetime is that you can always depend on things to change. When making the decision to reinvent herself and transition careers, Karen was determined and focused, which helped her remain confident in her decision. She also did her homework and went into the PhD program with her eyes open. While she didn't know exactly what jobs she would pursue after the degree, she knew the additional credentialing would empower her to break through the proverbial glass ceiling.

Karen has also experienced dramatic change on a personal level many times in her life. After an emotionally devastating divorce, she experienced clinical depression. Years later, Karen found the book: *The Cracker Factory*, a wonderful resource to better comprehend the healing and self-understanding required of those who suffer from depression. Five years after reading the book, her second husband was killed in an accident and Karen fell into another round of depression, which inspired the book she wrote, *The Second Chasm* (Wyatt-MacKenzie Publishing), which was published in January 2009.

A Journey of Hope

Karen's book is unique because it bridges two of the most common losses faced in the world: divorce and widowhood. Her stories of recovery offer a message of hope as she describes the journey from despair to healing. Not only did the book prove to be an emotional catharsis for Karen, it launched her freelance proofreading career as well. One would expect detail orientation from a scientist and Karen fits the bill working as a proofreader/editor consultant with Wyatt-MacKenzie Publishing.

It's clear that Karen has found a place of peace in her life and is pursuing a career with many facets that she enjoys. She encourages others considering a transition to do their due diligence and reflect upon what is meaningful for them. This research scientist hopes to bring a resolution to the work she has been doing on an HIV vaccine. She also plans to continue pursuing her work as an author and editor. There are several books floating around in her head, which Karen aims to write down some day. Indeed, it took courage to pursue a PhD in her forties and Karen Kibler is now thriving.

What's New?

Karen's incredibly important work in HIV continues. Her work in biosafety concluded, and her role broadened to encompass research safety. But not long after our follow up conversation, Karen would be returning to pure research, which has been the most exciting work for her. Human clinical trials for an HIV vaccine should start within a year.

It was interesting to hear the "scientific" reasoning Karen shared about her career transition. She had owned and run a business with her second husband, which she kept going for two years following his death in an accident. Then one day she decided "I'm not going to do this anymore," and started evaluating her options. She followed her business experience into an accounting role, but soon realized that she'd progressed as far as she could without additional education. If she was going to make a change, and if returning to school was on the table, she wanted to follow her life-long interest in science.

Karen told me that mentors really helped in her journey. Her mother was a great role model, as she completed her undergraduate degree at age 59. Her professors also helped; they encouraged her to hang in there when she felt like she was drowning in her first semester of graduate school.

If your work matches your values, your chance of happiness in a career goes way up. And this is certainly the case with Karen. She has always enjoyed connecting the dots, and unraveling mysteries – whether it be with numbers in her accounting job or with data in her research. She also enjoys feeling like she is a part of something bigger and more important than herself. "I'm a small part of a huge effort to make a difference in a biological challenge we face."

You can't help but learn about yourself when you navigate career transitions. Karen has learned that research takes forever and "I have no patience with people, but a lot of it with viruses!"

Looking forward, Karen wants to see her research through to phase three trials. Then she wants to "retire, clean up my house, and unpack boxes from 30 years ago." She will continue to edit, proofread, and write – but on her schedule. And with 10 grandchildren and more on the way, she wants to spend lots of time with family.

Karen's advice for those considering a career change is quite practical: If you are considering pursuing a degree, it's really important to know what your options and opportunities will be with it. Earning a degree is a lot of hard work and can be expensive; do your homework so you have a realistic picture of what you'll be able to do after you graduate. Returning to school as an adult can be much more difficult, but it can also be incredibly rewarding. Karen loved her journey to a PhD, and knows she had a much better attitude about the work because she brought maturity and life experience with her.

Karen's story is truly inspiring. If she could do this, just imagine what YOU could do!

Karen's Advice and Action Steps:

- Do your homework and research new career options to find your best match.
- Don't fear going back to school as an adult – it can be exhilarating.
- Embrace change.

- Don't give in to negativity – focus on the positive. Don't waste energy on self-doubt. You must believe in yourself.
- Pay attention to the special moments.

Resources:

The Second Chasm Book: www.thesecondchasm.com
Wyatt-MacKenzie Publishing: www.wymacpublishing.com/

> **"**Remember that love and friendship are gifts we give, with no requirement that they be earned.**"**
>
> –Karen's mantra

ᵒ⅌ ᵒ⅌ ᵒ⅌ ᵒ⅌

47. TAKE A STEP FORWARD

The women in this chapter show us that reigniting or reinventing a career is an ageless endeavor that can happen multiple times throughout our lives. It's never too late or too early to find a new calling.

Create Vision Board

As you will discover in the Chapter 8 *Reinvention Toolbox*, a portfolio is a powerful tool that can be used to showcase your skills and experiences to a new employer or during a promotion review. But before you interview for the dream job, you must come up with a vision that illustrates your future goals.

Magazines, websites, and newspapers are overflowing with stories and images of people, items, places, and experiences that just might ignite your passion. Clip stories and photos that motivate you and save them in a vision folder that you can look through for inspiration. If you respond to visual stimuli, use your favorite images to create a vision board to make a collage of the images that motivate you. The concept is to surround yourself with motivational descriptions of what you want. When you become inspired to act, then you will be more likely to find those people, places, careers and experiences in your real life.

Beverly Solomon used this technique very successfully when transitioning into her new career. It created the visualization she needed to move forward with her plan. Based on the law of attraction, design the vision you want to live. You can use the low-tech version with a cut out collage on a cardboard base and place it prominently in your living and/or work space. Or, you can opt for an online tool that helps you create a vision board. A tool I find appealing is Dream it Alive, (www.dreamitalive.com) which gives you step-by-step resources to create a dream or vision board. You can also communicate with like minded dreamers and even connect with funding sources to make your dream a reality.

Put Your Passion to Work

You've heard over and over from many different women in this book to identify your passion and put it to work. I'm thrilled that so many women have articulated this same theme since they were not prompted by me, don't know each other, and represent a diverse group of individuals from a variety of backgrounds and careers. The one thing they do have in common is career reinvention and the fact that they are now in careers they thoroughly enjoy. This should help you understand the importance of finding your passion.

If identifying your passion seems too daunting, start with what you really like and work your way towards what you love to do. Be more aware on a daily basis of what intrigues you, what brings you joy, and how you like to spend your time. It may be that an undiscovered passion is closer and more obvious than you think.

Identifying your passion is one thing **but the goal is to monetize it and make it part of your career path**. It may surprise you that some of the most successful people are the most ardent. They find ways to incorporate their personal passions into their day-to-day work. Start by integrating your passions into your current career and see if this leads to new opportunities that maximize the ability to use your passions.

For example:

- Passionate golfers take clients to the golf course and talk about business on the links. Many successful deals have been closed during a golf game.
- People who are passionate about photography never leave home without their camera. They take photos at work events and publish the images on the company website or newsletter whenever appropriate.
- Creative or imaginative people express their innovation regularly. They are constantly trying new approaches to old problems and finding clever solutions to daily tasks.
- Professionals who love to socialize attend networking events and make regular plans to have lunch with friends or colleagues.
- People who enjoy public speaking join organizations like Kiwanis, Rotary, and others, to take advantage of opportunities to address public groups on their favorite topics.

By taking baby steps and incorporating your passions into your current career, you will find ways to rejuvenate an existing position or, you can develop a new opportunity by playing to your passions more regularly.

Be Proactive and Recharge Your Career

People who incorporate passion into their career don't just fall into this situation. They very deliberately incorporate their passion into their jobs. If you like to write, volunteer to author content for the company website, newsletter, or intranet. If you are energized by people and enjoy travel, volunteer to attend every conference you can as a representative of your organization in the industry. The magic happens when your boss and your colleagues see you in your element, thriving and playing to your strengths. When you demonstrate success in what you like to do best, your managers will be more likely to find additional ways to let you shine.

Hang out with people who share your passions. Find the other artists, sports fans, writers, gardeners, theatre lovers, etc., and network with them just as you would in your career life. These passion connectors can lead to new career opportunities as well as newfound friends who share your interests.

Be curious and read a book or magazine about a topic you know nothing about. Wander the web and find sites and blogs that you never knew existed. Talk to people that you don't already know and learn something new as often as you can. New passions can arise in the most surprising places and when you find something that lights your fire, you just might consider this as a new career endeavor.

Retooling for a Change

Sometimes a career reinvention involves a new opportunity that is beyond your current skill set and experience. It's never too late to re-credential yourself, and Karen Kibler showed us this by earning a PhD in her forties. Whether earning a degree or pursuing workshop certifications to enable you to be eligible for new career opportunities, these additional credentials can often be the ticket to position eligibility.

Research wisely before you jump into a degree program. During a recession, graduate and professional school applications spike since people often find a safe harbor in an academic program when jobs are scarce. Investigate the field you are pursuing to learn if the degree you seek will enable you to find a job in that particular career sector. Just because you earn an MBA doesn't entitle you to a job in the business sector. You still need to be a full package candidate who can articulate why you are a value-add for an organization. The degree doesn't automatically mean you will find a job.

Finding your bliss, putting passion into your work life, and being proactive will help you gain career satisfaction. Passion is a career asset and if you read the biographies of people you admire you will often see how they integrate passion into their lives. If you need to add skills or credentials to your professional toolbox, first consider what you are working towards and make sure it corresponds with your goals. Career reinvention is timeless. I've had multiple career reinventions and I fully expect to have many more!

REINVENTION TOOLBOX

Use a Portfolio as Your Secret Weapon; Embrace Change

Fine artists have been using portfolios for decades to showcase examples of their work. This multidimensional tool is gaining popularity in the job market for other professions as well. By assembling an archive of your work, you can show employers why you will be a value-add to their organization.

Similar to the resume, the portfolio should be customized for each unique opportunity. You should include your resume and/or CV as well as letters of recommendation, quotes, or special comments from key constituents and examples of what you do well that is relevant to the new job opportunity. A mission statement can articulate why you want the job as well as why you are an excellent match for the position.

I like to include a list of my top skills with descriptions of how they will be applicable to the new job. A goals or future plans section can help you articulate how you will grow in a particular role in the organization. Employers will see you as a strong, long-term investment for their team.

If writing is a desired skill for the new job, include samples that showcase your best work and a variety of styles. Get creative and use graphics or photos for visual pop but keep text pithy and succinct using bullet points and tag phrases instead of long paragraphs.

Leave a Lasting Impression

I encourage my clients to bring the portfolio to the interview; walk your future boss through the document and leave it behind after the interview, which allows the hiring committee to have a lasting impression of you as a candidate.

Spiral-bind your portfolio so that the pages are secure,

and be sure your full name and contact information appear clearly on the cover page. While you want to show the breadth and depth of your experience, keep the portfolio brief so that the readers don't lose interest while viewing.

This secret weapon can set you apart from the competition. An added bonus of assembling a portfolio is the valuable self-reflection process that will put you in tip-top shape for your interview, giving you the opportunity to focus on your strengths in an articulate manner.

Can you Handle Change?

A transferable skill that tops the list of competencies which employers value most is the ability to handle change. While change is an essential element in life and career, most of us instinctively resist it. The ability to handle change requires ongoing attention and perseverance. In the career arena, learning to deal with change can be used to your best advantage.

Keeping an open mind when change is imminent in your place of work will help the powers-that-be to recognize that you are a true team player. When you look to grow, rather than focus on the possible negatives of change, the process becomes easier. If you adopt a negative attitude about change then your energy is wasted on this behavior, and your productivity decreases as well as your professional worth within the organization.

If you are in a position of authority in your organization or pursuing an entrepreneurial venture, be sure to motivate your team and help them through the growing pains of change. By rewarding success, you will create internal champions from among those who are higher risk takers and more aware of the value of new outcomes. Be enthusiastic and persistent with your team to help them re-boot the negative hard wiring that is often the first response to change.

The Power of Being a Change Agent

I know that sometimes change comes unmercifully with lay-offs and downsizing. I encourage you to let your feelings out and experience the full gamut of emotions since it's a vital part of catharsis and moving forward. When you resist your emotions you simply make them stronger. I have established a 24-hour pout period when I allow myself to rant and rave in the privacy of my own home about a disappointment – then I move forward and focus on what I can control.

I have seen many people make lemonade from the career lemons they have been dealt in this tumultuous economy. Believe in yourself and know that life is what you make it because **change is constant.**

- Write down the major changes you have handled with grace during the past year.
- Utilize these stories as part of your interview repertoire when pursuing a new job or pitching a proposal. The ability to handle change is a powerful asset.
- New leaders emerge during times of change so being nimble and positive may create an advancement opportunity with your name on it.

9

EVERYTHING HAS ITS PLACE: HOW TO FIND YOURS

The women in this chapter have capitalized on former career experiences to move forward with new opportunities. In this day and age, people change careers an average of five to seven times during their adult lives. I believe everything happens for a reason and with these women everything also had a time and a place.

48. KARI DiFABIO: SAY "CHEERS"... TO A NEW CAREER

Kari DiFabio had tears of joy in her eyes when she earned her Elementary Education degree and couldn't wait to get started on her career as a teacher. After teaching multiple grades in Arizona and Nevada she had a revelation that launched her personal career change. "Sitting in the teacher's lounge one day, my life flashed before my eyes and I saw myself 20 years down the road, unhappy and bitter if I stayed in this career." Following her intuition, Kari quit teaching, moved to California, and lived with her grandmother while she figured out what to do next.

A Transitional "Fun Job" That Turned Into a Career

As a way to generate income while she figured out her next career move, Kari took a part-time job at a winery in a small tasting room, earning just pennies above minimum wage.

"After I left teaching, I found the wine business by asking myself, 'If I have to get a job while I figure out what I want to do with my life, what menial job sounds like the most fun?' I believe I found something I enjoyed because I took the pressure off myself to find the *right* job."

Kari learned a lot in her first job in the winery tasting room by asking many questions and absorbing information from her coworkers. It was like learning a new language in the beginning, and visiting other vineyards expanded her industry acumen. While some family and friends thought she had jumped off the solid career bridge, Kari remained positive and enjoyed her new work experience in the winery. She loved the blend of science and art, intellect and creativity, and even though this was not a long-term job, Kari discovered it was a starting point and had tremendous growth potential. She moved on to sell wine to key accounts as a distributor in Los Angeles for several years.

"I realized early after I left teaching how many skills I had that I considered transferable. As a teacher, I was managing a team of 20-40 people (albeit "little" people) and had daily tasks that included sales, communications, PR (parents), staff management, and teaching. I decided I was just as equipped for the business world as anyone. So, during my first wine sales interview, the manager interviewed me. He was an old-timer of the business and looked it, kind of like an old cowboy who could eat you up and spit you out at breakfast. He looked over my resume and said almost with a sneer, 'So you were a teacher. What makes you think you can sell wine?' I looked at him and replied without blinking, 'I sold algebra to eight-year-olds. Do you really think selling wine is going to be hard for me?' I got the job."

As with any new career transition, Kari faced a lot of challenges. It was financially difficult since her first sales job was 100 percent commission in the lowest-producing territory and the thought of not being able to pay the rent was terrifying to her. Her grandmother always served as a mentor and inspiration and she encouraged Kari to persevere and ignore the naysayers.

The Power of Self-Reflection

As she progressed through different jobs in the wine industry, Kari moved to Napa and pursued a thoughtful self-reflection of her values, interests, personality, and skills to find a more meaningful position that was a good fit for her in the industry. She considered what a dream day would look like at work and started a list that included: working for someone she respected, working in a beautiful environment, being allowed to use all of her talents and abilities in one position, not being micromanaged, and having an opportunity to work from home.

On a whim, she logged onto a wine jobs website and found her current position at Sodaro Estate Winery. Her employer shared, "We knew immediately that Kari was the right fit for the position." The rest is history.

Although Kari has autonomy over her entire work day, self-motivation is essential. "The good part is that you are all by yourself, the bad part is also that you are all by yourself!" Sometimes she misses having an office environment to bounce ideas around and although the winery staff works independently, they are definitely a team.

With the world of social networking, Kari is learning to become adept at utilizing Twitter and Facebook to keep Sodaro Estate's wine in the limelight of a competitive industry. You have to be a Jill-of-all-trades in a smaller company. She's now a tech person, a marketing person, a sales person, a hospitality person, a VP business person, an accounting department, and an office manager all-in-one. Way to multitask, Kari – although she does have a part-time assistant who helps greatly.

Dare to Design Your Dream Job

She got all the dream job wishes on her list and now works from home as well as at the beautiful Sodaro Winery – a breathtaking landscape that reflects the stunning beauty and individuality of this estate. Working with renowned winemakers Bill and Dawnine Dyer and Don Sodaro, Kari is thrilled to have colleagues she respects.

Kari sees life as a continual journey and hopes to own her own business someday. For now, she is thrilled to hone her skills and work in this dream job at Sodaro Estate Winery, and is thankful she had the courage to admit that teaching was not a good fit. It's liberating to know that we can change our career minds as often as we wish and this teaches us all to trust our gut instincts. Cheers to Kari on her self-assessment and reinvention!

What's New?

I am happy to share that since my first conversation with Kari, she has expanded her role to include motherhood. She and her husband welcomed a son and a daughter to the family, in the span of less than two years.

With the birth of her son, Kari dropped from full-time to part-time in her role with the winery, and was able to work from home. Eventually, she knew that for her, the right thing was to leave work and focus on raising her son. "I remember trying to nurse him while I was on a conference call, and it was just too much. We looked at all our options – daycare, a nanny, staying home – but for me it was a value-based decision. The right thing for me now is to stay home to raise these beautiful children."

Kari admits that she wonders if she's done the right thing on the difficult days, but knows the alternative (leaving her children to return to the business world) isn't the right choice for her at this time. Kari describes herself as a person who's willing to jump off the proverbial cliff – "I have faith that things will work out." She took a leap of faith when she left education for the wine industry – and that was a great success. She took another leap of faith when she left work to raise her children. When she's ready to re-enter the workforce, Kari knows that the right opportunity will present itself at the right time.

In comparing her experience in the working world to her life now, Kari states unequivocally that staying home with two small children is the "hardest, craziest, most insanely difficult job" she's had yet. She misses intellectual conversation and being a part of the business community/world, but she is also learning skills she will bring back to the workforce. "I've learned a lot about customer service. When you have two very demanding 'customers' who won't listen to logic, you find other ways to solve problems! I've also taken multi-tasking to an entirely new level." Kari said she has learned to approach situations from a more intuitive and grounded perspective.

Looking forward, Kari is considering the option of home-school-ing, as this would allow her to tie-in her skills in education while meeting her children's needs. Looking back, Kari wouldn't change a thing. I asked what advice she would offer women in her situation: "If you want kids, do it, but be aware of what and how much they really need. Don't be afraid to leave the workforce if you choose to. You will come back to it a wiser, more valuable and resourceful person. My life is richer now than it ever was in the business world!

Kari's Advice and Action Steps:

- Follow your intuition no matter how quietly it speaks; follow what calls to you – no matter how crazy it sounds.
- Get specific about what you want – make a list and make it happen.
- Test drive different jobs/ideas until you find what suits you best.
- Make excellent mistakes – that is how you learn, and life is a journey.

Resources:

Sodaro Estate Winery: www.sodarowines.com
Savor the Success: www.savorthesuccess.com

⁶⁶Don't ask yourself what the world needs, ask yourself what makes you come alive and go do that. Because what this world needs are people who have come alive.⁹⁹

– Harry Thurman

ↄ ↄ ↄ ↄ

49. Debbie Waitkus: Hole in One

Always an athlete, Debbie Waitkus played on the soccer team at the University of Arizona. After graduate school, she went on to establish a thriving corporate career as president of a $130M private banking firm that had been around less than 40 years. She always attributed golf as one of her keys to success since she would take her clients on golf outings to establish and steward professional relationships and business deals. When the CEO of her firm implemented a new strategy that didn't follow suit with her professional values, Debbie knew it was time for a change. What better way to plan her reinvention than to leverage the game of golf in a new business?

The Power of a Personal Coach

Debbie utilized the expert resources of a personal and executive coach, Silver Rose, whom she first encountered when she brought in Silver as a consultant on a project while she was still working at the firm. Debbie hired Silver personally and began exploring an exit strategy and new options for her career future.

Her professional reinvention began with weekly one-on-one calls with Silver and detailed homework assignments on self-assessment and personal tracking. She conducted informational interviews with business peers and joined a mastermind group that works as an advisory board of sorts to provide motivation and accountability – all under the tutelage of her coach. Debbie also joined Toastmasters and a few networking groups for outreach, education, and personal growth purposes.

Silver gave Debbie permission to explore, and she realized that golf – her passion – was also an educational tool and a business opportunity ripe for developing. Her knowledge about how to generate business through golf made Debbie a valuable resource others wanted to learn from. She also saw a tremendous opportunity to build confidence in businesswomen through strategies incorporating golf.

Move Over Boys – Women Are Playing Golf, Too!

According to Debbie:

"It's a known fact that women, as a group, don't participate in the game of golf to the extent that men do. For the most part, they see the game of golf as a mystery to which only men hold the key. Yet, the message businesswomen hear today is that golf is a widely accepted playing field for conducting business and they are missing out on opportunities by not participating. The golf community has created women-only golf clinics targeting the female executive. Statistically, women are the largest new group coming to the game of golf today. Yet, often frustrated with their skill-set, they are also the largest group that leaves the game and does not return."

So Debbie capitalized on demystifying this critical business skill that can be used successfully on the golf course. Her business, **Golf for Cause™**, teaches women (and men) how to use golf as a business tool, to create opportunities, and to forward relationships because it's more than just about going out and hitting golf balls. **Golf for Cause™** provides the keys and the tools to demystify the game.

In her new role, Debbie enjoys being 100 percent responsible for the success and failure of each strategic decision in her company. She has control over her schedule; her work product matches her integrity and is a more accurate and rewarding reflection of who she is and what she wants out of a career. Debbie also appreciates the opportunity to set a positive example for her children by doing something that makes a difference and by giving back to her community.

Making Money Playing Golf

While the new career sounds too good to be true, Debbie has learned a lot over the years. Her initial business plan was not realistic and included programming that does not fit her business model today. The plan required some tweaking and adjusting over time. With a small staff of only two (including Debbie) she doesn't have a large team to rely on as she did back at the firm. Debbie has learned that she can only control so much and that delegation is not always an option. A perfectionist by nature, Debbie also learned that delivering the perfect program was unrealistic. "At some point you need to step up to the ball and hit it off the tee!"

Since golf is now her livelihood, another important lesson learned was to identify which programs work well and which generate meaningful revenue. The economy has also been a challenge and the meeting and events industry has taken a particularly hard hit. Many companies have cut training and professional development budgets entirely. Debbie learned quickly that she needed to stay flexible and remain open to new ideas and partnerships in order to grow her business.

A personal goal for Debbie was to keep her schedule free enough to travel with her daughter, a student athlete, to national tournaments and college recruiting trips. This was a liberty she gave herself with the new business that would not have been possible at the firm. She also set up administrative systems to enable the business to run smoothly in her absence.

> "I set up systems such that I have an assistant who works remotely and maintains my database, follows up on various tasks as needed, brings forward ideas, keeps me on task, etc. Finding the right person was an incredible challenge as I spent a lot of time and money getting systems in place and then checking, redoing, and re-educating. With the right person in place – I'm free to work 'on' the business and not 'in' the business."

Mission Accomplished

The mission of **Golf for Cause™** as an organization is to develop and deliver products and services that move others to use golf as a dynamic strategy to achieve their objectives, focusing primarily on business professionals new to the game, especially women.

While Debbie benefited from the expert counsel of her coach, Silver Rose, she also suggests that women seeking a career change develop a support network to help stay properly focused on goals and to provide a level of accountability.

She suggests that new entrepreneurs work with a good accountant from the start to better understand which strategies are effective and meaningful tax-wise for the business.

Birdies and Bogeys Lead to Great Business

Debbie's repertoire of golf educational opportunities provides a myriad of topics such as:

- The secrets even successful business owners and managers don't know
- Create an even more rewarding business environment
- See how your business success and your golf game are a reflection of who you are
- How to improve both your business and your golf score

Participants usually spend half the day in the classroom using golf as a metaphor to learn what differentiates being an entrepreneur, manager, or technician, and how this applies to the business world. After the classroom session, participants hit the course and play nine holes of golf in a strategic format. All levels can participate, even beginners who have never played before. The day ends with a facilitated debriefing session, awards, and refreshments. An ideal group size is 6 to 40 participants, and Debbie customizes programs to fit an organization or individual's needs.

The reviews are in and Debbie consistently scores big with her clients! The programs are experiential and golf anchors the learning. Debbie's repertoire of golf educational opportunities provides a myriad of topics such as:

Mental Mulligans: A fun and enlightening team-building workshop for your group that reveals how you present yourself both in and out of the office, on and off the golf course. Learn to understand different behavior styles on the golf course and how they impact your game and your success in business!

Get in the Game – Business Golf with On-Course Mentoring: A great way for business professionals to add golf to their business tool boxes.

Tee Off Program: A half-day outing designed to prepare the newer golfer (or non-golfer) who wants to make a positive impression when playing in a charity or industry golf tournament.

Nine and Wine: A golf mentoring program offering a casual golf experience, designed especially for new golfers (men and women) to help them feel at ease on the tees. Golf up to nine holes with a mentor, with a facilitated debriefing, networking, and hosted happy hour after golf ("wine" not "whine!").

Birdies, Bogeys and Business – Success On and Off the Course: a program that Debbie co-created and delivers with Joyce Friel from Peak Performance Consulting (www.peakperformancecorp.com). This half-day program uses golf as a metaphor to learn what differentiates being an entrepreneur, manager, and technician – and the implications for you and your business. Explore your ownership mentality and create an even more successful business environment.

By discovering new fairways and approach shots for defining business objectives, relationship development, and marketing strategies, Debbie Waitkus has turned golf into gold.

What's New?

A few years after our initial conversation, I asked Debbie what she would change given the benefit of hindsight. "Nothing! Everything happens for a reason, and you just have to go through the learning. I've learned I can jump in quickly, then may have to back-pedal a little..." But even with an occasional back-pedal, Debbie has continued to take great strides forward in her dream.

Debbie described her business as reaching a new level. "First I was focused on visibility, then on credibility, and now on profitability." Recent years have held great milestones for Debbie's endeavors and Golf for Cause®. The new website is up and running, and Debbie's first book *"Get Your Golf On! Your Guide to Getting in the Game"* was published.

Keeping a new business growing during the economic downturn wasn't easy. Debbie shared that she had to "turn on" a different part of the business by focusing on consulting to organizations about how to raise funds through golf. In addition, **Golf for Cause®** has developed successful partnerships with three women's organizations. A true advocate of the sport, Debbie is a co-founder and partner of the National Women's Golf Alliance – evaluating and certifying golf facilities for how well they "Roll Out the Green Carpet™" for women, and a past-president of Women in the Golf Industry. Debbie also donates a portion of the proceeds of her book to the Marilynn Smith Scholarship Fund, advancing the opportunity for girls to play golf in college.

When I asked Debbie to reflect on her career change, she became thoughtful. "Looking back, I had great support from my family. I knew I could always go 'get a job' but they supported me as I moved from being all about the money, to helping non-profits. This work matches my values. Sometimes I miss the taste of the deal, but I still use the skill set I developed in my corporate career. I felt like such a newbie – a guest – in the golf industry, but that helped me be respectful of others. I still feel like a kid in a candy store!"

Career changes often teach us a lot about ourselves. Debbie said she learned she can sometimes be too controlling, and may have too much going on at once. "I can have too many plates spinning, but I've learned when to ask for help. I get so excited that I often want to share something before it's ready. And I've learned that I'm good at what I do!"

The future looks strong for Debbie. Her plans include getting more engagements as a motivational speaker, and empowering more women through golf. She intends to continue her association with the National Women's Golf Alliance, and hopes to see an increase in the number of facilities that welcome women.

Debbie has advice for women who are considering a career change: Find others who have done what you want to do, but in a different industry... it helps to know that "if she can do it, so can I!" Also, it helps to find a group to support you by holding you accountable to your plans and goals. And when you need extra hands to help, consider leveraging interns from a local university. They are bright, eager, resourceful, and anxious to have meaningful experience on their resumes! This is great advice to consider as you "play through" your career transformation!

Debbie's Advice and Action Steps:

- For all the perfectionists – let go already and just do it!
- Consider a professional career coach and/or a resource team to assist you.
- Find a good accountant early on if you begin a new business.
- Really think about what you are passionate about doing – your next career may be right under your nose.

Resources:

Golf for Cause: www.golfforcause.com
Silver Rose, Coach: www.silverspeaks.com

> **"**The bad news is time flies. The good news is that you're the pilot.**"**
>
> – Michael Althsuler

∾ ∾ ∾ ∾

50. STACY BREUERS: FROM M&A TO CABERNET

I am convinced that "six degrees of separation" is getting smaller every day and I met Stacy through a classic example of this phenomenon. My Mom attended a charity fundraiser at a wonderful restaurant in New Jersey, and Stacy supplied the wine. In the spirit of networking, and always on the lookout for women's great reinvention stories, my Mom connected me to Stacy and the rest will unfold in her story below. Cheers to you, Mom for introducing me to Stacy – she is a great addition to the book.

Stacy Breuers spent 18 years in the banking and finance industry. This high-powered career met her values at the time. She held a myriad of positions from consulting on Mergers & Acquisitions to working for an Executive Search firm managing operations and marketing, and later worked in secondary markets on the lending side of the financial coin.

As you would expect, these kinds of positions required long hours and constant travel. Eventually Stacy decided that she did not want to spend all of her time on the road. She enrolled in a wine immersion course at the Culinary Institute of America (CIA) while on a vacation in California, which whet her appetite (and her thirst!) to learn more about the wine industry.

Taste Test

Stacy had a giddy excitement about the class and realized that she had never felt as much passion for the banking industry.

The first CIA course taught her about different facets of the wine industry and later she was referred to the *Wine & Spirits Education Trust* (WSET) run out of London. Since the commute to England for the course was appealing but not feasible with her day job, Stacy opted for a 10-week East Coast class, which was closer to home.

She breezed through the beginner level classes quickly. Intermediate and advanced wine curriculum covered wines from around the world, delving into viticulture and vinification - the business of wine and what makes these wines what they are today. After an additional three years, Stacy earned a Diploma of Wine & Spirits and focused on building her expertise in the trade side of the wine industry.

When You Least Expect It

Two years into her program, the financial market crashed and Stacy was laid off from her job. She got a meager severance and this gave her an incentive to consider all of her options.

With some deep thought and some really good wine for inspiration, Stacy decided to take the plunge and begin a career in the wine industry. She left the financial world behind.

It was a leap of faith, but one that Stacy never regretted. The WSET diploma empowered her with a marketable skill set, even in a difficult economy. She started with a managerial job in a retail wine store and then moved on to a distribution role. Currently, Stacy is a Sales Representative for one of the premier distributors of fine wines from around the world with a diverse portfolio of quality products from the world's most prestigious regions. In addition, Stacy now teaches some of the WSET classes to students in Philadelphia at Philly Wine.

She sells to stores and restaurants and works with Sommeliers, individual clients, and chefs. With a portfolio of over 2,000 wines, Stacy travels around New Jersey, loving her new career and thriving in her new role.

Good to the Last Drop

Stacy shared that the distributors are the middlemen in the industry who work with restaurants and retailers as well as with suppliers and importers. She loves talking about wine with her customers and has traveled to learn more about many of the distinct wine regions including those in Italy, France, Spain, Portugal, Austria, New Zealand, Canada, and California. She loves the continuing education aspect of the wine industry that allows for constant professional development. While taking vacations, she often schedules visits to wineries.

Sometimes it's hard to remember her old life in the financial sector because Stacy is so well matched to her new career. A self-described foodie, she lives to eat and enjoys pairing great wines with great food. While she admits to never getting a bottle of wine as a hostess gift since her friends are afraid to make a wine selection for her, she is happy to share her wine wisdom with friends as well as clients.

Stacy is on-call to many friends who need a wine suggestion for a special occasion meal or gift and is more than happy to oblige.

Cup Half Full

The passion is palpable in Stacy's voice and she lives each day with a sense of adventure that is infectious. While the transition was very scary at first and she had to tap some of her savings, it was well worth the risk in the long run. She recalls a few moments when she thought, "What did I do?" after starting from scratch, but Stacy is playing to her strengths and truly monetizing a new passion.

Although a rookie in this new career field, Stacy is very happy to utilize her creative strengths and knows she has the potential to make the same kind of money she once made in the financial sector. She has come to terms with the need to be patient and persistent and is enjoying every day at work in this new role.

Future plans may steer her towards the management side of the business but for now she is soaking up all she can to experience the world of wine and the opportunities that are available to her. An eternal optimist, Stacy's cup is not only half full – but overflowing with great opportunities.

Being a Rookie Again

When I got back in touch with Stacy, she'd been in her new career for about 6 years, and had gained some interesting insights during that time.

"When you go through a change like this, you think you know what it will be like. But you need to have an open mind because it can be very different from what you think or what you've experienced in the past." Stacy came out of a very structured, corporate environment, and the contrast was a bit jarring. "I wish I'd talked to more people and understood more about the differences before I made the leap."

Changing careers is challenging, and Stacy faces these trials head-on. "A big challenge for me was having patience. When you make a move like this, you're starting all over in a brand new field. You can't look back and think 'this is where I was 6 years ago'. Sometimes it's hard accepting that you're a rookie again."

Building a whole new network is challenging. "You must have a personal support network when you make a change like this. But you also have to start over in building a professional network. I learned that I should have kept in touch more with my previous professional contacts, because they could have been helpful in all kinds of ways."

"For example, I have my moments when I wonder if I should return to my previous field of work – usually when I'm thinking about income. If I'd kept in touch with my old network, a quick conversation could reveal that 'the financial industry is the same as when you left' – and then I could stop wondering…"

Stacy reflects on her new industry – "in wine, there will always be some aspect of sales. Not every company has the same positions, and there is much less structure in this industry. Very few teaching and training roles exist..." and she is very excited that she recently accepted one of these hard-to-find roles.

Stacy is thriving in her new role as Director of Learning and Development with one of the largest wine and spirits distributors in New Jersey. She is busy helping educate associates who serve as the critical link between wine and spirit suppliers, and the retail outlets where alcoholic beverage brands are legally and responsibly sold and enjoyed. Stacy also enjoys working with the management team to help them learn and improve their coaching skills.

This role is a bit of a mix between her old career and her last position. Now that she's part of a larger company, the environment is a little more corporate, and there's more structure in the position. But in the end, Stacy is still happy with her new career field. Her advice for others is clear: "It's hard to make a change like this, but a support network helps. Go ahead and take the risk, or you'll always wonder 'what if'... and if it doesn't work, you can try something new."

Stacy's Advice and Action Steps:

- Remember the importance of your network and the power of relationship building.
- See how your current network can be transferable to a different industry.
- Make a plan and figure out what it takes to make that succeed.
- Take a class in something you are really interested in – it may spark a new career opportunity.
- Take a risk so you can move forward.

Resources:

CIA: www.ciaprochef.com/winestudies
Wine & Spirit Education Trust: www.wsetglobal.com

❝I can and I will succeed!❞

– Stacy Breuers

☞ ☞ ☞ ☞

51. KIM DALY: THE URBANE CONCIERGE

Kim Daly has worn many hats during her professional career, from an Executive Briefing Program Manger to the Director of Global Travel Operations. In her previous life, Kim was working a full 40-hour week and spending 20 additional hours running errands and doing a plethora of other miscellaneous tasks. Her free time was hardly spent doing the things she wanted to do. She soon discovered that there were many people in the same position – their lives were lost to mundane chores.

So, Kim created The Urbane Concierge for people like her. But rather than simply start a personal assistant service, she wanted to offer something special. For 30+ years Kim worked as an event planner and global travel arranger, and her clients demanded a unique experience. And that's what she vowed her new company would offer. Kim's concierges are experts at delivering intangibles beyond simply serving your needs. They become an extension of yourself, anticipating your requirements and accomplishing tasks the way you would want them to be done. That's why all her services are customized and Kim wouldn't have it any other way. Many people start businesses out of necessity, and that is certainly the case with The Urbane Concierge. Kim was ready for a change.

Wanted: Chief of Staff for Your Life

The very definition of an urbane concierge is: affable, balanced, cosmopolitan, courteous, cultivated, gracious and mannerly. These days, hiring the equivalent of a "Chief of Staff " is more common than you might think for everyone from business owners to corporate managers and stay-at-home moms. Yet, as our lives get more complicated, the role of personal assistant has grown in scope to include highly sensitive and confidential tasks such as project managing for small business owners, paying bills, managing the individual services for your home (i.e. gardening, housekeeping, remodeling), personal and business travel arrangements, even overseeing your social calendar. There are tremendous benefits to having someone within arm's reach who can juggle what you never have time to do.

Kim believes that in reality, work time is intermixed with personal time. Her clients need far more than a junior assistant: they need a trusted adviser, a concierge who is standing by 24/7. The Urbane Concierge provides customized packages so that clients can focus on their core competencies and strengths and leave what they don't enjoy doing in the capable hands of a concierge. In return, life is simplified and clients can have more balance to enjoy non-work time with friends and family.

I Can't Get No Satisfaction

Kim started her business after 30 years in the corporate sector because she was extremely unhappy in her professional life. She felt as if she was selling her soul to her employers and had to compromise her values to make a good living. In March of 2007, she quit her job and began to research what else was out there.

She knew her strengths: she enjoyed the organizational and detail-orientation skills that came naturally to her, and she also enjoyed helping others. But she wanted to utilize her skills on her own terms. Kim was a frequent conference attendee at the Professional Business Women of California (PBWC) events and became inspired to branch out on her own after attending a PBWC program that had an entrepreneurs track.

With the input of a SCORE (Counselors to America's Small Businesses) advisor, Kim quickly developed a business plan, a web design logo, and applied for a tax ID number. Soon after, she assembled an amazing team of women whom she knew and trusted from her professional contacts, and the business officially launched in October of 2007.

She chose the name The Urbane Concierge because she wanted to reflect the unique services offered that distinguished her from other personal assistant companies out there. Branding is especially important for a new business and Kim did a lot of self-reflection and research to consider what her special sauce would be in this service industry.

A Very Special Valley Girl

Demographic research was also very important when Kim approached the question of where to focus her business. She has captured a niche market in Silicon Valley and the San Francisco region. The vast majority, 95% of her clients are men and 90% come from within the San Francisco area. These young professionals are very busy and career-focused, so they need The Urbane Concierge services to handle their multifaceted lives. This high-end clientele is the definition of urbane and they see having a personal concierge as a status symbol as well as a necessity, and that's good for business.

In her business, Kim often has access to a client's personal bills and medical records, etc., so discretion and confidentiality is of the utmost importance for her and her staff. Kim relies on having a stellar reputation as well as positive recommendations from clients. This is the number one way that her business grows.

The old adage – The customer is always right! – is alive and well. However, according to Kim, there are some clients that just can't be helped; she has learned that in some cases she must turn down a client if she thinks it won't be a good fit for her or her staff. This is the beauty of running your own shop – you can say no to business you don't want.

Über Organized

In some cases, Kim talks about working herself out of a job because she gets a client so organized that they don't need her anymore. But that is usually a good thing because it results in a strong referral and the original client most often comes back for another service down the road.

While being organized is what Kim does best, she admits that some clients seem to have monumental tasks to accomplish. She trains her staff to keep their game faces on and to remember that "fear breeds courage" and to persevere at all costs. Since her team is made up 100 percent of contractors, she hand picks which concierges on her staff are best suited for particular assignments. Kim does the original client intake to build trust and determine how The Urbane Concierge can best help.

At the end of the day, Kim now values that she is completely accountable and responsible for the satisfaction of her clientele. She runs her business on integrity and trust and believes she is making a contribution in the lives of real people that she gets to know very well. Developing these strong professional relationships has given her a newfound satisfaction on the job and she enjoys being her own boss.

One-Stop Shop

The goal is to make the client aware that a concierge is a one-stop shop for all of their needs. Kim offers customized packages and pricing for each client based on what they require. A sampling of services includes, but is not limited to:

- Appointment setting
- Home life organizer
- Help small business owners manage projects
- Travel and event planner
- Personal shopper
- Errand runner/courier
- Home greeter
- Pet care
- Project Manager

Your Wish is My Command

Kim has developed numerous packages and customized services for individual and corporate clients, so the possibilities are endless depending on what a person needs. The first question in an intake is usually about cost. Why should they employ someone to do what they usually do for free? Kim has them fill out her Urbane Concierge Time/Cost Assessment, something she encourages clients to do before they even make an initial appointment. Suddenly, their mindset changes and they realize they actually need a concierge because Kim adeptly shows them that their time is valuable and time equals money.

Here is an example from one of Kim's customers. The client billed $300/hour as a business coach. She also estimated she spent 10 hours per week running errands, shopping, and so on. That is $3,000 per week at her billing rate, or $156,000 a year! After employing The Urbane Concierge, she not only saved money and time, but also found she had more energy to devote to both her business and her personal life.

Studies have shown that 75 percent of employees handle personal responsibilities while on the job. To make matters worse, 92 percent of employees admit to taking personal time off just to keep on top of their errands and personal responsibilities. Kim's business mission is to take care of people's needs so that they can focus on their core competencies and enjoy life more.

Time Flies

The business launch in October of 2007 seems like more than three years ago and Kim is thriving as a business owner. In 2009, she was named one of the Top 50 Women Entrepreneurs by Savor the Success. In 2010, Kim was awarded a full scholarship by Wells Fargo for the Fearless Entrepreneur Program. Future goals include continuing to build her clientele as well as her team of experienced concierges so that she can focus more on growing the business and handling select clients. She is conscious about staying on top of current trends, techniques, and technologies to better serve her clients.

Kim is now living her philosophy that time is money and she appreciates having control over her own time now. She has numerous client testimonials on her site that endorse The Urbane Concierge and validate that Kim's career reinvention was well worth it!

What's New?

Many small businesses are affected by economic downturns, and The Urbane Concierge is no exception. A few years after our first discussion, Kim shared that in response to the economy, she started to focus more of her services on helping international employees relocate to her area. She also shifted to a solo-preneur model, to focus on the one-to-one relationships with her customers. After all, people hire an *individual* for something as important as personal concierge services; they want to know the person they talk with is the person who will take care of their needs.

Looking back, Kim said there are some things she misses about a corporate setting, such as affordable health insurance and socialization with co-workers. But one thing she made clear – going back to a corporate job "is not going to happen!" She often felt that her corporate job required that she compromise her personal values, and that her standards of integrity didn't match those around her. She is not willing to get in that situation again.

Providing concierge services can be typical – arranging travel, running errands, paying bills – but it can also be unpredictable. For example, one offbeat request came from a financial executive who wanted some In & Out burgers brought in for a lunch meeting. And there was the ad agency that quickly needed a man in a tuxedo and white gloves to deliver an iPad in person. These odd requests were handled as if these services were provided every day, and the customers were very happy.

The cash flow that comes with a business like this can be unpredictable as well, but Kim met this challenge head-on. Early on, she charged a flat, hourly rate, but learned that the cash flow slowed down in the summer when many of her customers went on vacation.

So she shifted her model to sell hours in packages with a service agreement, and receives payment prior to providing services. Her income is no longer tied directly to how many hours she works in one week or one month.

Kim loves owning her business because it lets her use her planning and project management skills, while providing outstanding customer service. Kim said about once a year, she will interview with someone who is looking for a full time personal assistant. And each time, she realizes she is very happy where she is – she is able to make a living doing what she loves, and still have a personal life.

If you are considering going into business for yourself, Kim suggests you know the competition. This knowledge can help you define how your company will be different, which forms the basis of your unique brand. Also, she said it's a good idea to help each other out – a client that doesn't fit your company may work for theirs, and vice versa. In the end, significant business growth comes from one person telling another person that you do a good job. To be successful, make sure you provide the level of service that will earn a referral – whether from a customer or your competition!

Kim's Advice and Action Steps:

- Find the right people when building your staff.
- Be tenacious for what you really want.
- Realize that some clients can't be helped and that is no reflection on you – simply move on.
- Use technology to your best advantage. Keep abreast of new gadgets, programs and features that can help you in your work and life.

Resource:

The Urbane Concierge: www.theurbane concierge.com

Savor the Success: www.savorthesuccess.com

Professional Business Women of California: www.pbwc.org/

SCORE: www.score.org/index.html

Wells Fargo Fearless Entrepreneur Program:
www.futurewomenleaders.net/entrepreneurship-program

66 People have hired me because of me. 99

– Kim Daly

ﾌ ﾌ ﾌ ﾌ

52. JEANNIE MONTAGANO: SOUTH PAW BECOMES A PROFESSOR

I came to know Jeannie because I served as a career coach to her son, Chris when he was a student in law school. Chris was so proud of his Mom and shared her career reinvention story with such enthusiasm that I knew we were destined to connect. With no surprise, Jeannie and I hit it off famously and her energy and wisdom were palpable. I especially love her story because it shows us that reinvention is possible at any point in life and can also happen when we least expect it. I'm so pleased to include her in the second edition.

For 20 years, Jeannie Montagano enjoyed her career as a school psychologist. Part of her job was to supervise and mentor interns. At age 54, she had an epiphany and realized that she could play to her strengths even more by influencing students to become practitioners if she taught at the university level. This was the part of her job that she loved the most and so the quest to earn her PhD began.

The Stigma of the South Paw

It's important to take you back a bit farther to explain what initiated Jeannie's passion for education and student advocacy. Growing up, Jeannie had an archaic teacher in grade school that believed (as many did at the time) that left-handed kids were not good. It shows you how far we have come in our pedagogical views because Jeannie was actually singled out by this teacher who encouraged the other children in the class to point at and chastise Jeannie for using her left hand to write.

The peer pressure was unbearable and Jeannie was forced to try and change her dominant functions to her right hand. Luckily, Jeannie's mom spoke with the principal who intervened. At the end of that year the teacher retired and Jeannie has been happily left-hand dominant ever since. We can only hope that this teacher would have felt differently after reading about Dr. Alan Searleman of St. Lawrence University in New York and his study that found left-handers can be considerably more intellectually gifted.

From that point on, Jeannie was committed to defending the underdog and was drawn to studying social work in college because she wanted to help people.

It's Not the Destination but the Journey

At age 23, Jeannie remembered boldly applying for her ideal position as a school psychologist with the ink barely dry on her undergraduate diploma in social work. The search committee was encouraging but shared the news that an advanced degree was required. So Jeannie set out on a mission to earn her Masters of Science in School Psychology to empower herself for this dream career path.

The journey to earn the Master's degree was not fast as Jeannie and her husband were busy following the promotions, moving six times in seven years. But in 1980 she minted the degree and took on the role of school psychologist at Chattanooga Public Schools. That same year, her first son, Michael, was born so Jeannie was a busy woman to say the least.

As Jeannie raised her kids and grew her career, her husband continued to earn promotions and new career opportunities. As the family moved geographically and grew, with the addition of her second son, Christopher, Jeannie took on new roles in private practice and later as a school psychologist in northeastern Indiana.

No Roadblocks

A lifelong learner who craves intellectual stimulation, Jeannie noticed that her interns were talking about brain functions and other cutting edge industry disciplines that she found compelling. This also inspired her to consider the PhD. Jeannie is goal-oriented and knew the next degree would open up additional opportunities to take her to a new career level.

A firm believer in the power of mentorship, Jeannie is thankful for the great advisors in her life who have inspired and counseled her along the way. She was ready to take this leap and enroll in the doctoral program but the closest university offering a degree in her field was an hour away at Andrews University in Michigan.

Jeannie had the full support of her husband and two sons who applauded her decision. Since the kids were in college and high school at the time, and more independent, it was a good time to transition to a new endeavor that would require even more of her professional time.

With a *no roadblocks* mindset, Jeannie was off and running towards earning the PhD. Her two sons have absorbed her passion and work ethic in their lives and careers, and the energy in the Montagano family is palpable.

The Power of Stubbornness

Work/life integration was a challenge but Jeannie is proud that she never missed a single tennis match her son played during the time she was pursuing her PhD course work. She continued to work part-time as a school psychologist and took two classes each semester over a three-year period. With an hour-long commute each way, she took class from 6:30-9:30 pm, twice a week.

We talked about life balance, and Jeannie felt her "just do it" attitude and pure stubbornness was part of her drive towards achieving a goal. She was happy to share that she never missed out on anything during this time because she took control over what she chose to do. Jeannie also believes that you must "put your oxygen mask on first before you help your child" (just like the airplane flight attendant's spiel) because you must carve out time for yourself to rejuvenate, re-energize, and focus on what you need most, especially if you are a caregiver.

Was it easy? No way! Was it worth it? Absolutely!

As any PhD holder will attest, the course work is demanding but writing the dissertation is herculean. The next four years were spent writing the dissertation, and during the combined almost decade of course work and document writing, Jeannie recalls high school and college graduations, law school graduation, her son's US congressional campaign and a wedding! While Jeannie admits that her quest was sometimes slowed down so she could participate in these important life events, it was never discarded.

She recalled walking in over 31 parades during her son's congressional campaign and would not have traded a minute of it to earn the PhD any faster. Jeannie has mastered the art of realistic expectations and designed a life that is flexible so she can do what she wants to without sacrificing her personal goals.

Her Doctor of Philosophy in Educational Psychology was minted in 2010 and Dr. Montagano has made over 14 presentations to conferences including the American Psychological Association, the National Association of School Psychologists, and the International Association of Psychologists at Trinity College in Dublin, Ireland in her first year as a PhD holder. Her research interest focuses on the nature of math anxiety, test anxiety, and social anxiety in elementary students.

Jeannie is now influencing young minds as an associate professor at Andrews University and is accomplishing things that she had never imagined.

How to Live an Effective Life

Jeannie has long subscribed to Dr. William Glasser's Choice Theory, which postulates that what we do, think, and feel reflects our efforts to meet the basic psychological needs of love/belonging, fun, freedom, recognition, and faith. But at times the behaviors we choose to meet those needs are not very helpful - and may even sabotage our happiness! Over 10 years ago, with a longtime girlfriend, Jeannie came up with the idea to offer getaway weekends for women who were facing challenging transitions in life, teach them how to get these needs met, and remain balanced and happy throughout the process.

The business "**Insync**" is about to be rejuvenated with weekend events planned to provide these much needed resources for women in transition. These relaxing retreats will provide a supportive and energizing environment for women to come together in community and learn from each other. They are designed to teach women how to live happier lives. The concept is simple - take them out of their routine, teach some simple strategies, shop a little, sip a little, and laugh a little.

I'm Not Done

When Jeannie was a child, she had a wonderful teeter-totter in the backyard that she spent hours riding with her older sister and, sometimes, alone. When flying solo, she would place bricks on the other side of the teeter-totter and patiently adjust their weight, until it was balanced.

> "I always view my life as a teeter-totter, all my to-do things are on one side and I am on the other. When I find myself higher than the other side, then I know I have to adjust the fulcrum, otherwise I feel vulnerable, and well, high and dry! So, I return to those basic needs and take a quick inventory of how I am neglecting or meeting each one."

This is a perfect illustration of how Jeannie has integrated her personal and professional life – by adjusting. Balance is a relative state and she has achieved so much in her life by adjusting to each scenario accordingly.

With a passion to pay-it-forward to a younger generation in her new role as a professor, and to women in transition in her business venture, Jeannie is not done with her career growth. She wants to continue to contribute to the world as an advocate and a mentor and will always focus on satisfying her basic needs of fun, love, freedom, recognition, and faith.

A true artist in designing her future, Jeannie Montagano is an inspiration for career reinvention. I'm eager to see where her journey takes her next.

Learning to Fly Solo

When I caught up with Jeannie almost three years after our first conversation, much had changed. Less than a week after I first published Jeannie's story online, her husband Joseph "Papa Joe" Montagano passed away unexpectedly at age 61. Joe was Jeannie's high school sweetheart ever since their first date at age 16. In a few short moments, Jeannie's world was turned upside down.

Jeannie suddenly found herself responsible for her husband's business and his estate, and was not prepared to manage it all. "I had no experience with finances, no business experience – nothing." On top of all this, Jeannie was struggling with immense grief. Suddenly, this well-balanced career dynamo was lost.

"But I did it. I was at a point that was so low, I knew I needed to set very small goals, and there were some things I needed to make decisions about concerning the business." Just before Joe's death, Jeannie had signed on to teach more classes at Andrews University. She wanted to pull out, but her colleagues wouldn't let her quit. She's grateful for their tenacity and support, because having to pull it together to teach gave her some much needed structure. She has also had tremendous support from her kids throughout this transition.

In the midst of this tragic grief, Jeannie's first grandchild was born just 2 weeks after Joe's death. He is named Joey in honor of Joe. "We had to move forward." Jeannie enjoys a very close family, and delights in seeing Joey every chance she gets.

Joe's death "took away fear and barriers" for Jeannie. For the last 2 ½ years, she chose to "not say no to anything" and took several adventures. On the one-year anniversary of Joe's passing, she climbed a mountain on the island of St. Vincent. She recently decided to take flying lessons. "You know why? Because WHY NOT?!" It is one more fear for her to face.

When looking back, Jeannie acknowledges that her decision to return to graduate school to earn her PhD did not come at a convenient time. She essentially had to retire to make the time for it, and Joe wasn't really happy with that. Yet that decision saved her in the long run. Going back to school at age 50 caused her to redefine her self-perception, and made her proactive in her own transition. And she's grateful that she did it – "Where would I be now without the PhD?"

Jeannie's professional focus has shifted a bit. Instead of pursing Insync as a business model, she shifted her focus to studying math anxiety in children and the contributing factors in autism spectrum disorders. She created a 10-item survey for school psychologists across the nation, and is speaking across the country about the results. She is also coordinating the first university school psychology program in Trinidad. To date, she's given more than 40 presentations, nationally and internationally at organizations including the American Psychological Association (APA), American Psychological Science (APS), the

National Association of School Psychology (NASP), and the International School Psychology Association (ISPA),

The future for Jeannie is reshaping. She's considering selling the house that she and her husband built, and perhaps relocating. And because of her recent academic work, she plans to spend time in the Caribbean.

I asked Jeannie what she's learned that she would share with other career changers. Her advice: "Be assertive. Get the information about finances and know what you've got." Because you never know what's around the corner.

Jeannie's Advice and Action Steps:

- Tap into the power of great mentors and assemble your resource team.
- See yourself as timeless so you can embrace each new phase of your life as a new beginning.
- Life is never easy but it is manageable if you know what you want.
- Adjust to create balance.

Resources:

Andrews University: www.andrews.edu

<blockquote>

"Bloom where you are planted!"

– Bishop of Geneva, St. Francis de Sales
</blockquote>

∽ ∽ ∽ ∽

53. Take a Step Forward

Learning to find your unique place in the career world does not have to be a daunting task. The exploration process will help you learn what is out there so that you can find a new opportunity that aligns with your VIPS – values, interests, personality and skills. The women in this chapter all took a deep look inside themselves to discover what made them tick. Kari DiFabio honored her values and decided to off ramp from the career world while she raises her children. Stacy Breuers' emerging wine career has taken a few twists and turns and has now evolved into a role that includes teaching, which plays to her strengths. Kim Daly and Debbie Waitkus have been nimble in adapting and growing their respective businesses during less than stellar economic times. Jeannie Montagano has taken on opportunities she never would have considered several years ago.

Even small and incremental steps on a regular basis will help you move forward towards your goals. Often, the first step in a career reinvention is gathering information so you know what possibilities exist that honor your VIPS.

Inquiring Minds Want to Know

The informational interview is a nonthreatening way to ask professionals in your industry of choice for advice, guidance and most importantly, for information about their career field. It's very difficult to learn about a job just by reading a position description. By talking with people in the field you can get the skinny about work tasks, company culture, salary and benefits, and many of the off-limits questions that are not appropriate to ask during an actual job interview.

Keep in mind that you always need to bring your professional best to an informational interview. Dress the part and behave like a future employee. These sessions can lead the interviewing professionals to inquire about your career future, which opens the door to discussing how they might be of assistance, or to what degree they are willing to make network referrals.

Don't forget to thank the people with whom you meet by sending a hand-written thank-you note. Keep in touch regularly, as needs change in an organization frequently. If you made a positive impression you may be the first on their list when a position becomes vacant that you are well suited to fill.

Lastly, ask your connections if there is anything you can do for them in return. Make the networking a two-way street and be willing to pay-it-forward and help when you are able.

Volunteer Your Way into a Job

By giving away your skills in the form of volunteerism you can showcase your value to others while doing a good deed. Get involved in your community and take on a leadership role. Amazing things can happen when people give of themselves to a worthy cause. They learn important skills and form powerful and positive relationships that often lead to future opportunities. Feeling good about the work you provide as a volunteer is energizing, and can be the motivation needed to get you into the public eye so that you are not a well-kept secret.

Scratching the Entrepreneurial Itch

Many of the women I interviewed moved from careers in an organization to an entrepreneurial venture. Debbie Waitkus, and Kim Daly in this chapter, started their own businesses to enjoy the freedom, flexibility and independence of being their own boss. They found a way to monetize their passion. But these ladies can attest to the fact that business owners have total accountability for the success and failure of every task they pursue. Great risk is required to create a successful new product or service and to develop a brand that is unique and desirable.

Keep in mind that you don't have to jump ship and head out to sea on your own to scratch the entrepreneurial itch. There are numerous opportunities inside existing organizations for exercising the intrapreneurial muscles you may have. Take a closer look inside before you move outside to make sure that you have exhausted all the resources at your disposal in your current workplace. You might be surprised at the opportunities available down your own company hallway. Sometimes you just need to change roles in an organization to find career satisfaction. Consider having a confidential heart-to-heart with a Human Resources Manager or a mentor whom you can trust to give you sound internal career advice in your organization.

When to Quit the Day Job

Studies indicate that nearly eight out of every ten women are actively seeking new positions or are considering starting their own business due to career dissatisfaction in their current role. That's a very large percentage of the workforce. My strongest bit of advice is not to leave a job until you have another position to go to. Besides the financial risk of not having a steady income, you are far more employable when you are employed than when you are looking for a new job without a current position.

I encourage the career-changing women I coach to ease incrementally from a job they don't like until they can secure a new position, or start to earn income with their new business venture. Consider working part-time to be able to devote more time to career exploration or job interviews but still have some money coming in and a fresh reference from a current employer. Phasing out of one job and into another can often ease the stress of transition.

REINVENTION TOOLBOX

The Art of Self-promotion; Leadership Lessons; Play Nice in the Career Sandbox

It's not enough to just do your job well anymore. Professionals need to distinguish themselves in the workplace in order to earn promotions and recognition within an organization. Entrepreneurs have to take control of their own career advocacy to be noticed and stay competitive in the marketplace. The art of self-promotion is a necessity but walking the line between humble confidence and inflated ego can be difficult.

Here are some strategies to help you get more recognition on the job:

1) **Be a Social Butterfly** – Don't just work in isolation. You need to socialize with people, have emotional intelligence,

and social awareness in your organization. Your visibility at work is just as important as your competency. Your positive attitude will take you places, and colleagues at all levels of the organization should be aware of what you are accomplishing for the company.

2) **Understand Company Culture** – It is very important that you understand the culture of your organization. It's all about how you fit in and assimilate into your career environment. You don't need to change who you are, but you should identify the potential to grow your career and mold yourself accordingly. Company culture ranges from fashion style and quitting time at the end of a workday to going above and beyond for a special project. Adapting to your firm's culture will empower you to be recognized as a team player.

3) **Develop an Expertise** – In addition to having a broad span of transferable skills, develop a niche skill that is unique in the company and you will quickly become the go-to person for this much-needed proficiency.

4) **Embrace Your Humble Confidence** – Nobody likes an egotistical bragger, but if you can learn to talk with humble confidence about the accomplishments you earned, you will quickly become an asset to your organization. It's necessary to be able to talk about what you do well in performance reviews so keep a record of what you have accomplished during a given time period and be ready to discuss this if your boss asks what you are doing, at any time. *Manage Up* in-between performance reviews so your boss knows the value you bring to the organization at all times.

5) **Be a Team Player** – You can rarely accomplish anything solo in an organization. Being a team player not only provides you a holistic picture about the task but also helps you broaden your skill set. Teamwork is an opportunity to be connected to people from other groups and divisions in your organization. This enhances your chances to move up in your company and increases your visibility throughout the organization.

6) **Network, Seek Feedback, and Have Mentors** – Build your personal Board of Directors at work and seek feedback and constructive criticism regularly. Don't wait for a performance review to ask for pointers; be pro-active and seek out mentors within and beyond your organization. Earn the backing of a Sponsor who will put their professional reputation on the line and recommend you for advancement because of the great work you have accomplished.

7) **Make an Impact** – The impact can be on the company's bottom line or significant work you do in the community. Be an influencer; give back or pay-it-forward to ramp up your visibility at work.

You are in the driver's seat when it comes to your career self-promotion. Learning to be your own best advocate will help you achieve your goals within an organization and beyond. It takes practice and a conscious mindset, but the art of self-promotion is doable for all.

Women Leaders

Former Secretary of State Madeleine Albright is paving the way for the future women leaders of the world and unlocking the door to the proverbial good old boys' club. At Wellesley College, Ms. Albright's alma mater, an Institute for Global Affairs named after her offers students around the world access to nonpartisan lectures, seminars, and internships, with topics ranging from political science and economics to religion. The goal is to address the issues at the core of international societies and empower women leaders with an opportunity to make a difference.

Albright believes that women see the human part of issues and pursue power in order to do something with it, not just to have power for the sake of having it. With less than 20% of women holding cabinet positions worldwide, Albright is on a mission to groom the next generation of women leaders.

Here are some key competencies for leadership success:

- Good leaders should foster the potential of others in an organization.
- Optimistic leaders are more effective.
- Effective leaders learn to be assertive and not aggressive.
- Strong leaders are comfortable in their own skin and lead by being authentic and true to themselves.
- Successful leaders understand human motivation.
- Valuable leaders give their team the space to work autonomously.

Playing Nice in the Career Sandbox

I have learned that there is nothing stronger than the power of women in community and that women can be inspirational resources in the professional arena. But I also know the reality of being a woman in the professional world and how we often struggle with owning a strong, confident persona while maintaining our authenticity and honoring our femininity at work.

Learning to play nicely in the proverbial work sandbox does not have to be that difficult. Here are some strategies that will help you become a good team player but still empower you to stand out and make your mark on the job to earn the recognition you deserve.

- **Preparation equals credibility.** It's that simple: be prepared and you will earn the respect of your colleagues and impress the powers that be.
- **Pick your battles.** There will be difficult situations, but don't fall on your sword for every cause. Be mindful of your values and what is really important to you as well as what will empower you to advance in the organization to achieve your goals.

- **Own your confidence.** In order to succeed you must believe in yourself and your abilities. By tapping into your humble confidence you can project an image of self-reliance, poise, and assurance that will give your team faith that you can get the job done.

- **Be aware of your surroundings but focus on you.** On a team you must be cooperative, but at the end of the day, you have to be your own best advocate and be ready to take charge of your career future. Don't wait for a boss or supervisor to groom you for greater things; be proactive and strategize about ways to upgrade your standing in the organization.

- **Don't gossip.** The old adage, "If you don't have anything nice to say, don't say anything at all," still rings true. Avoid hallway gossip and treat your colleagues with courtesy and respect. What goes around comes around and you should expect the same professional treatment from others.

- **Honor your values.** It always comes back to who you are, what you value, and how you want to show up in the world. Take stock of how you want to make your mark and align your personal and professional values so they are validated for you at work.

10

A CALL TO NURTURE

From rallying community resources to finding a cure for cancer, these women have turned taking care of others into a career.

54. JACQUELINE EDELBERG: HARNESSING THE GOODNESS OF HER NEIGHBORHOOD

An academic by training, Jacqueline Edelberg earned her PhD in Political Science and taught at the University of Osnabrück in Germany as a Fulbright scholar. After the international teaching stint, Jacqueline returned to her beloved Chicago with her husband, Andrew, ready to give birth to their first child. After a very complicated and difficult delivery, Jacqueline was relieved and fortunate to have a healthy baby. The experience ignited her maternal instincts and she wanted to focus completely on nurturing her infant daughter for the next six months.

While Jacqueline relished her new role as a mother, the pangs of career guilt began to set in for this professor-turned-mom who craved intellectual stimulation and challenge. Struggling with the proverbial question of "What do I want to be when I grow up?", Jacqueline took the advice of a dear relative who shared that raising a child is a special time in a mother's life, and a very short one at that. She cautioned Jacqueline to enjoy this time with her daughter and to be confident that the work would always be there when she was ready to go back. Little did Jacqueline know that her future career would be to mobilize a grass roots movement rehabilitating neighborhood schools in her Chicago community and across the nation.

Mother Knows Best

Jacqueline took this wisdom to heart and started to believe that her skills would not go away and that her role as a mom was very important. In addition to her training as a professor, Jacqueline is also a fine artist, a painter who specializes in ketubahs: distinctive Jewish marriage agreements which have become a significant form of Jewish ceremonial art. Painting was something she continued to enjoy while pursuing the full-time career of being a mother.

From the time her daughter was an infant, Jacqueline's husband Andrew agreed to pursue the research about where their daughter would attend school. However, Chicago parents, like parents across the country, face the same sobering reality: given the scarcity of spots, it's extremely difficult to get your child into an expensive private school. Entry into a respected public magnet school isn't any easier. In fact, Jacqueline points out that it's statistically easier to get your high school kid into Harvard than to get your kindergartener into a selective enrollment magnet school. In Chicago, most middle-class parents believe that their non-selective neighborhood public school is not a viable option.

Many parents assemble portfolios with glossy brochures and work with consultant recommendations to figure out where to send their kids to kindergarten and beyond. Andrew passed the baton to Jacqueline and the school research became her responsibility. Finding a suitable school for her daughter, Maya (and son Zack, who was on the way), was a top priority.

The Power of the Roscoe Park Eight

Struck with the possibility of moving out of Boystown, her fabulous Chicago neighborhood known for its architectural charm, rich culture, diversity, and tolerance, Jacqueline convinced her friend Nicole to come with her to check out Nettelhorst, her neighborhood's underutilized and struggling public elementary school. After a 3-hour tour of the 110-year-old building, the new principal, Susan Kurland, asked what it would take for them to enroll their children. Stunned by her candor, they returned the next day armed with an extensive wishlist. Susan read their list and said "Well, let's get started, girls! It's going to be a busy year..."

And so the journey from Roscoe Park to the school began. Jacqueline and Nicole recruited six more park friends to join the cause. The women called themselves the Roscoe Park Eight, and met once a week in a Boystown diner, to plan how to fix Nettelhorst so their kids could walk to school.

Eight Women in a Diner

This meeting of the minds may have started humbly in a diner, but never underestimate the power of mothers on a mission. The talent pool within the mommy brigade was deep, ranging from lawyers and executives to artists and bankers. They decided to call their group, The Nettelhorst Parents' Co-op, with the motto "We do more during nap-time then most people do all day!"

The Roscoe Park Eight set an ambitious goal: the Parents' Co-op had just nine months to reinvigorate Nettelhorst. These women were scrappy, creative and spirited, and as Jacqueline admits, too naïve and green to know how difficult this endeavor really was.

Running on infectious energy, each park mom captained a Co-op team: infrastructure, public relations, marketing, special events, fundraising and curricula. Each woman was assigned a task that best met her skill set and experience, and each team had to succeed concurrently. The team captains then set out to recruit as many families as they could to join their fledgling cause.

Mommy Moxie

How could the Co-op refurbish a school with a budget of nothing? The moms began cold calling people to solicit services, supplies, and volunteers with skills and an interest in the project. In the beginning, fundraising efforts were futile since nobody wanted to contribute to a failing city school. The development team was disbanded and efforts were refocused on getting the necessary goods and services donated for the cause.

In a matter of months, the community donated over half a million dollars in goods and services, contributed inch-by-inch and a gallon of paint at a time. The beauty of this project was that anything you had to offer for the cause was perfect. If you had a gallon of neon yellow paint, great! Nothing was turned down and nothing was wasted. The community joined in, and now there isn't an inch of the school that hasn't been touched by a neighborhood artist. The whole school is an inspiration!

The community buy-in was extraordinary and people started calling from distant parts of the city to contribute to the reinvention of Nettelhorst. The Roscoe Park Eight truly harnessed the goodness of a neighborhood. The story has been featured on *Oprah & Friends*, *NPR*, *CNN*, *60 Minutes*, *Education Weekly*, and in the local Chicago media.

Sustaining the Cause

Eight years into the project of fixing Nettelhorst, Jacqueline wrote a book about her experience: *How to Walk to School: Blueprint for a Neighborhood School Renaissance* (Foreword by Arne Duncan and Afterword by Rahm Emanuel). The book chronicles the highs and lows of motivated neighborhood parents galvanizing and then organizing an entire community to take a leap of faith to transform a challenged urban school. They successfully turned Nettelhorst into one of Chicago's best schools, virtually overnight. Jacqueline proved that the fate of public education is not beyond our control. In the book, she provides an accessible and honest blueprint for reclaiming the great public schools our children deserve.

The original eight moms wanted to create a sustainable school that could thrive into the future, and now, Nettelhorst is one of the most desirable schools in Chicago. Enrollment has doubled; test scores have tripled; and parent involvement is off the charts. The teachers and administrators are also thriving and proud to be part of the school's renaissance.

The original fundraising committee may have been unsuccessful at first, but now that the school is thriving, development efforts are a well-oiled machine. For example, parents forged a deep, mutually beneficial partnership with the Stanley Cup-winning Chicago Blackhawks. With a $210,000 donation, the Blackhawks built a state-of-the-art fitness center in the school and an outdoor hockey field. Players, coaches, and team managers frequent the school, teaching kids about sportsmanship, discipline, and maintaining healthy lifestyles.

Thanks to the work of driven parents, the school now has the financial wherewithal to maintain the building, and to provide innovative programming to enhance an already solid curriculum.

Labor of Love

While the moms contributed sweat equity to this cause eight years ago, and did all the work pro bono, Jacqueline is still on a mission to continue with the renaissance of neighborhood schools nationwide. America is based on the neighborhood school model, and that model succeeded in this country for over a century. Jacqueline is obsessed with sparking the national grass roots movement since so many of America's neighborhood schools are now in sad shape. According to Jacqueline, "If everyone just fixed their own neighborhood school, we could see real, systemic change across the country."

Jacqueline has led workshops for the Community Schools Initiative, Northside Parents Network, and Chicago Public Schools on how public schools and reformers can stimulate communities to improve public education. She has consulted with schools and neighborhood groups on issues of strategy and organizational development. Her goal is to have these ideas become part of the national dialogue about education in America.

The story is inspiring on so many levels, but in addition to reinventing a school that was literally falling apart at the seams, Jacqueline reinvented herself in the process and established a brand new career. Harnessing her transferable skills from the academic and artistic arena, this mom has a passion for changing neighborhood schools across the country, so that kids can walk to school in their own communities.

Take Back the Schools

The next step for Jacqueline is to generate a steady income as a change agent consultant for neighborhood school reform. As the story of Nettelhorst spreads, she's gaining momentum on a national level. If you have an interest in reforming your neighborhood school, be sure to contact Jacqueline. How to Walk to School provides a blueprint that any community can duplicate – with a little elbow grease and a lot of passion.

While doing a good deed that would enable her own children to walk to school, Jacqueline unearthed an accidental career that has inspired her to continue this work in other communities. Her success proves that good things do happen, often when you least expect them.

What's New?

All the foundational work that Jacqueline and the Roscoe Park Eight did is paying off. Four years later, the school is thriving. It is full of kids who live in the neighborhood, and student test scores are "through the roof." The school has developed such a strong reputation that "in the Nettelhorst school district" is frequently seen in local real estate listings.

Nettelhorst is a thriving community school, and it's leading the way in social justice, too. Despite the school's reputation for inclusiveness, a few years ago, some Nettelhorst students bullied a gay substitute teacher and a few classmates of same-sex parents. While the principal reacted to each incident swiftly and appropriately, concerned parents organized a diversity committee to help Nettelhorst foster a culture of tolerance and respect, not just for gay kids, or kids of gay parents, but for *all* kids.

With a new diversity curriculum in place, the committee co-opted the school's annual Fabric Fence public art project to help drive the point home. At the end of the school year, parents, teachers, and students installed the piece on the playground fence as usual, but this time, they arranged the colored fabric strips into the pride rainbow sequence, and posted this sign:

> "Each Nettelhorst student has tied a piece of fabric to the fence as a tangible sign of his or her personal intention to create a better world. As Nettelhorst, we've also made a collective intention: that each of us becomes kinder, gentler, and more tolerant. Here, the rainbow colors of gay pride are a visible sign of our respect for the neighborhood of which we are a part,

and the diversity of families that we serve. Nettelhorst was the first public school to walk in Chicago's Gay Pride Parade. We believe family means everybody.

Twenty thousand people pass by Nettelhorst's playground every single weekend. Many of them stopped, smiled, high-fived, tweeted and posted; some even cried. But Jacqueline never could have anticipated that the rag-tag public civics lesson would have inspired such a deeply personal, neighborhood catharsis.

The mainstream media praised Nettelhorst for fighting the good fight, and sadly, Nettelhorst landed on every hate blog in the country. It was an extremely difficult time for the community, the parents, and the school. But their struggle became crystal clear: if the school community couldn't take a stand against discrimination, what kind of example were they setting?

And, so it was, that on a sun-soaked summer afternoon, 200 Nettelhorst families – both gay and straight – marched in the parade; in fact, they led it. The outpouring of support from the 140,000-strong crowd was like nothing Jacqueline has ever experienced. Chicago's first openly gay Alderman, Tom Tunney, also marched in the parade proudly wearing his Nettelhorst Pride t-shirt. "Time will show," he professed, "on this day, Nettelhorst was on the right side of history."

The following year, Nettelhorst marched in the Parade once again, only this time, with employees from U.S. Cellular, another elementary school, and the openly gay Chicago Public Schools' CEO, Ron Huberman, pushing his baby in a stroller; flanked by the Governor, and the Chicago Blackhawks, hoisting aloft their hard-earned Stanley Cup. In what seemed impossible just twelve months earlier, the establishment stood with the Nettelhorst families to say, out loud, in one strong voice: Every school should be a safe place to learn, where all kids feel free to be wholly themselves.

As Jacqueline navigates her ongoing career journey, she tries to "feel free to be wholly herself." In fact, she "had an epiphany" about what it means to be true to herself. In her words:

> "It was almost fifty degrees, a real rarity for April, so I decided it was a good morning to separate the fabric that my daughter and I had bought at the Textile Outlet in Pilsen. In two weeks'

time, 70 volunteers from the IGLTA were coming to the school to help tear it into strips for our annual Pride Fence.

After an hour or so, I stuffed the makings of a rainbow back into garbage bags, and hauled it back into the school to a low storage room. The sole light had burned-out, but even in the darkness, I still knew my way around: pipes on the left; twenty-two radio flyer tricycles on the right; and a mysterious drop-staircase to somewhere straight ahead. I shoved the bags along the wall, hoping to leave enough room so that the kindergarteners could wheel their tricycles in and out. I made a mental note to remind the building engineer to replace the light bulb. I also tried to remember that we would need to gather at least five pairs of good scissors for the LGLTA event or else we'd be stuck with dull kiddie scissors from the art room.

There, rummaging around on my knees in the darkness, it hit me:

I am doing exactly what I am supposed to be doing.

...I'm doing right by my kids, and I'm being true to what I want to be doing in the world. In the pachinko game of life, we make all these decisions, and then we wake up one day and say: "This is Who I Am." Would I like to make money off the work I do? Sure. Would I like to be more famous or successful? Of course. But that is the response to work--not the work itself.

The gift of meaningful work is more work.

I own the choices I've made. I am doing what I'm doing because I think it's important and I find it sustaining."

Think about it. Do you own your choices? Do you find your work important? Does it sustain you? Are you doing exactly what you are supposed to be doing? We can all learn from Jacqueline's journey.

Jacqueline's Action Steps for Reforming Your Neighborhood School:

1. Form a group of core parents.
2. Find a Principal you can work with.
3. Find a pro-bono lawyer.
4. Get the school spruced up.
5. Start a public relations program.
6. Enroll your own kids in the school.
7. Get the community involved in the school.
8. Settle in for three or more years of open houses and fundraisers, volunteering at the school, and meetings out the wazoo.
9. Acknowledge you're not going to get any breaks.

Resources

How to Walk to School the Book & Blog:
　　　www.howtowalktoschool.com/
Nettelhorst School Video: www.youtube.com/watch?v=XPZr6BYJSGc

"Never doubt that a group of small thoughtful citizens can change the world. Indeed, it's the only thing that ever has."

— Margaret Mead

ᘏ ᘏ ᘏ ᘏ

55. JOYCE BOYD: THERE IS MORE TO LIFE THAN BEING THE MAYTAG WOMAN

Joyce's story came to my attention through a family friend. I was especially intrigued about her interest in reinventing after success in a competitive job sector that required years of specialized training and study. Joyce's reinvention was extreme. Her self-discovery and reinvention journey is inspiring to anyone who ever felt stuck in their line of work. You can always redesign your career destiny and Joyce is a role model for finding a new passion that unlocked her nurturing self and honored her authentic professional values. I'm pleased to include her in the second edition of my book.

As an undergraduate at the University of Virginia, Joyce loved math and earned a degree in Electrical Engineering. She was one of a few women in her academic discipline and this held true even in the professional world. She landed a competitive and prestigious spot in a fast tracked, entry-level engineering program at an important Fortune 500 company designed to mold the industry leaders of the future.

This program included a full scholarship for Joyce to earn her Master's degree in Electrical Engineering. Working as a Systems Engineer, she loved her job with the company and discovered she was better suited for program management than for the theoretical design of engineering.

The Maytag Woman

Joyce worked in high profile defense corporations over the next several years, testing engine and flight control systems for various aircraft. She was responsible for identifying and isolating problems, failure analysis, and working with engineers on possible fixes. She reported that while on field assignment, she often felt like the Maytag Woman, searching for things to do at work since there were rarely problems to report on the fully developed system. She worked with other organizations that used the same system on their flight simulator and forged a new opportunity for the company in the area of field engineering support.

Joyce longed for more challenges at work and also yearned to be closer to her family in Virginia, since her job at the time kept her in upstate New York. She left the avionics industry to work with sonar systems on submarines. Later she moved into the corporate sector, again looking for a better fit.

The Tipping Point

Joyce did all the right things trying to overcome the typical corporate promotion hurdles. She networked, earned stellar performance reviews, and even had an internal sponsor to help advocate on her behalf. Joyce shared that even though she had significant experience, the educational pedigree, and the commitment to grow within the company, she was never taken seriously, nor did she feel fulfilled in her career.

That was the catalyst that made Joyce seriously reflect upon her future and her options. For years, the idea of medical school was gnawing at her psyche. Joyce was a nurturer and often took care of family and friends when they were sick. But could she leave a lucrative position, go back to school, and start over?

A consummate planner, Joyce decided to explore the medical world before she made any rash decisions about leaving the technical field. She joined the local Fire Department as an Emergency Medical Technician (EMT) volunteer. She attended Fire Academy at night after work to train for her EMT certification and eventually began volunteering nights and weekends.

Joyce shared that her stress relief was going to the fire station and working EMT shifts. She loved the new adventure, camaraderie, and often slept at the station, showered, and then went off to her day job as program manager. Sometimes after a full day in engineering, she immediately reported to the fire station energized to work another EMT shift

The World is Your Oyster

Up until this point, Joyce's newfound desire to be a nurse was a secret she kept from her colleagues. But the light bulb moment finally happened when Joyce had the courage to say out loud: "I care about people!" She was more interested in working with people and focusing on the holistic care of mind/body/spirit than in fixing engineering/management problems. Joyce unlocked her true passion and enrolled in nursing school.

She grappled with the idea of medical school instead of nursing, but realized her strengths were in taking care of people, instead of focusing on the disease or injury, as physicians do. A woman of strong faith, Joyce has always relied on her spiritual convictions to guide her and she believes this decision was part of a divine guidance and provision.

Leaving a secure position and salary was a scary proposition, so Joyce worked hard to save money before she took the plunge. She learned to live modestly and budgeted for a Bachelor of Science in Nursing degree and completed the pre-requisite courses she needed before even starting the program.

Joyce knew her initial earnings potential as a nurse would be much less than what she was making as a program manager. She learned to budget based on what she truly needed versus what she wanted, and realized with planning, faith, and God's provision she could make things work financially.

Have No Fear

With her faith and the support of her family and friends, Joyce passed the 15-month academic nursing program with flying colors. Her EMT training really helped her in school and with the hands-on practical training of the nursing profession. She was passionate, regimented, and committed to helping others. Interestingly, Joyce was in good company as many of her fellow nursing students were also career changers.

When graduation came, the economy was in a full recession and the job market had changed from when she had started the program 15 months earlier. Luckily, some nursing jobs were still available. Joyce was a top student with EMT experience, and she had the professional savvy of a career reinvention to distinguish herself as a candidate. Her top three choices were to work in intensive care, an operating room, or an emergency room environment.

Joyce took her dream job with a local hospital emergency department and thrived in her new role. Still a consummate planner, Joyce is already envisioning her future career journey in the medical profession and is considering becoming a nurse practitioner.

Although she is the new rookie nurse, Joyce is enjoying her new profession. She doesn't worry about tomorrow since she is doing what she loves and believes God is on her side. For the first time in her professional life she is working with mostly women and enjoying the camaraderie of her co-workers.

Joyce knows she made the right decision every day when she works with patients who look up at her and say, "Thank you for being here," with a knowing glance without even uttering a word.

Where I am Supposed to Be

I caught up with Joyce a few years later, and was happy to hear that her career was continuing to grow and change.

Looking back, Joyce reflected on her first career decision to go into engineering. "There were two tracks I was considering: engineering and nursing. When anyone was sick, I was the one by his or her bedside. I cared for my grandfather when I was 15, and he would call me 'nurse.' But the financial prospects with engineering seemed stronger, and it seemed like a more secure career." Although she gave it her all and excelled in the engineering field, Joyce told me that engineering never really met her values, especially when politics came into play.

The first time she considered becoming an EMT, her brother talked her out of it, reminding her that although she could handle the sight of blood, she was squeamish about broken bones. It was 10 years later that she finally followed that dream and became an EMT. But this time, she didn't tell anyone about it first; she didn't want them to talk her out of it, or urge her to go to medical school instead.

Joyce doesn't regret the delay in following her dream of a career in medicine. "Who knows? If I'd gone into nursing right out of college, I may be burnt out by now. You end up where you're supposed to be."

There were several people who assisted Joyce along the way. She appreciates the help of her fellow firefighters, Fire Chief, her sisters, brothers and father, her study partner, and the President of the

Fire Department (who happened to be a woman) in supporting her through the application process and nursing school. "Once I made the decision to become a nurse, all these doors opened up. I knew if I acted on faith, I would get there."

After working in the emergency room for two years, Joyce had the opportunity to work in a cardiac catheterization lab where she learned a lot, but struggled with the hours and the commute. Currently, she is a contract nurse and has travels to assignments throughout Virginia. Through the agency, her favorite assignment is being a clinical and lab instructor at a local nursing college. More recently, Joyce was accepted into George Mason University's Doctor of Nursing Practice program and is working towards earning her licensure as an Adult Gerontology Nurse Practitioner.

Joyce's story illustrates the power that outside opinions can have on our decision-making process, and the importance of being true to yourself. It's your life, and your career, so it's critical that you get still and really listen to what's in your heart. Seek the advice of others, weigh it carefully, and follow the path that's right for you.

Joyce is inspired by the following scripture passages to get her through good days and bad.

- Psalm 23:1 – The Lord is my shepherd, I shall not want.
- Matthew 6:34 (NIV) – Therefore do not worry about tomorrow, for tomorrow will worry about itself. Each day has enough trouble of its own.
- Proverbs 3:5-6 – Trust in the Lord with all your heart and lean not on your own understanding; in all your ways acknowledge him, and he will make your paths straight.

"Make sure your career is something that will fulfill you. Don't get distracted by obstacles in your way. Be prepared and keep your eye on the prize. Find what you love and do it!"

– Joyce Boyd

♂ ♂ ♂ ♂

56. Ellen Palmer: Tap Into your feminine Side

I first ran Ellen's story on my blog and it generated so many comments that I knew it struck a chord with my readers. We all long for work/life integration and those opportunities to pamper ourselves with some quiet time or a special spa treatment. Ellen teaches a valuable lesson about how important it is to honor your body since it's the only one you have and I'm very excited to include her story in the second edition of my book.

After seven years with Cigna Insurance, Ellen Palmer jumped off the corporate train and decided to pursue a Masters degree in Education. A lucrative position beckoned and Ellen left her academic program to build a subsidiary for Cigna. In the new company, she started as employee number three and left two years later, after she brought on significant clients and built a sales pipeline which helped the company grow to 143 employees during that short time.

Making a conscious decision to leave that job and get married, Ellen Palmer left her corporate career to take control of her life. Throughout her professional life she helped other companies get their businesses started, so she worked as a consultant when her kids were young doing just that. One day it dawned on her that she could start her own business and over the next five years, she created three: **Spoil me Spa, Ellen Palmer Wellness and Create Your Perfect Day™**.

Good Health and Conscious Living

Ellen works with individuals and groups to help them take control of their health, nutrition, and fitness - naturally and holistically. She believes that it is our gift to feel great inside and out and she thoroughly enjoys helping people get back on track to looking great and feeling their best. Ellen works with clients struggling with weight loss and fertility, as well as degenerative diseases such as Diabetes, Arthritis, Candida, Fibromyalgia, ADD, ADHD, and others. She counsels her clients about natural approaches to overcoming challenges by designing a unique plan to suit their needs.

Ellen admits that for the first time in her life she is living her purpose and enjoys the work/life balance she craved during her corporate years. She is on a mission to help other people live fuller, healthier lives and designed her businesses on the philosophy of self-improvement as an empowerment tool. Ellen shared: "The positive ripple effect that people share with their families and colleagues is amazing when they take control of their health and their lives."

The healthy approach is also something Ellen believes is applicable as a business model. Her company - Create Your Perfect Day Business Coaching™ is a coaching service for Women Wellness Practitioners and Entrepreneurs. She helps other women create meaningful and profitable businesses that blend with their unique family goals.

Ellen designed the program to reveal your true gifts so you can apply them to your business in an authentic way that best suits your personality and your desires. It provides a level of accountability that many women need to follow through on tasks to keep them moving towards their goals. Ellen and her team help their clients navigate the inevitable potholes and detours that come up in both life and your business!

Detoxing Your Life

The desire to help others lead healthier lives came from Ellen's personal wellness transformation. After a lifetime of suffering from digestive conditions, reproductive issues, and allergies, Ellen had a conversation one day with her General Practitioner that changed her life. She was tired of years of medications, and procedures and surgeries that didn't seem to be helping. Ellen went to her doctor's office with a thick file of research she had done and asked her to go through it with her to try and understand why was she sick. Ellen's doctor was very rushed and instead of discussing her condition and the research, she prescribed yet another medication.

Ellen pleaded that she didn't want to treat the symptoms - she wanted to get to the bottom of why she had the symptoms in the first place. Her doctor was very frustrated and said, "That isn't my science and I can't help you." It all made sense to Ellen then. It wasn't that her doctor didn't want to help, she wasn't trained in medical school about how to heal, just how to treat symptoms, which is only enough in the short term. If Ellen wanted to get well forever, she needed to take control of her health. Ellen says that for the rest of her life, she will be grateful for her doctor because that experience launched her wellness journey.

Your Body is Brilliant

Ellen received her formal training to practice Health Counseling at the Institute for Integrative Nutrition in New York City. It is the only nutrition school integrating over 200 traditional dietary theories with modern concepts such as the USDA Food Pyramid, The Glycemic Index, The Zone, Raw Foods, Gluten Free and Superfoods. It was there that she had the unique opportunity to learn directly from leaders in the medical and holistic health field such as Dr. Andrew Weil, Deepak Chopra, Dr. Mark Hyman, Dr. Marion Nestle, David Wolfe, and Paul Pitchford.

She also earned advanced certification with M'lis Corporation, a longstanding international leader in natural, holistic health and skin care solutions.

"The body has an amazing ability to heal itself and it is here that this belief was solidified for me. Through detoxification, cleansing, food, and lifestyle changes, people can take control of their health and return to symptom free living! I believe that life is an amazing gift and everyone deserves to live it with great energy and joy."

After learning what her body needed nutritionally, emotionally, and physically, Ellen is happier and healthier than she has ever been. She is also on a quest to share her passion for wellness with others. She is now a woman in charge of her own wellness.

Tap into Your Feminine Side

Taking her wellness training and putting it into practice with Ellen Palmer Wellness, Spoil me Spa and Create Your Perfect Day™ was difficult at first. Ellen was used to the corporate culture and what she calls the masculine model of doing business. She built her businesses on her own feminine model of nurturing and creating an authentic environment that would focus on positivity and helping people.

She admits to a crisis of confidence at first since all she knew was the corporate environment, but she was sure she did not want to re-create that in her new endeavors. Just as she healed her body, she was determined to build healthy businesses that would reflect her values. Authenticity was not negotiable.

Her distinct businesses serve different populations. **Spoil Me Spa** is a talented team of spa professionals who deliver an entire spa experience to you at your home, hotel, bridal location, or corporate event. Based in Connecticut, Ellen's clients are often people who simply do not have a lot of free time. Hectic schedules, juggling family and career.... **Spoil Me Spa** was created for them. Ellen's team can transform a location into a relaxing environment where you can enjoy an array of spa services including massage, facials, manicures, sugar hand scrubs, personal training sessions, hairstyling, makeup, and more. Whether clients are taking time for themselves, planning a special occasion, spa party, or rewarding their employees, **Spoil Me Spa** has something for everyone.

Ellen Palmer Wellness offers 1:1 and group coaching and work-shops on wellness topics including nutrition and personal develop-ment, transformation for mothers, detoxing your life, and health is wealth. Ellen also writes a newsletter with helpful tips and best practic-es, and sells a line of internal body care products by M'lis Corporation.

Create Your Perfect Day™ is a coaching service for women wellness practitioners and entrepreneurs. Ellen and her team help other women create meaningful and profitable businesses that re-flect their unique family values and personal goals. Ellen will be expanding this brand to include other *Create Your Perfect Day™* modules for different transition stages in women's lives such as *Cre-ate Your Perfect Day on Campus™, Create Your Perfect Day for New Moms™*, and others.

Build Your Community

Ellen has learned a lot about herself developing her businesses and advises women who are considering any type of change in life or career to listen to themselves. Take the time to be quiet and slow down to discover the new roles you can play. She also believes that women have a natural intuition, which is a gift, and encourages us all to open up that unique and personal present.

Both businesses have given Ellen an opportunity to build communities. She enjoys bringing women together and teaching them how to live optimized lives with great health and great joy. Clearly her teaching world has come full circle from the days she left her Master's program to return to a career in the corporate world.

Ellen believes everyone has the opportunity to hit the restart button on life and design a new role that fits them better. Her quest is to help others utilize a unique toolbox for their individual body so they can take control of their personal development in a more healthy way.

While Ellen's business background and corporate experience was certainly a plus as she launched her new businesses, she also used *Savor the Success*, a premium business network for women entrepreneurs, to promote her companies and tap into the power of the women's network.

Let it Shine

After many years of struggling with health problems, Ellen is now in control of her wellness and energized to help others do the same. She is hosting wellness renewal retreats, writing a journal/workbook, and hosting a tele-seminar series to help women connect with their passion, create their perfect day, and transition to more peace, joy, health and happiness. Everybody deserves a little pampering and whether you are interested in a spa day, a wellness business, or a healthy living overhaul, Ellen is prepared to help make your life shine. It is the journey and not the destination and Ellen is proof of that.

Learning to Be Patient

When Ellen went through her career transition from the corporate world to the world of health and wellness, she learned many lessons. In the time since our first interview, her learning increased exponentially.

Running two businesses – **Spoil Me Spa** and **Ellen Palmer Wellness** – made it difficult for Ellen to focus and stay grounded in the moment. One day, as she was walking and checking her cell phone, she slipped on a slick rock at the beach with her family. Ellen fell and hit her head, and suffered a major concussion.

For a week after the accident, she tried to push through, but really couldn't function. A close friend "called her out" for not following her own health advice about slowing down to allow healing. Ellen said she "felt like the universe had hit me on the head and said 'pay attention'!" For two months, she couldn't tolerate anything – no TV, no phone, no friends, not even reading. She had two months to do nothing but think.

> "This gave me such clarity. I realized how loud and crazy the world is. I needed to return to basics. This became a beautiful time in my life." Ellen had to close her coaching practice for a few months. She had also been trying to sell her successful business **Spoil Me Spa**, but decided to simply close it. "The universe made the decision."

Now Ellen cherishes her clarity – about how to spend her time, and with whom. Her goals for her business became clear, and she was able to distill her work into manageable, impactful pieces. She still focuses on "all things holistic wellness" through one-on-one and group coaching programs. She's working toward certification as a corporate wellness specialist, holds "Best You Retreats" and online webinars including a program she developed called "Once And For All Weight Loss ™".

Ellen's future goals center on being more accessible to those who need help. She's doing this by creating additional group programs, webinars, and live events to help people come together to understand what food, exercise, and self-care lifestyle changes will help them create lasting change in their health and their happiness. This will be available to schools, universities, communities, and corporations. She's also collaborating with other women to create powerful programs for children to integrate real food for peak performance at school, in their activities, and sports and to create opportunities for success in the future.

When we talked about her current challenges, Ellen was quick to say that she "prefers to look at 'opportunities' instead of 'challenges.'" She is still working on managing priorities, but she's much more mindful of this and is using her skills to be successful.

I asked if, with the benefit of hindsight, she would have done anything differently in her first career transition. "I wouldn't have had a race to get it all done immediately. I wouldn't have had such intensity around it. That (sense of urgency) was leftover from the corporate environment. I wouldn't have created so much stress for myself! Even with something that you're passionate and excited about, it can be too much. Now, there's a settling in, an acceptance, and patience."

With her new outlook, it's been easier for Ellen to collaborate. She told me she's shifted from "I'm on my own to get this done" to being open to the help of others. And this is the advice she offers others – "enlist help. We are meant to be a community, and to collaborate."

Ellen's story is amazing – we never can know what's around the corner, nor how our lives might change in the next moment. Spend time being still. Listen to your inner voice. Then focus on your goals, while staying grounded in the moment. And watch the universe open to you!

Ellen's Advice and Action Steps:

- Have faith in yourself.
- Tap into your feminine side, especially if you have been working in a masculine career environment. Take the time for self-care and for silence.
- Tap into your transferable skills to synthesize new opportunities.
- Believe in your body – it will tell you what it needs. It's the only one you have.

Resources:

Ellen Palmer Wellness www.ellenpalmerwellness.com
Savor the Success www.savorthesuccess.com

❝Nurture yourself.❞

– Ellen Palmer

ൟ ൟ ൟ ൟ

57. CAROL COVIN: A CURE FOR CANCER IN HER DESK

For 25 years Carol Covin enjoyed a career in the computer industry as a software engineer, but in 1997, something significant happened that would change the course of her career dramatically. Carol's colleague, struggling with inoperable stomach cancer, found an obscure cancer treatment developed by a scientist in the late 1970s. It was held by a private scientific library the scientist endowed to hold his papers before he died in 1986. Carol's friend followed the scientist's suggested cancer treatment protocol and his 30-pound tumor was gone in six weeks.

Her friend handed Carol a copy of the protocol and said "This works – I am living proof!" His concern was that it would never be patented because it was all natural and he feared that it would never make it to clinical trials due to lack of funding and serious interest by the medical community. Carol's friend died shortly afterwards of liver damage sustained during the five-year growth of his tumor but his body was cancer free.

Clean out Your Junk Drawer

The cancer treatment protocol remained in Carol's desk for seven years while her career took several different turns. Carol quit the computer company where she had worked for eight years and started a publishing company and flourished, publishing her sixth book with her new company following five others with a previous publisher. But the cancer protocol sitting in her desk drawer kept haunting her and eventually prompted her to seek out the scientific library where the protocol was archived. Carol is quick to point out that she is not a doctor or a scientist but she got so involved in the research, she started telling people that she was working on a cure for cancer. Nobody laughed, and many offered to help.

Eventually the networking stars aligned and Carol was introduced to a pediatric oncologist, who used to work at the FDA, the NCI, and a major pharmaceutical company. This doctor was experienced in fraud detection and interested in alternative treatments and has been guiding Carol's research ever since. Today Carol is incorporated and the President of her own company: Sky Blue Pharmaceuticals, LLC. She is seeking funding to conduct a Phase I clinical trial for the cancer treatment protocol.

A Sense of Urgency

It's not often that you meet someone working on a cure for cancer. I asked Carol if she was excited to get up every morning to work on this profound new career path and she said that she is extremely focused but also feels a sense of urgency to accomplish her goal.

"I went to a memorial service last summer for a friend's daughter. She died after her breast cancer recurred. I was reacquainted with her two high school children – their mom had baby-sat for my younger son. I left with a renewed sense of urgency to make this cancer treatment protocol a reality."

Everyone knows someone who has been affected by cancer. Every minute, of every hour, of every day, someone will die of cancer and Carol Covin is on a mission to cut that number down considerably, knowing the ones she misses will be somebody's loved ones.

Identify Your Purpose in Life

The mission to cure cancer sounds noble but how does a non-scientist even begin to tackle this herculean task? Carol chose this path thoughtfully and with the support of her family. Initially, Carol set aside $5,000 from money she inherited from her mother to hire a consultant to assess her scientific literature review. Carol had gone to the National Library of Medicine on the campus of the National Institutes of Health (NIH) to gather information that had already been written on this topic and read the citations of those sources to educate herself and others on this approach.

Her goal is to find out if the treatment works and if it does, to tell people about it. Ultimately she wants to take the treatment to market.

But before she can do any of this she must take the protocol through clinical trials, to prove the claim that it has some effect on cancer.

The Sky Blue Pharmaceuticals team of two includes Carol and the pediatric oncologist who is guiding her research efforts. Carol has not yet had access to grants so she is relying on private funding, and clinical trials are not cheap. Ultimately, she hopes a pharmaceutical company will offer to license her product and take it to market; but the Phase I, and possibly Phase II clinical trials must happen first.

Trials and Tribulations

The cancer treatment protocol will be taken by the patient in the form of a pill on a 30-day regimen. It takes about three to six months to manufacture the pill and the full Phase I clinical trial will take about a year with 1 to 2 months of treatment and then observation, and follow-up testing. The recipe and production of the protocol will cost approximately $500,000 and another $3 million to facilitate the clinical trial.

Carol has a business plan and a line item budget and she is looking for investors to help underwrite the cost of the clinical trial. Venture capitalists will be pitched after the trials, so for now, she is living off her 401K which looks more like a 201K in the current economy.

She is networking like mad, connecting with entrepreneurs and women's business organizations as well as people who are living with cancer. Sky Blue Pharmaceuticals is truly a labor of love since there is no money coming in for Carol, but she considers this her full-time career and she is committed to meeting her goal of bringing this protocol to market.

Carol has learned that you need to identify what you need and then ask for it. This was a lesson that took a while to sink in, but Carol can say with confidence now that her life has purpose and she is unflappable in the face of adversity.

Assembling a resource team was crucial for Carol and she works with a team of advisors who are helping her make the clinical trial goal a reality. She is learning the art of fundraising and is perfecting the subtleties of "the ask" since at the end of the day, what she needs most is financial support.

Seek and You Will Find

Research has become one of Carol's top transferable skills these days. She found an online message board and unearthed discussions among people who had tried the protocol. She posted a message to ask if they were willing to be interviewed about their experience, and, if possible, supply supporting medical documentation. This has resulted in 15 case studies, including seven who supplied medical documentation, from people who had actually utilized the protocol successfully to treat their cancerous tumors. This information is now documented in a brief that will be part of the clinical trial application.

This particular protocol is unique because it is a treatment for cancerous tumors and not a preventive measure. But preparing for government application for a clinical trial has been a lesson in patience and perseverance. Carol has a 50-year plan for the rest of her life that she breaks down into 10-year chunks. She predicts it will take 8 to 10 years to get the protocol to market and she is in it for the long haul.

No One Else is Going to Do It

In the last nine months, Carol has added another advisor to her team and is talking with a law firm about a promising road map to a patent. She also won the STEM Award (Science, Technology, Engineering and Math) for a case study called The Hot Mommas Project. Carol submitted the study to George Washington University's Business School and presented a poster on the project at the Annual 2010 Multinational Development for Women in Technology (MD-WIT) conference.

Nobody expects a software engineer to cure cancer but Carol has taken this on as a personal mission. She has always put herself into challenging situations and thrives on intellectual stimulation. While some people are dubious about her efforts to cure cancer, more are applauding her and sharing personal stories of people in their lives affected by cancer. These connections have offered Carol hope and inspiration to tackle the monumental challenge she has dedicated her life to pursue.

Blue Skies

Carol left the security of a steady career to pursue a very risky venture because it speaks to her heart. Many years ago, her husband had a cancer scare but he is alive and well today; Carol lost a former college roommate to cancer, who left behind three young children; there are countless others who have been robbed of life by this selfish disease, including the colleague who gave her the business-launching protocol.

When someone asks Carol Covin at a cocktail party, "What do you do for a living?" – she answers with confidence, "I am working on a cure for cancer!" And she really means it.

Joining The Cancer Warriors

When Carol and I spoke several years later, her determination was even stronger. She'd learned several lessons that led her to adjust her approach to achieving her goal. Early in her efforts, Carol gathered all the scientific literature she could, then focused on collecting case studies from patients. She has shifted her approach to focus on securing a patent, because this will be necessary to attract funds for development. The big challenge in getting a patent is that the idea was in the public domain. So Carol is looking at licensing proprietary excipients (chemicals that are added to a pill for the purpose of extending its shelf life or making it easier to digest, for example) or manufacturing techniques. This would allow her to claim intellectual property rights and open the way for raising funds.

Carol is also learning from the successful cancer warriors who've come before her. After reading *Dr. Folkman's War: Angiogenesis and the Struggle to Defeat Cancer* by Robert Cooke, she took note of Dr. Folkman's approach to a problem. He had noticed the importance of vasculature to tumors, and thought there could be a cure lurking in this observation. His method of research was to list all the assumptions necessary to determine if his observation could be used to affect tumor growth, then his graduate assistants would pick an assumption and devise methods to test its veracity.

So, Carol is following this elegantly simple method. She hopes to work with scientists who would help her develop the list, ask "is there reason to believe this is true?" and, if so, determine how one would test it. She hopes to gain help in prioritizing the list, also.

Funding remains the number one challenge in Carol's project, and she is taking a new approach to that as well. "I know how to write books," Carol said, so she is using this talent to fund her life's work of bringing a cancer treatment to market. Like her previous, tech-focused books, her new writing topic is directly influenced by her personal life.

After becoming a new Grandmother, a friend proposed that Carol refer to herself as "Glamma" – a tongue-in-cheek combination of Glamorous and Grandma – but she received surprising pushback from the parents on that idea. Carol talked to her friends about this, and discovered there was a lot to learn about this issue. She started asking mothers "what can't you say to Grandma?" and asking her friends "what can't you say to your grandchildren's parents?" The result was a series of essays looking at both sides of the generational disconnects, and it was a hit.

Carol ran with the idea, and published *Who Gets to Name Grandma? The Wisdom of Mothers and Grandmothers,* an Amazon best-seller. It answers questions like, should Grandma spank her grandchild? How do you keep Grandma from sneaking in candy treats? How do you teach your daughter to feed her children healthy food? What does safety mean to Grandma? To Mom? How do you keep Grandma out of trouble when she is just trying to help? How do you stay involved in your grandchildren's lives at a distance? This book is based on 40 interviews with mothers and grandmothers who answered the question, "What advice would you like to give the other generation about the grandchildren?" Carol is also blogging about grandmothers, and incorporates great ideas like "10 minute activities" you can do with the grandkids. Her future plans include gathering some of the activities she has described on her blog into a new book, *10-Minute Science to Delight Your Grandchildren.*

Carol's dedication to her mission is unwavering. As she encounters obstacles, she finds a way to adjust her approach. She isn't afraid to ask for help, or to take on something big. Her focus and courage are inspiring. What a great example she sets for all of us. Stop and consider: What are your priorities in life, and are you as fearless in your approach?

Carol's Advice and Action Steps:

- Reflect on how you want to make a difference in the world. What is the imprint you will leave?
- Look to the end goal and keep your eye on the prize.
- Assemble a great team early in your venture.

Resources:

The Hot Mommas Project: www.hotmommasproject.org

> ❝Identify what you need and then ask for it!❞
>
> – Carol Covin

ↄ ↄ ↄ ↄ

58. HOLLY LEMON BATTERTON: A CIRCUITOUS ROUTE TO CAREER BLISS

My editor for this edition, Amy Hume helped me update all of these wonderful stories. She also brought to my attention a new story that we wanted to include. This is about a woman who had the courage to change her career completely, and the strength to succeed in all the steps along the way. Holly Lemon Batterton has had a wild career ride, and she's not done yet! The key to her success has been in finding the time, and the space, to really listen to herself. And then having the courage to course-correct along the way. Perhaps you'll recognize something of yourself in Holly's story.

Holly's story starts at age 16, when she first became a certified lifeguard. This role was much more than a way to earn summer income – lifeguarding quickly became a passion with Holly, and she still lifeguards today. "My parents were swimmers, and I fell in love with lifeguarding. Ever since, I've been in some position with the American Red Cross. I love first aid, and emergency medicine. I train first responders, and have taught individuals with a fear of water and/or disabilities about water safety." This passion was the first clue in her career journey.

In college, Holly studied journalism and marketing, and she continued to enjoy lifeguarding. The first few years after college were a bit bumpy, so when the opportunity to help her sister in New Orleans came up, she took it. "I got a job teaching swimming at the local club, and I started to go to art gallery openings for fun." Holly has a wonderful, open, and bubbly personality, so it wasn't long before she made friends. The gallery owner noticed Holly's natural talent, and offered her a 100% commission sales position selling art in the French Quarter.

Holly went for it, and with the help of a wonderful mentor, did exceptionally well. Things were starting to click. With her new life and new success, Holly decided that she didn't want to date for a while so she could focus on getting her feet under her. Fate had another plan. One evening while out with friends, Holly literally ran into her future husband. "We fell in love and that was it." Not one to hesitate, Holly was soon married.

Meanwhile, her art career was skyrocketing. "The artists are so inspirational, especially those building their careers." Holly enjoyed world travel and a strong circle of artist friends. Those friends urged her to open her own gallery – so she did! And she loved it. She found it easy to sell art that moved her so. But it was not meant to last.

When Holly's father fell ill, she returned to her home in Louisville to care for him, and she decided to sell the gallery. Her father had a long successful career in insurance, and owned his own agency. To keep things rolling, Holly became an insurance agent. "Boy did life change! Going from the French Quarter arts scene to working for an all-male company, wearing suits and panty hose, I even learned to play golf – and I hate golf."

Holly shares that she thought she was successful because she made a lot of money. "Honestly, I hate selling insurance. But I did it for 22 years because I was good at it – I was the top producer in the country and won lots of trips. I 'drank the Kool-Aid' and believed in the product. And the money I earned kept me into my family." Soon Holly was promoted to Vice President.

After the birth of her first baby, the company didn't fit her so well anymore. Things got very stressful at work as Holly continued to be a stand out success in a male-dominated company. The stress started to take a physical toll, and Holly opted to stay home for a while. After her second baby was born, Holly became very ill and needed a long recovery period. Through all this, she continued with her love of swimming and life-guarding , and she really enjoyed being a mom.

When her husband was offered a job that allowed them to move anywhere, they chose a tiny town in Texas that has a lot of river access. Of course, Holly started learning about boating and river safety. In caring for her health, Holly was going to many doctors "I never knew about" and she was doing a lot of research. And when she found herself pregnant at age 40, she got a job at a hospital-based workout facility where she was in charge of safety and did all the training. "I got to know all the EMTs – and I was inspired, but still too scared to act on this strong interest of mine."

Finally, at age 45, Holly started to look at what it would take to get into emergency medicine and to be a first responder. Faced with the daunting requirements, she said, "that's not going to happen" and returned to insurance. At this point in time, Holly was selling property and casualty insurance to school districts, traveling the state of Texas. This redirection didn't last long, however; a change in the state laws put the branch out of business.

Meanwhile, Holly faced the largest health crisis of her life. After a ruptured appendix, she required 5 surgeries, each two weeks apart. The recuperation took months, and this gave her a lot of time to think about what she wanted to do next. She met with a career counselor. She considered going back to being an insurance agent – and she finally knew that wasn't a fit any more.

Following her love of medicine and health, Holly looked into becoming a Physician Assistant, and enrolled at the University of Texas San Antonio (UTSA). There were two full years of pre-requisite courses she had to take. "I had a panic attack in my first chemistry exam."

This is a woman who was used to not just succeeding, but surpassing all expectations; the pressure she put on herself was enormous. "My grades were okay, then great, and then I started to make *friends*. I joined the pre-med group, and it all started to be real. I knew I could achieve it. They even asked me to tutor in general chemistry. When I started in the program, I didn't even remember what a periodic table was!"

After a meeting with her Physician Assistant advisor, she learned that it would require another four years of course work before she could get into the program. So, she started looking into what was required to become a nurse. "Nursing is not what I wanted to do. But I found out I can work as a nurse and make money while working toward becoming a Nurse Practitioner." Holly landed a job as a scribe in the emergency room, and fell in love. As soon as she could, she started nursing school, and has finished her first year.

Holly has made important friendships throughout her career journey. "Now my best friend is a 23 year-old fellow student… we have a maternal/friend relationship and support each other every step of the way. We have had what each other needed on many troubled days, and I'm so grateful for her, and for our relationship." Holly is also inspired by the "ninja nurses" who run the program and with whom she works with in the Baptist Emergency Department. "Nurses are a breed of human I cannot explain. They work until exhaustion daily and yet will still take precious time to help anyone and everyone. They 'care' more deeply for mankind in a way I could not fathom until now."

Finally, Holly is following her heart into her career and will soon be a Nurse Practitioner. Looking back, she's amazed at what she's achieved. "It took me a full year to get over my exam nerves. I'm not good at math – "X" and I don't have a good relationship; I could never find "X"! But she followed all the clues along the way to the career that plays to her strengths, and that makes her heart sing.

Holly's Advice and Action Steps:

• Don't wait. Fear is your enemy. Face it and be active in your own success.

• There will always be a way to succeed on your new journey. Look behind the trees and under the rocks - there are people and programs in every career to help you succeed!

- It is always easier said than done, otherwise 'everyone would do it.'
- No matter what, just do it!

❝My father used to warn me, 'Be careful on which course you travel, changing it is like turning a ship without a rudder.' Funny thing, had I listened more closely, I may have travelled a straighter line, but I would be so much less grateful for the results.❞

– Holly Lemon Batterton

ℒ ℒ ℒ ℒ

59. Take a Step Forward

We spend nearly half our lives and most of our waking hours in the workplace. So we owe it to ourselves to create enriching experiences during those hours that are meaningful and gratifying. Some of these opportunities come unexpectedly and others are carefully planned; but the career reinventions for Jacqueline Edelberg, Joyce Boyd, Holly Lemon Batterton, Ellen Palmer and Carol Covin happened because these women had the courage to try something new.

Tapping Your Inner Indiana Jones

Say yes more often and be willing to explore new things at work. Many people discover their calling by the moves they make at work. If you are open to new experiences, assignments, projects, travel, and training, for example – you just might find something you love to do that you are very good at that was previously unknown to you. By saying yes to new things passionately you will show your boss that you are the go-to person to be counted on and this could lead to new opportunities.

I have always been willing to take a risk and have tried many new things beyond my operatic career. By trial and error I was able to determine what I really loved and what I wanted to spend more time and energy pursuing. I have many more things on my future career wish list that I am eager to try in the near future. Taking a risk can often lead to a reward, but you will never know if you don't try.

Don't be Afraid to Fail

Experiencing failure is a reality for each of us in our careers. Some employers won't hire you, others won't promote you, and some dream jobs will be disappointing. Congratulations – welcome to the human race. We are all fallible and once you have experienced failure, you will be better at knowing how to recover the next time around. I embrace the concept of failing forward so I always learn something useful from an experience that didn't go as expected.

Failure can be painful, but we learn valuable lessons when things don't go as planned. The real failure comes from never trying something in the first place. In the moving words of author Gail Sheehy:

"If we don't change, we don't grow.

If we don't grow, we are not really living.

Growth demands a temporary surrender of security."

Show Your Enthusiasm

I can say with humility and appreciation that I have been recruited for many positions throughout my professional life. I take pride in doing my job to the best of my ability and I always try to show a genuine enthusiasm and sincere interest in taking the job above and beyond the call of duty. Perhaps ambition is in my DNA. I have a strong work ethic that gives me great satisfaction in doing a job well and overcoming challenges. This has served me well, as others have recognized my competencies and invited me to take advantage of new careers that they believed would be a good fit.

Be cognizant of the fact that other people with hiring authority may poach you away for a new career, and that can be a very exciting thing. Don't be a well-kept secret in your job success. Perform to the best of your abilities and let others know that you are open to new adventures!

The Barter and Trade System

You may have a tremendous skill that is in great demand from others, and likewise you may have friends and colleagues with an expertise you need but don't have in your personal toolbox. Consider the barter or trade system to swap what you have for what you need.

Let's say you are interested in creating a website for a freelance business that could turn your hobby into a full-time career if it takes off. You have a graphic design background and can create images and a logo for the business but you need a web programmer to create the technical code for the site and a copywriter to help you flesh out the written content. Look to your network to see if you can swap services with someone else who needs something you do well.

Swapping goes back for centuries as a way to make payment for services rendered. Now you can tap into the vast Internet network for online swapping sites like BarterQuest.com, SwapTree.com, and Swap.net to find people who have exactly what you need for an equally measured swap. I often trade my coaching services with fellow entrepreneurs who have services and products I find valuable.

Don't Be Limited by Your Education

Many people fear pursuing a career change because they don't have a degree in what they believe is the requisite field. Except for some very specialized fields, such as medicine and law, many careers rely more on your transferable skills, your willingness to learn, and your emotional intelligence than your degree qualifications. And don't forget, the recovering lawyers in Chapter 5 were able to put their transferable skills to great use beyond the legal sector in new careers.

Did you know that Mick Jagger was an Economics major at the rigorous London School of Economics before becoming an iconic rock star? Michelle Obama studied sociology and African-American studies at Princeton University before heading to Harvard Law.

They each developed core skills and a specific knowledge base from their respective disciplines, but these high profile individuals went on to develop careers that were not limited to the academic choices they made in school.

REINVENTION TOOLBOX

Using a Coach – Best Practices; Honor Your SELF

Olympians and professional athletes at the top of their game have been utilizing coaches for decades so why is it that professionals in the world-of-work have taken so long to catch up? A coach stands on the sidelines and gives you input and objectivity that you cannot effectively produce yourself. You should hire a coach because you want to get better at what you are already good at.

A good coach will help you discover what you need and will provide you with a strategic action plan, motivation, and accountability to accomplish your goals. While change in the workplace is inevitable, suffering is optional; a coach can help you unlock what you are passionate about and help you move forward if you are contemplating a career transition or professional reinvention.

Coaches can provide you with opportunities to own your self-confidence and play to your strengths. A great coach once told me that individuals bloom when they decide to ride their horse in the direction it is already going.

Are Your Coachable?

Shop wisely for a coach and be aware that the industry standard is to provide a free consultation to learn about their services and to determine if it's a good fit for you. Use your intuitive and perceptive senses to gut-check whether a prospective coach is a good match for what you need. This is an investment in your career and your life, so look for someone you can trust, that comes well recommended (check references), and provides a complimentary consultation so that you can get to know each other before you sign up.

Coaches specialize in a wide variety of services, including personal branding, executive and leadership development, communications, entrepreneurial ventures, social media, and leadership enhancement, to name just a few. Be sure to find a coach that specializes in what you need most. There is a niche market ripe with coaches dedicated to all areas of expertise. Find one who is a specialist and not a Jack-of-all-trades to get the most focused coaching experience possible.

If you are considering the services of a coach, I am happy to help get you started on your quest for the best fit. Please contact me through my website www.carolinedowdhiggins.com.

A Lesson from Tracy Robbins

Jane Austen, the English novelist was known for her biting social commentary in the 1800s. I believe she would have been an avid blogger if she was alive today with hundreds of connections on her LinkedIn profile. As much as I adore Jane Austen's work, whenever I re-read her novels or watch a movie or mini-series, it makes me appreciate the modern times in which I live.

Jane's plots, although often comedic, highlight the dependence of women on marriage to secure social standing and economic security. She was a rare bird to be a female published author in her day. Thankfully, times have changed and modern women can make their way in the world, with or without a significant other in their lives. Women today have choices and have been empowered to lead authentic lives and forge careers that are meaningful to us as individuals.

Jane Austen would have been inspired by Tracy Robbins, the highest-ranking woman and Executive Vice President of

Global Human Resources for Intercontinental Hotels Group, PLC. In an interview with Pink Magazine, Tracy shared four tips for honoring yourself and finding success.

Stretch Yourself – take on projects that have potential to make a big impact on your career and your life. Make those accomplishments visible and find authentic, effective ways to promote your achievements.

Be Yourself – be genuine in your life and career choices. Don't fake it to fit in or get ahead on the job. Honoring your values and passions will reap greater rewards in the long run.

Have Fun – laughter breaks down boundaries. Add some levity to each day and don't take yourself too seriously. Develop your sense of humor and enjoy a good hearty laugh – it's good for your health.

Develop Your Team – be relentless, caring, and tenacious about developing your team. Surround yourself with great people who do what you can't and support them and encourage them to achieve success together.

11

THE FORCE OF THE SISTERHOOD

60. EMPOWERMENT, OPTIMISM, AND HUMBLE CONFIDENCE

After my own personal reinvention I feel empowered to do a great many things in my career. I believe that I have many professional lives ahead of me and I will continue to reinvent myself again and again as my values and interests change over time, and I utilize the variety of skills in my professional toolbox.

Empowerment is a buzz word in our culture that refers to increasing the spiritual, political, social, or economic strength of individuals and communities. Ideally, the empowered develop confidence in their capabilities. I am on a quest to help women own their strengths and become empowered in the workplace so that they can thrive, and can earn equal pay commensurate to their male counterparts!

The reinvention stories of these amazing women have inspired me to pay-it-forward to help women in the workforce own their strengths and gain confidence on the road to empowerment.

A Cup Half Full

Positivity and optimism are powerful tools for us to employ daily. It's easy to focus on the negative and get depressed about what we can't control. But I urge you to be a cup half-full person and focus on what you **can** control. Celebrate that you can be the change agent for your career destiny. Positivity is infectious, so be the one in your organization who sets the tone for the work environment.

Now that you are feeling empowered and positive, let's talk about confidence. Historically, women have been taught not to brag or be boastful about their accomplishments. As a result, we are often uncomfortable promoting ourselves and we miss out on career opportunities because we don't sing our own praises in a performance review or job interview, let alone a networking conversation.

Practice embracing your humble confidence. This should be a blend of owning your strengths and celebrating the accomplishments you have earned and doing so in an authentic way that is professional and palatable for you and your audience.

Picture the woman in your network that walks tall with humble confidence. She owns the space she occupies in a room and she speaks with conviction. She attracts people to her with a positive energy and she is respected and well known for her accomplishments. We all know someone like this and we have great admiration for this woman in our respective networks. Think of her as a role model and channel her when you begin to put into practice your humble confidence.

61. RUNNING YOUR CAREER MARATHON

It's rare to have a single job with an organization for your entire professional career. Part of that is because work culture has changed and organizations don't incentivize company loyalty as they did years ago. Statistically, people change career fields (not just jobs) an average of 5 to 7 times during their adult lives.

Career reinvention is on the rise so you are in good company. I believe the career transition phenomenon is widespread because people are becoming more aware of what they value. They want to work in environments where they are challenged, stimulated, and gratified. The millennial generation now entering the work force is clearly articulating that they want work/life balance. While this is unsettling for the old guard, it just may revolutionize how companies view part-time employment, flexible work schedules, work-from-home options, and longer vacation periods.

I hope the concept of the career marathon brings you comfort and helps you think of the long run in your full career life. Alma Bond is certainly not considering retirement yet and she is in her 80s. Bottom line, you always have a choice. Take stock of what mile marker you are currently at. Perhaps you are taking it slow because you are raising young children, or maybe you are ramping it up because you are eager to seek new promotional opportunities. Consider your life milestones and plan your career marathon accordingly.

62. SETTING AND ACHIEVING GOALS

Having dreams and goals for the future is a wonderful way to focus on what you want in your life and career. A wise mentor once told me it's not enough to just think about your goals – you must write them down. Putting your wishes on paper helps you articulate things more clearly and gives you accountability for achieving your goals.

Carol Covin has set out a 50-year plan for her career goal of taking a product to market that will cure cancer. Her project is massive in every respect since she must first take the cancer-curing protocol through a series of clinical trials that will literally take years to accomplish. You need not carve out a 50-year plan, but I urge you to take a close look at the next 90 days and write down what you want to accomplish. You can always change your mind and adjust your game plan, but dig deep to think about what you really want. Dream BIG because you deserve it!

First, Take Baby Steps

Split your 90-day goal into smaller, attainable actions and chop it into manageable baby steps. Writing down your goals can be a secret weapon to help you focus on your objectives.

This is also a good time to look to your posse, your personal Board of Directors, or your resource team to assemble the masterminds that will help you reach your target. Identify your solutions instead of focusing on the problems; seek information and help from your advisors.

It's easy to get bogged down with over ambitious to-do lists. The point of the exercise is to manage the workflow into reasonable and attainable increments. Reaching a goal is extremely gratifying so set small, attainable goals for each day and work incrementally towards the big finale. Studies tell us that you are 90 times more likely to accomplish a goal when it is written down. What are you waiting for... grab a pen and write down your goals!

Keep Your Eye on the Prize

Once you visualize your bigger career goals, keep the focus and reward yourself for all the accomplishments you achieve along the way. Celebrate small milestones like increasing your network, pursuing informational interviews, or taking on a new assignment at work. You must reward your successes to motivate yourself to reach the end goal. Have someone on your resource team be your accountability master to hold your feet to the fire for deadlines and difficult tasks in your career plan. This person could be a friend, mentor, or a coach who can really give you the push you need to move forward, especially when times are tough.

Opportunity knocks when we least expect it so always be at-the-ready to consider and take advantage of new breaks. If you can seize the moment and come to the rescue for a difficult challenge at work – you just might be the next go-to person when it comes time for a promotion. Being well prepared is a skill in and of itself.

63. WORK/LIFE BALANCE AND MAKING CHOICES

One of the most common questions from young millennial aged professionals is: How will I maintain work/life balance if I land a competitive job in the cutting edge corporate world? I can honestly report that most of those organizations are not hiring young associates and paying them mega salaries so they can enjoy work/life balance. They feed you breakfast, lunch, and dinner at the office, not because it's a perk, but because they don't want you to leave the building!

You must have realistic expectations about what you value and what it requires in your work environment. I'm not saying that if you make a lot of money you won't ever have work/life balance, but I am saying that you will have to work very long hours to earn that jumbo pay check.

It's really all about making choices and looking for careers and organizations that honor what you value. If work/life balance is important to you because you want to spend time with your family, then look for companies and careers that celebrate those values.

You can have it all but it might not be all at the same time. Many of the women in this book left a corporate environment because they wanted to be more in control of their own time. The entrepreneurs love being their own boss but they know that often it takes 24/7 work to get everything done – especially for a start-up business. You can design your life around your job or design your job around your life. Neither is better or worse – but it is **your** choice.

64. CELEBRATE THE NEW YOU: RECHARGED, REIGNITED AND REINVENTED

Since we spend over half our lives in the workplace, we owe it to ourselves to be happy in our careers. We should create enriching experiences that stimulate and challenge us. I urge you to consider at least one thing you can do TODAY to turn the career you didn't order into one that you love.

Thank you for coming on this career reinvention journey with me and the women showcased in this book. I have learned so much from these amazing women and I am inspired by their courage, their strength, and their passion for life. Whether you are recharging and reigniting an existing career with some new strategies or reinventing yourself entirely, you have the power to do great things. Be sure to share your reinvention stories with me and perhaps I will feature you in my next book.

My offer remains to help you with your individual career transformation goals. I have dedicated my career coaching practice to helping others own their strengths and embrace their confidence. You can learn more at www.carolinedowdhiggins.com – I hope to hear from you!

In addition to the resources suggested by the women featured in this book, I have included a list of some of my favorite books and websites that you may also find helpful on your career development journey.

RESOURCES

As a coach, I firmly believe in sharing great resources. Here are some of my favorite websites and books that have helped me navigate my continuing career and life journey. I believe they will be wonderful additions to your growing professional toolbox and I hope you will share them with others who are also on a quest for career and life satisfaction.

- Caroline Dowd-Higgins' website: www.carolinedowdhiggins.com
- She Negotiates: www.shenegotiates.com
- Ellevate Invest in Women Network: www.ellevatenetwork.com
- The Wage Project: www.wageproject.org
- Myers-Briggs Foundation: www.myersbriggs.org
- StrengthsFinder 2.0 by Tom Rath
- *Thrive: The Third Metric to Redefining Success and Creating a Life of Well-Being, Wisdom, and Wonder* by Arianna Huffington
- *Daring: My Passages: A Memoir* by Gail Sheehy
- *Are You Ready to Be a Thought Leader? How to Increase Your Influence, Impact, and Success* by Denise Brosseau
- *The Confidence Code: The Science and Art of Self-Assurance What Women Should Know* by Katty Kay and Claire Shipman
- *Don't Let 'Em Treat You Like a Girl: A Woman's Guide to Leadership Success* by Liz Weber
- *Something Needs to Change Around Here: The Five Stages to Leveraging Your Leadership* by Liz Weber

- *The Invitation: When You're Ready to Take Your Next Step* by Mary LoVerde
- *Brag! The Art of Tooting Your Own Horn without Blowing It* by PeggyKlaus
- *The Hard Truth About Soft Skills: Workplace Lessons Smart People Wish They'd Learned Sooner* by Peggy Klaus
- *Nice Girls Don't Get The Corner Office: Unconscious Mistakes Women Make That Sabotage Their Careers* by Dr. Lois P. Frankel
- *See Jane Lead: 99 Ways for Women to Take Charge at Work* by Dr. Lois P.Frankel
- *This Is Not the Life I Ordered: 50 Ways to Keep Your Head Above Water When Life Keeps Dragging You Down* by Deborah Collins Stephens, Michealene Cristini Risley, Jackie Speier, and Jan Yanehiro
- *What Color is Your Parachute?* by Richard N. Bolles
- *Knock 'em Dead: The Ultimate Job Search Guide* by Martin Yate
- *Knock 'em Dead: Social Networking for Job Search and Professional Success* by Martin Yate
- *Heed Your Call: Integrating Myth, Science, Spirituality and Business* by David M. Howitt
- *What Got You Here Won't Get You There* by Marshall Goldsmith
- *The Fine Art of Small Talk: How to Start a Conversation, Keep it Going, Build Rapport and Leave a Positive Impression* by Debra Fine
- *The Fine Art of the Big Talk: How to Win Clients, Deliver Great Presentations, and Solve Conflicts at Work* by Debra Fine

ABOUT THE AUTHOR

With over a decade of career and professional development experience, Caroline Dowd-Higgins has a desire to empower and energize women to achieve their personal goals. Her coaching style is engaging, high energy, and positive with a focus on unlocking the self-advocate within you.

In her capacity as a Director of Professional Enrichment for the Indiana University Alumni Association, she leads an expanded alumni career enhancement and leadership development program based on a lifetime engagement model. Caroline served for six years as Director of Career & Professional Development at Indiana University Maurer School of Law where she helped thousands of newly minted attorneys and seasoned alumni to navigate their careers in the legal arena and beyond. She is a member of the American Counseling Association, National Speaker's Association and the International Speaker's Network. She also serves on the Advisory Board for the Indiana Governor's Conference for Women.

Caroline's passion is to empower women, so it's unsurprising that her first book *This Is Not the Career I Ordered*® focuses on women who have experienced a career transition and reinvented themselves in the job world. The book and blog of the same name serve as a resource and an inspiration for women who have survived a career change brought about by choice or necessity. With a social media reach of 81 million, Caroline also writes for the *Huffington Post, America Online,* CNN Money, London based online magazine – *The Rouse*, and More magazine in addition to a column for *The Chronicle* newspaper in Indiana. Her articles are distributed internationally and she is a sought after guest for career themed broadcasts.

As a testimony to the power of transferable skills, prior to establishing her consulting practice, Caroline worked as a professional opera singer in Europe and the United States. She knows the power of career transformation and is adept at helping individuals fine-tune their communication skills to improve their professional public image and effectiveness in the workplace. Her many years singing on the

professional stage have helped her hone the art of personal branding and authentic communication. Caroline is a Marshall Goldsmith
Stakeholder Centered certified Executive Coach.

For two years, she hosted the nationally acclaimed talk-radio
show *Career Coach Caroline* on CBS Radio. Her podcast series, *Your
Working Life* has an international audience featuring interviews with
thought leaders and inspiring topics about thriving in life and career.
Caroline's mantra is: *Enjoy Your Career. Love Your Life!* www.caroline
dowdhiggins.com

CPSIA information can be obtained at www.ICGtesting.com
Printed in the USA
LVOW04s1127101214

418147LV00001B/3/P